PRAISE FOR *EATING DIRT*

"It is hard to say why a book that is full of mould, sodden clothing, overdoses of sugar and carbs, bad weather, grizzly bears, cream and crud, broken-down trucks, blisters and tiny seedlings shoved into the ground should be engaging, rewarding and full of knowledge, but it is... Gill's is a book you can live in. You come to speak its language and to feel as she feels."

WILLIAM BRYANT LOGAN,
author of *Dirt: The Ecstatic Skin of the Earth*

"An engrossing account of not only tree planting's unique culture, but of the role it plays in the larger industrial enterprise that surrounds it."

NATIONAL POST

"Gill's story of a life spent planting seedlings for pay, mandated in Canada's clear-cut forests, is entrancing if horrifying. The dirt, physical pain, loneliness, camaraderie and primordial awe are elbowing for space in Gill's remarkable memoir of an awful job."

TORONTO STAR

"Her prose style suits the subject: short, stabbing sentences like tree trunks or mosquito bites."

MONTREAL GAZETTE

"[For Charlotte Gill] there are no more hips bruised from carrying bags of trees, no more blistered heels, legs rubbed hairless from chafing, no more encounters with bears sniffing at the wild air, no more falling into blurry, wine-dark taverns in lumber towns, but for readers, there is this book, this experience, this gift."

VANCOUVER SUN

"In her new book, *Eating Dirt*, [Charlotte Gill] questions whether the intricate relationships between species that have developed over centuries in old-growth forests can be replaced through the efforts of an army of shovels."

CANADIAN GEOGRAPHIC

"A beautifully written and absorbing book."

FINDING SOLUTIONS

"Gill gracefully guides us through the world of the tree planter from the beginning to the end of a season, dedicating plenty of attention to the details of bush life. And nestled among her personal experiences is her perspective on the world behind the industry: the politics, science and history of forestry around the globe. Gill's strength lies in describing the people she has met ... They practically jump off the page, thanks to her beautiful prose and sensitivity to detail."

WINNIPEG FREE PRESS

"The book is like a forest itself. It's very rich and the writing is lush, and full of imagery. Gill allows the reader to see the landscapes that she is travelling through. She is able to take the reader into the forest, and into the brutal tree-planting experience."

DAILY HERALD-TRIBUNE

"*Eating Dirt* will endure as a testament to the vital but often overlooked actual and symbolic role that forests, tree planters and tree planting continue to play in our times."

THE TYEE

"In the hands of this wordsmith, the mundane becomes magical ... With *Eating Dirt*, Gill has produced a winner. Not all of the two million seedlings she planted during her two decades in the wild will have thrived, but this book will."

QUILL & QUIRE

"A joy of a book! *Eating Dirt* romps through the grime, the pain, and the legendary, eccentric lifestyles of the tribe of tree planters. In this natural history of tree planting, Charlotte Gill discovers beauty even in the clear-cuts of our thrashed forests, and the often-deranged culture that works to protect the remnants of a noble environment."

BRIAN BRETT,
author of *Trauma Farm: A Rebel History of Rural Life*

"In the same spare, unflinching prose that brought her such acclaim for her short stories, Gill takes us into the remote and rarely seen world of the tree planter, immersing us in the unique combination of sweat, fog, heartache, and humor that distinguishes it from all other labors."

JOHN VAILLANT,
author of *The Tiger: A True Story of Vengeance and Survival*

EATING DIRT

CHARLOTTE GILL

DEEP FORESTS, BIG TIMBER,
and LIFE *with the*
TREE-PLANTING TRIBE

David Suzuki Foundation

GREYSTONE BOOKS
D&M PUBLISHERS INC.
Vancouver/Toronto/Berkeley

Greystone Books
An imprint of D&M Publishers Inc.
2323 Quebec Street, Suite 201
Vancouver BC Canada V5T 4S7
www.greystonebooks.com

David Suzuki Foundation
219–2211 West 4th Avenue
Vancouver BC Canada V6K 4S2

Cataloguing data available from Library and Archives Canada
ISBN 978-1-55365-977-8 (cloth)
ISBN 978-1-55365-792-7 (pbk.)
ISBN 978-1-55365-793-4 (ebook)

Editing by Nancy Flight
Copyediting by Lara Kordic
Cover and text design by Naomi MacDougall
Cover photograph © Hugh Stimson
Printed and bound in Canada by Friesens
Distributed in the U.S. by Publishers Group West

We gratefully acknowledge the financial support of the Canada Council
for the Arts, the British Columbia Arts Council, the Province of
British Columbia through the Book Publishing Tax Credit, and the Government
of Canada through the Canada Book Fund for our publishing activities.

Greystone Books is committed to reducing the
consumption of old-growth forests in the books it publishes.
This book is one step towards that goal.

For the people of the tribe

I made a shift to go forward, till I came to a part of the field where the corn had been laid by the rain and wind. Here it was impossible for me to advance a step; for the stalks were so interwoven, that I could not creep through, and the beards of the fallen ears so strong and pointed, that they pierced through my clothes into my flesh. At the same time I heard the reapers not a hundred yards behind me.

JONATHAN SWIFT, *Gulliver's Travels*, "A Voyage to Brobdingnag"

. . . . .

He was a work-beast. He had no mental life whatever; yet deep down in the crypts of his mind, unknown to him, were being weighed and sifted every hour of his toil, every movement of his hands, every twitch of his muscles, and preparations were making for a future course of action that would amaze him and all his little world.

JACK LONDON, "The Apostate"

Contents

{ 1 }

the LAST PLACE *on* EARTH

WE FALL OUT of bed and into our rags, still crusted with the grime of yesterday. We're earth stained on our thighs and shoulders, and muddy bands circle our waists, like grunge rings on the sides of a bathtub. *Permadirt*, we call it. Disposable clothes, too dirty for the laundry.

The sun comes up with the strength of a dingy light bulb, dousing the landscape in shades of gray. The clouds are bruised and swollen. We stand in a gravel lot, a clearing hacked from the forest. Heavy logging machinery sits dormant all around, skidders and yarders like hulking metallic crabs. The weather sets in as it always does, as soon as we venture outdoors. Our raincoats are glossy with it. The air hisses. Already we feel the drips down the backs of our necks, the dribbles down the thighs of our pants. We're professional tree planters. It's February, and our wheels have barely begun to grind.

We stand around in huddles of three and four with tooth-paste at the corners of our mouths, sleep still encrusted in our eyes. We stuff our hands down into our pockets and shrug our shoulders up around our ears. We wear polypropylene and fleece and old pants that flap apart at the seams. We sport the grown-out remains of our last haircuts and a rampant facial shagginess, since mostly we are men.

We crack dark, miserable jokes.

Oh, run me over. Go get the truck. I'll just lie down here in this puddle.

If I run over your legs, who will run over mine?

We shuffle from foot to foot, feeding on breakfast buns wrapped in aluminum foil. We drink coffee from old spaghetti sauce jars. We exhale steam. Around here you can hang a towel over a clothesline in November, and it will drip until April.

Adam and Brian are our sergeants. They are exactly the same height and wear matching utility vests made of red canvas. Heads bent together, they embroil themselves in what they call "a meeting of the minds," turning topographical maps this way and that, testing the hand-held radios to ascertain which ones have run out of juice. Their lips barely move when they talk. Their shoulders collect the rain. We wait for their plan of attack as if it is an actual attack, a kind of green guerrilla warfare.

At the stroke of seven, we climb up into big Ford pickup trucks with mud-chewing tires and long radio antennae. We slide across the bench seats, shoving ourselves in together. Five diesel engines roar to life.

Adam sits at the wheel. He has an angular face, hair and skin turned tawny by the outdoor life, arresting eyes the color of mint mouthwash. He pulls out at the head of our small convoy. His pupils zip back and forth over the road's unpaved surface. He drives like a man on a suicide mission. No one complains. Speed is the jet fuel that runs our business.

While he drives, Adam wraps his lips around the unwashed lid of a commuter mug. He slides aluminum clipboards in and out of his bag and calls out our kilometers on the truck-to-truck radio. Logging trucks barrel down these roads, laden with bounty like land-borne supertankers. Adam slides his maps into various forms of plastic weatherproofing. Multitasking is his only speed—as it is for all of us—too fast, too much, and all at once. We're pieceworkers, here to make money, a lot of it, in a hurry. Earning our keep can feel like picking quarters off a sidewalk, and it can feel like an emergency.

Logging routes are like human arteries, main lines branching out into fine traceries. We pass from civilization to wilderness on a road with muddy ruts. Old snow decomposes along the shoulder. The land around here is jaggedly three-dimensional, fissured with gullies and brush-choked ravines. Mountains bulge from the seashore. We zoom through stands of tall Douglas-firs, conifers bearded with lichen. A green blaze, we're driving so fast, skimming along the surface of our known world.

Most of us are veterans. *Crusty*, we call each other, like those Special Ops who crawl from war-ravaged mountains with wild hair, matted beards, and battle-mad glints in their eyes. Sean and Pierre were doing this job, they sometimes remind us, when the rest of us were in diapers. Pierre is fifty-five. He tells us he has a resting pulse rate lower than Lance Armstrong's. He tells us a hundred things, every day, in great detail. He shows us the display screen of his digital camera. He shows us photos of ravens and skunk cabbage. Snapshots from his civilian life—his faraway kids, his foxy lady friends.

Sean is both wiry and muscular. He has a titanium hip. Some of his clothes are as old as his tree-planting career—threadbare, unraveling around the edges. He plants trees for half the year and windsurfs the remaining portions. His lips and cheeks are speckled with liver spots from a life in the sun. But like Pierre, he's still going.

Jake, at twenty-one, is the youngest. Jake calls Pierre Old Man. He refers to himself as Elfie, in the third person.

Elfie's not digging this action, he says. Elfie thinks this is fucked up.

Oakley and Jake are best pals. Jake is short and muscular, and he talks in rowdy shouts. Oakley is tall and sturdy. We always know where he's working, because his lunch box is a plastic tub that once contained a body-building supplement. Find the Mega Milk on the side of the road and you know Oakley's beavering away behind the rise. Oakley and Jake play Hacky Sack for hours every evening, and Pierre documents this, too, with his digicam.

We spend a lot of time in trucks, and it's here we get to know one another. The crew cabs are our living rooms, the bench seats our sofas. Nick is redheaded. He reminds us of Richie Cunningham. He doesn't drink. He says he used to. Some call him Risky, like the business. Carmen knits. She's a single mom. Her boys are at home with her parents. On commutes she clicks away with her needles at socks the size of kiwi fruits.

Sean has more seniority than anyone, and he has an inexhaustible supply of jokes to prove it.

How many tree planters does it take to screw in a light bulb?

One. But you'll find five bulbs in the socket.

What do you call a tree planter without a girlfriend?

Homeless.

No one is offended. We're unisex guys, the men of mandays. The work wears us down and lifts us up, everyone together, equally. Sometimes we glance sideways at the old-timers and we wonder just how long we'll keep doing this job. We think: *Take me out before I end up old and battered and stooped like Quasimodo.* But we're halfway there already. It feels as if we've been doing this job for a thousand years, and our bodies are rusted with it.

I nestle among my work comrades as I have done for nearly twenty years. The rituals and routines of planting trees are as familiar to me as boiling water or brushing my teeth. But February always shocks me. Usually, I'm unfit after a lazy, indoor winter. So is K.T. He's my boyfriend and also my co-worker. We've made a life of it—city dwellers in the winter, tree planters come spring. Now, after one week on the job, even my eyelids feel sore. My palms and heels are blistered. I still yearn for the comforts of home. The ease of the easy chair, the depths of my own downy bed.

Soon enough these cravings will evaporate. In eight hours I'll be too tired to care. To say planting trees is my day job is not quite right, because to do such work is to give one's whole life, albeit temporarily. There's no room for taking notes. When I plant trees, both hands are entirely spoken for.

When Adam hurtles us around the bends we slide into one another. Our toes bump against a heavy-duty jack, coffee mugs with broken handles, a soggy wool sock, an empty sandwich bag smeared with mayonnaise. Our breath clouds the windshield. The blower can't keep up. Someone farts silently, and the smell creeps out among us. We veer down branches and forks. Fat drops tap the windshield, shed from the arms of the trees. We crash through puddles that look like chocolate milk.

Nowhere beyond the village is there a single paved road. No signage, no radar enforcements, nothing to tell us to slow down for the children. There are no bed-and-breakfasts. No cell phone reception. Where are we going at such heedless velocity? We couldn't point to a map with any certainty and name the road, the creek, the bridge. Most of the time we have no idea where the hell we are.

VANCOUVER ISLAND, a three-hundred-mile stretch of land hovering off the British Columbia coast. Locals call it merely The Island, as if it is self-evident, as if everyone should already know its name. Its southernmost portion dips below the 49th parallel, like a toe, into American waters. Less than a million people live here, most of them clustered on the south end, which is pretty as a postcard—sunny, mild, and bustling with tourists. Shopping malls, hanging flower baskets, hippies in Birkenstocks and crocheted toques, alternative-healing centers and covert marijuana farms. Marinas bristle with yacht masts. Halfway up the island, the temperature drops and the clouds sock in, even at the height of summer. The North End, Up-Island. The kind of raw geography Hollywood seeks out for movies about warriors in furred robes who wield maces and battle-axes. Cold, pewter-toned lakes. Cedar trees with dead spires like sharpened joists rising from the forest. Bald eagles filling the air by the dozens, circling on thermal currents.

Vancouver Island lies in the middle of a region known, in theory anyway, as Cascadia. It's an area defined not by national borders but by a shared climate and a history of geographic isolation. A strip of land that tilts toward the sea as if nudged to the water's edge by the coastal ranges. It begins at the 40th parallel at Cape Mendocino in California. It encompasses Oregon and Washington State, as well as portions of Montana and Idaho. It runs north along the coast of British Columbia all the way to the

Gulf of Alaska. In popular imagination this is the landscape of the Pacific Northwest, defined by ocean, mountains, and rain.

Weather systems skid toward the coast in spiraling pinwheels, picking up moisture along the way. They make landfall, dumping up to thirteen feet of rain a year. If you were born in the desert or raised in the heat, the monsoons are a form of water torture. The chill works its way under sweaters and scarves. It whistles under the doors. Winter here is a monotonous gloaming of cloud and puddles, a soul-craving for the sun. Mist-loving plants creep in around the edges of civilization. Rooftops, lawns, even cars grow moss. The air smells of mushrooms and compost. Rain seeps into every pore.

Snow seldom persists. Fires rarely burn. The soil is unctuous, like brown shortening. The conditions are perfect for temperate plant life and for several species of decadent tree. In the forests there is nowhere to look without a plant in the way, without ferns and moss and branchy lattices. Chlorophyll proliferates with a patient aggression. The canopy blots out the sky. Sometimes the only sound, besides the dripping, is the silent roar of matter breaking down and melting back into the soil. Amid the huge trunks and sunless rot, one can easily believe that the forests are winning.

Perhaps it's no surprise that the population of Cascadia is relatively small. It takes all three of the region's major urban centers—Vancouver, Seattle, and Portland—to make a population rivaling that of New York City. Until the mid-nineteenth century, this corner of the continent wasn't part of any territory or confederation. It had no European laws or government. Cascadia was little more than an unexplored possibility, a mercantile interest shared between Britain, Russia, and the United States. No infrastructure existed except for the services provided by missionaries and the Hudson's Bay Company. The United States had declared itself a free country for seventy-two years by the time the Oregon Territory attained any official status. British Columbia joined Canada more than three hundred years after Jacques Cartier stuck a cross on the shores of the Gaspé Peninsula.

European explorers once sailed the long way around to get here, an eleven-thousand-mile voyage around Cape Horn. The trip was so long and stormy and bereft of provisioned harbors that many ships turned back, their crews plagued by scurvy, their rigging battered and in need of extensive repairs. The only other route to the west coast involved an overland journey through what are now eight provinces and ten states—by wagon, horse, and canoe and on foot. So arduous was this trip that a century passed before newcomers began to trickle west from Atlantic to Pacific. The same journey one can make today in an airbus without even needing to eat on the way.

The Pacific Northwest was once the edge of the known world, shielded to the east by snowy ranges. By non-navigable rivers that plunged from dizzying heights into canyons and seething gorges. To the west lay unfathomable sheets of ocean. To get here, you had to be obsessed, greedy, insane, or perhaps a touch of all three—qualities, you might say, that still linger in the air today.

For most of its colonial history, Cascadia was a wet, woodsy hinterland. But behind the geographic challenges lay a gold mine in waiting, a superabundance of natural resources. The Pacific coast has a mild climate and, once upon a time, had a teeming fishery. In pre-Columbian times land and sea fed more people than anywhere else in North America. Since then, Cascadia has supplied the world with bulk ingredients. Furs, fish, metals, and not least, lumber.

Euro-American immigrants didn't begin to arrive in any serious numbers until the nineteenth century. They came via the Oregon Trail, a grueling two-thousand-mile trek from the Missouri River to Oregon City, now a town on the outskirts of Portland. The journey involved a months-long expedition by covered wagon along a wild, rutted, and frequently muddy track. In some spots the route was so precariously steep that wagons had to be hauled up or lowered down with ropes. When a wheeled conveyance—containing belongings and food rations—bogged down or broke apart it was left by the roadside to weather and disintegrate. For many this was a one-way trip. The mountain grades were so intense they proved impossible to scale in the opposite direction. Departure did not guarantee arrival. Travelers faced snowstorms, floods, wild animals, and disease. Accidents and death due to primitive, trailside medical care. Starvation and even cannibalism. And yet they came in droves. They'd succumbed to the allure of prosperity, a fresh start on the emerald coast.

Perhaps nothing captures these aspirations better than the trees themselves, which grow so prodigiously it defies the imagination. Some of the tallest trees in the world can still be found here. The mighty redwoods of California. The cedars and Douglas-firs of British Columbia. The Sitka spruce, the state tree of Alaska. Some trees are as old as the Magna Carta. They look dead on their feet, rotten hearted. Their growth rings tell of countless droughts and deluges.

The coastal region supports more biomass per square foot than any of the planet's tropical rainforests. There is simply more living matter breathing, dying, and metamorphosing here than anywhere else. But these are fragmented glades, the remnants of a forest that once spanned, virtually uninterrupted, through twenty degrees of latitude, nearly half the length of the North American continent. Most of the original forests of California, Oregon, and Washington are now gone. The big tracts that remain grow north of the 50th parallel—the world's last great temperate rainforest by the sea.

OUR TRUCKS climb the nameless mountains the way airplanes ascend, nosing up at the sky. We switch up and back along steep, cobbled surfaces, flattened shards of white rock chiseled from the mountain by road crews who dig and dynamite their way through. We climb into the belly of a cloud. The light brightens; the view widens. Before long, we find ourselves in the middle of a clearing. It feels like relief, this release from the canopy's darkened tent. Big trees surround us at the edge of the clearing, what's left of an old, gnarled forest. Storm-battered firs with flattened bonsai crowns. Gnarled cedars with bleached wood tusks protruding from lofty, lime-green foliage. Trees with mileage, like big old whales with harpoons stuck in their flanks. Handkerchiefs of mist drift among them.

We tumble out of our trucks like clothes from a dryer. Fog clings to the warp and weft of our tatters, the fine hairs on our cheekbones. Cigarettes are lit before feet hit the ground. Our smoke drifts up in a communal cloud. Most of us smoke. Brad has a way of making it look delicious, of holding a cigarette high in the crook of his fingers and putting his whole hand to his face. Those who don't wish they could, just for the portable comfort.

We gear up for the daily grind, grope around in our vinyl backpacks for wetsuit shirts and watertight containers. Gear hijacked from other sports—shin pads, knee braces made of hinged aluminum and Neoprene. We slide our feet down into tall leather boots with spiked soles. Loggers' boots, made for walking on bark and slick logs, made to bite down and stick. We lace ourselves tight. We slip our hands into heavy-duty gloves. We tug it all on in preparation for battle. We're proud, and yet ashamed.

There is something bovine about our crew. Brian threads his way around between us. He has a wavy thatch of side-parted hair, freckles, and a devious grin. He is a rapid-fire talker. He barks out a bunch of words so compressed and contracted they sound like a foreign language. We let ourselves be herded this way and that. At the same time we hate to be told what to do. We slide waxed boxes from the backs of the trucks and fling them down at the road. *Handle with Care,* the boxes read. *Forests for the Future.* Nothing about this phrase is a lie, but neither is it wholly true.

We chortle darkly, rubbing our palms together. There is nowhere to hide from the cold. No inside to duck into for warmth. A buzz develops all at once and out of nothing at all, the way bees begin to vibrate when they're about to flee a hive. Box upon box lined up on the side of the road, each one filled with 240 trees. Ready for us, by the hundreds and thousands, lined up together like bullets. A box of seedlings is ripped open. A paper bag torn. Bundles of plastic-wrapped seedlings tumble out. The stems are as long as a forearm, the roots grown in Styrofoam tubules to fit in the palms of our hands. We like this idea, since it lends a kind of clout—trees grown to our ergonomic specifications. Tree planters: little trees plus human beings, two nouns that don't seem to want to come apart.

Boot spikes crunch around in the gravel. A runaway seedling rolls down the road. We jostle around one another, hungry for the day that awaits us. We throw down our tree-planting bags and kneel next to them and cram them with trees. We do it with practiced slapdash, as cashiers drop groceries into white plastic bags. We bump shoulders, quick fingered and competitive, like grannies at a bargain bin. As if there weren't enough, thousands and thousands, to go around.

Before long we abandon the scene, an explosion of brown paper and Saran Wrap snaking around on the road. We stomp out in every direction, right and left, up and down the mountain. We lean into the next minute and the next like runners in blocks. We don't know how to do our work without pitting ourselves against one another, without turning it into an amazing race. Otherwise piecework is grindingly relentless, tiny objects passing negligibly through human hands. An inaudible gun goes off over our heads, and the day begins. Somewhere behind the clouds the sun is our pace clock in the sky.

We came as one, and now the space between us stretches like the filaments of a web. Adam doles out my work space, a hectare of clear-cut hillside. As he points out the boundaries of my daily turf I watch our breath puff out in clouds. And then he launches into his fervent, head-down walk, leaving me to the twists of the day.

At the lip of the road I peer out at the land. My tree-planting bags ride heavy on my thighs. Human saddlebags, one pouch in the back and one on each side. Every day, they turn gravity up a few notches. In my dreams they have sentient, subservient lives, like the magic broomsticks in *The Sorcerer's Apprentice*. They fill themselves up, I whistle them to life, and they trot out to do the job on their own.

Until someone invents a tree-planting robot, a plane that shoots seedlings from the sky, it's just me and my speed spade— a gardening trowel with a long plastic neck and a D-handle, a stainless steel blade shaved down with a grinder to resemble a big spoon. It feels in my hand the way spears must to Masai tribesmen, not merely a tool but something like an emblem, an extension of the hand and limb.

I'm not too bad at planting trees, if only because of the practice. I have climbed the flanks of a hundred mountains and hoisted my limbs over countless logs and stumps. I've stuck a million seedlings in the ground. I've met quite a few people who've doubled and even tripled this number. Or so they claim. I don't mind reading bush maps or flying around in helicopters or driving big pickup trucks. I hardly ever get cold in the rain. But I am not a natural tree planter. I have the hands of a typist. Being filthy and clammy makes me hate myself. And most of all I'd rather plant a pretty tree than a fast one. Which is one thing a tree planter should never do if she intends to earn a living.

My mornings are hours of reluctance and loathing. I size up the clouds and decide if it will rain or not and if I am wearing the right kind of clothes. I swallow one last cookie. I blow warm air into my fists and scope out the job that looms before me. I eye it up the way rock climbers stand at the bottom of cliff faces pondering spatial puzzles of slope and texture and rock. How many people are doing just this right now, somewhere in the world? Planning and plotting and putting off chores of epic proportions. A hundred boxes of file folders. A great wall of dirty dishes. A graduate thesis. A long row of toilets to attack with just a scrub brush and a can of cleanser. The body recoils. It feels wrong in my cells. My neck hair stands on end.

Planting trees isn't hard. As any veteran will tell you, it isn't the act of sowing itself but the ambient complications. It comes with snow pellets. Or clouds of biting insects so thick and furious it is possible to end a day with your eyelids swollen shut and blood trickling from your ears. There are swaying fields of venomous plants like devil's club and stinging nettle. There are sunburns and hornets. There are swamps rimmed with algal sludge to fall into up to the armpits. There are leeches and ticks, bears and cougars. There are infections and chafe and boils and trench foot. It's possible to be so cold you feel dreamily warm and so hot you fall into shivers. Over time the work has the bodily effect of a car crash in extreme slow motion. Sometimes our bosses make off to Mexico with all the money. Besides that, the task itself is thankless and boring, which is to say it is plain and silent. It is also one of the dirtiest jobs left in the modern world.

What could compel a person to make a career of such a thing? I have always wanted to find out.

AIRLINERS GLIDE through the skies on their way to Asia. We vanish like fleas into the fur of the land. We look for moss and signs of dirt, searing holes in the ground with our eyes. We find spots, and we stab as if to wound them, throwing our weight behind our shovels. If we're lucky our blades penetrate slickly, as knives slide into melon. If not, we've got roots, rock, wood, grass—barriers to chip at with the blades of our shovels in search of elusive earth. We dig around in our left-hand bags and come out with the trees, one by one by one.

I push into my shovel as if it were a heavy door. A square of earth breaks open at my feet and sighs a moldy breath. I bend at the waist and slide the roots down the back of my spade. My job is to find these trees new one-hundred-year homes, though I seldom think of it that way. Douglas-firs with slick, wet needles, twigs dressed in green whiskers. I tuck them in with a punch of my fist. I haven't stood up and I'm already walking. Bend. Plant.

Stand up. Move on. The work is simply this, multiplied by a thousand, two thousand, or more. Twenty-five cents a tree.

Goodbye, little bastard. Have a nice life.

A rainforest, minus the forest. On wet February days our lives are tinged with dread, a low-grade Sisyphean despair. Moisture comes down in every degree of slushiness. In every shape from mist to deluge, so loud we have to shout over its pattering din. It descends sideways, and it slithers in long strings. We've even seen rain fall *up*, propelled by ocean gusts. There is no way at all to stay dry, despite our rain gear, which comes with intrepid names like Wetskins, Pioneer, and The North Face. The wetness envelops. It begins at the scalp and dribbles down the back of the neck, all the way down the spine until our boots fill up with water.

Some days we're like bugs crawling around in Velcro. Grubbers in the soil, incapable of dreams. In this gigantic landscape it's easy to feel small, as if we could flake away from the land and splash down in the open ocean. Sweat trickles between our shoulder blades. We do a lot of gazing down.

Do you like work? we ask one another during the moments in between.

Not really, we agree.

The days go by in intricate visuals and bodily sensation and zooming clouds and hundreds of schlepping movements accompanied by five-second shreds of thought. We look out, at the end of the day, at our fields of seedlings. They shimmy in the wind. *There*, we say. We did this with our hands. We didn't make millions, and we didn't cure AIDS. But at least a thousand new trees are breathing.

{ 2 }

a KIND *of* TRIBE

TREE PLANTERS OBSERVE a different calendar, not a year highlighted by summer vacations and Christmas holidays, but one aligned with the seasons. We head out to the fields when winter gives way, when the woods are still dormant but the ground is shovel ready—around Valentine's Day on Vancouver Island. February is our New Year, a time of preparation and departure and excitement mingled with dread.

I spend my Januarys gazing through windows at the mountains, waiting for the snow line to edge upwards. Then, just when the flowering plum trees push out their first blossoms, I start drumming my fingers and cleaning out the perishables in the fridge. I listen to the weather forecast. When I drag out my caulk boots from storage, they fill my apartment with that old familiar smell of mold, sweat, and petroleum. I oil up my boot leather and screw the soles with brand-new gleaming spikes. I make my trips to the forestry supply store and Mountain Equipment Co-op in the hopes of finding some glove, some supersock that might save me from the impending miseries of outdoor life. It's high time to head out to the cut blocks. I wait for the phone to ring.

The forest has its seasons, too. In winter it sleeps. In spring, when the temperature rises just the right amount above freezing, the soil begins to wake up. The plant world gathers strength. Soon it begins its underground work, knitting and probing and girding itself for the summer's big push. We plant trees in this window, to give our seedlings time to get used to their new environs before the thirsty months set in.

A northern forest must take advantage of the short beneficence of fair weather. And so, too, must we. Like fruit pickers we are a migratory work force. When spring turns to summer we'll travel inland and northward, where the thaw comes later and the snows are more persistent. By Labor Day we'll find our way back to the coast. By late fall the trees harden off in preparation for another winter. The ground frosts over again. It is possible to work as a tree planter from February until October, which nearly negates the need for a home at all. But now we prepare for the rush of work, a new chapter for the arboreal humans, whose lives are measured out not in days or work weeks but in silvicultural increments: seed lots and hectares. Of sleeps and wake-ups. Measured out not in nine-to-fives but in diurnal phases.

A season in the lives of rainforest planters. We have a million trees and then some to plant before the end of spring. Sixty days, says the boss, between us and the solstice. How much is a million trees besides just a number? It's a tower of tree boxes more than one mile high. With the contents, we could forest five hundred Manhattan city blocks. Silviculture is a business of tiny things rolled out in big numbers, like grains of rice, like leaves of tea in China.

THE NORTHERN tip of Vancouver Island, with its rugged folds
and its light dusting of residents, has a history of abandonment.
A century ago the Danes arrived, but a decade later they fled.
Then other Europeans, Canadians, and Americans came. A
hundred years of coming and going, waves of immigrants failing
in their various ways to scrape a living from the rain-soaked land
and the broody, cold ocean. Here nothing wants to grow but
trees. Even the aboriginal peoples have dwindled down, done
their own kind of surviving. They are now called the Nahwitti,
at least by anthropologists. What would they say if we called this
our office, our corner of the world to bash around in?

Far from glinting steel buildings and cappuccino foam and
the breath of a million idling cars. The trip from Vancouver
involves a ferry, four hours of driving, and, finally, a long, winding gravel road over a mountain pass, pocked with holes in the
summer and clotted with snow in winter. A dune of white to
climb with tire chains and snow tires.

On the other side is Holberg, a tiny village of woodcutters.
For our first job of the season we are headquartered here. Houses
nudge up to the jutting inlet amid the tall firs. Trees, trees, trees.
From the snowy peaks right down to the tide line, where sea-
weed often dangles from the lower branches. You could feel
pushed out to the edge of the storm-hammered shore. You could
lose yourself among them.

The village itself is no more than a primary school, a postal
station, a pub, and a convenience store where it is possible to pay
three dollars for a small handful of Gummi Bears. The houses
here are slapped with remaindered paint in peanut-brown, in
the green of Wrigley's Doublemint. In the center of town sits the
biggest stump we have ever seen, hauled from the guts of the
bush. It serves as civic sculpture. Like other logging settlements

on the island, this town grew up in uneasy permanence, built to be dismantled, as if the entire village could decamp any second.

There are twenty of us, and since there is no facility big enough to house us all, we're billeted, like a sports team. Some of us live in rented houses peppered throughout the village. Some of us live in the old logging barracks, known by its somewhat correctional name, E Bunk. The exterior is painted a linty shade of gray. There are no flowers and no birdhouses. E Bunk is a long modular building, the kind common to logging camps, mining operations, and industrial sites everywhere. A long hallway lit by fluorescent tubes, insect carcasses trapped behind pebbled plastic panels. Old lino on the floor, grimed with Rorschachs where our liquids have been spilled and emitted and dripped and tracked in and left to dry.

The kitchen is a communal arrangement. Empty beer vessels rest on every horizontal surface. Half-crumpled cans of Pacific beer, craft-brewed bottles of nut-brown ale. A microwave, three fridges, and an old stove encrusted with hardened goo. Dirty dishes stacked up in the sink. A tea bag with the tag slung over the counter. And behind one of the fridges, quite a few strands of spaghetti are stuck to the wall. The bathroom houses a bank of showers and a short row of toilets, the porcelain enrobed in a fur of dust and pubic hair. There's a sign, written on loose-leaf in black Magic Marker, above one of the toilets that reads: *Poo Bandit: We Are Watching You!*

What use is there for shaving and hygiene and cleanliness when we're only going to get dirty again, when fresh rounds of soiling await us? Besides, with the shortage of women, the lack of civilized company, there is no one to impress. Pot smoke, warm beer, musty footwear. The air is thick with male craving. It condenses and runs down the walls.

Despite all of this, the space is friendly and unabashed. A party all are welcome to join if they can look past the proprietary filth. A long row of private quarters. Ten-foot rooms furnished with single mattresses, in-built desks, and orange chairs made of plastic with ovoid cutouts in the seats. Here we fling ourselves into all kinds of oblivion, tangling our legs in the covers. House-keeping laxity camouflages workday mania. Call us anything but lazy hippies.

WE CAME together at the start of the season, an undifferentiated group of faces. As the early days tick by, names come to mean something—complexions and hair color, our laughs, the way we throw back our lunches, in avid bites or all at once. We get to know the talkers and the joke tellers from the silent observers. Nick. Jake. Brad. Neil. Fin. Jon. The grown-up boys with mono-syllabic names.

Soon our men will grow beards, their last decent haircuts pushing out into long shags. Their faces will become wind burnished. The skin of men who toil outdoors, dawn to dusk, tanned in the blunt light of winter. For now our femaleness is limited. We are just two—Carmen and me—in the early days, when the sun drops from the sky before our workday is even over, plunging us into twilight. Other women are rumored to arrive, and we look forward to that day, because until then we are invisi-ble and outnumbered. Or perhaps we are too visible. We endure the talk of rampaging lust, of toilet habits. We get used to the sweaty tang of them, these dudes who surround us on all sides. Like those crewmen on Circe's island, metamorphosed into pigs.

But, as with families and weather and bad tattoos, what we can't change we learn to love. We work next to these men, plant-ing trees when the wind stirs the forest around like palm trees in a hurricane. When the wind blows our snot sideways from our nostrils. Together we bend and shove trees into the ground when the rain turns to sleet. When the hail comes down like icy BBs. And when our fingers finally give up, freeze into numb things at the end of our wrists, we ask to thaw our hands in their armpits, and they agree. We stand together, in the field, with our hands tucked under their wings, our hoods pulled tight. We gaze into their faces and see that their brute behavior is just a cover. They've been tenderized by inconvenience, the weather pulsing through their hair, running over their scalps, and down the backs of their necks. After all this tapping and needling, their defenses whittle down. What remains is pure personality, turned out, as plain as day. And if it's happening to them, it must be happening to us, too.

Enter Doug, with his wool beret and his temples rutted with wrinkles. His pensive brow and sloe eyes, his voice sweet and creosotey as sauce sizzled down the back of a barbecue. There's K.T., whose nickname derives from the way he scribbles his initials on our daily tally sheets. Enter olive-faced Jon. Tall, with the build of a decathlete and the gentle demeanor of Ferdinand the Bull. He has the kind of eyelashes that make women groan with jealousy. Fin, with his sunbaked blonde hair and his perennial surfer tan. Whose name, he tells us, is spelled like the end of a French movie. When he talks he sounds like Grover from *Sesame Street*.

After just two weeks we know exactly who's disciplined and who's lazy. And who, left half-alone, would pick our gritty pockets clean. You can tell a lot about people—everything, you might say—by how they look over their shoulder when you come up behind them. How they bend down into their work.

Enter the French Canadians, Pierre and Sylvain. They make a code of their crazy Quebec argot. Even though many of us speak rudimentary French, they know we won't understand them. In return we take a name as poetically apt as Sylvain and anglicize it to Sly.

There are the men with matching names, the Daves, the Steves, the Chrisses. And so we resort to surnames, as it goes in the military. Maguire. Davidson. Then Oakley, whose name, like his shape, reminds us of a tree.

Some of us have known each other for years, since the days of pimples and cowlicks. Every year we bumble into each other's company. It's a loose, coincidental friendship. We Facebook in the winter but seldom call, since we've seen too much of one another, overdosed on our common life of planting trees. We've known each other through all kinds of vicissitudes. Through long hair and short hair. Through boom and bust. Through girlfriends and boyfriends, through spouses and children and divorce. All these circumstances somehow figuring from a distance, like a moon hugs the oceans of a planet.

A HORSESHOE of mountains, checkered with clear-cuts. A finger of inlet pushes into the land. In the morning we drive out on the valley main lines, climbing the elevation lines. Young trees dot the valley the way hair grows in after a transplant. The loggers crawl the mountains. We see them across the valley. Their trucks budge around in the distance, like white bars of soap carried by ants. Trucks going up, trucks going down. The tidal motions of bush work, up to the peaks in the morning, down to the main lines in the evenings. Sleep in the valley, toil in the sky.

Logging roads cross-cut the landscape like old surgical scars. Few residents but plenty of business. Every crag and knoll cruised, engineered, divvied up, high-graded, surveyed from the air. *Creamed*, as we are fond of saying. The term is always the same. No matter the province, no matter the branch of the clan. *Cream.* An absence of impediments to the eyes, hands, and feet. Breezy money, soil as open and inviting as beach sand. The more complete the devastation, the more a clear-cut resembles a lunar surface, the bigger our financial slice. We're conflicted about this, if only on the bottom shelves of our minds.

Cream can extend to anything in this world—people, food, love—just like the Dutch word *lekker* refers to all things alluring and delicious. In contrast, we have as many different words for garbage-work as the Inuit use for snow: *snarb, schwag, chud, cack.* Clipped, Germanic nonsense words, uttered from the back of the throat.

The area surrounding Holberg features mountains rolling down to the Pacific like the soft folds of a blanket tossed over a bed. Nobody has ever logged or ever planted back here before, and the forest floor is untrammeled. The soil is cushy with wine-dark humus built up by hundreds of years of forest creatures growing and dying and dispersing back down into dirt. This job, despite our complaints, is a cream show. Perhaps we complain *because* it's a cream show. If we pause in our bitching about the tree prices, the accommodation, or the weather, maybe someone will whisk our good fortunes away. We believe the good times will never end, like Niagara Falls will never end.

But there's a catch. It's a crapshoot.

Today we drive our trucks into a new cut block, ripping new ruts in the road. We stop abruptly at a broad crack in the gravel surface where a culvert has been dug out by a backhoe. We get out and prepare to walk the rest of the way. We peer out over jumbles of logs on the roadside's downward slough. Our noses work the air for the smell of fresh soil, of fragrant mineral rot. Our eyes skim the land for the story of our day's wages, a hint about our upcoming fortunes. We catch sight of a stretch of beautiful dream-cream. Fresh logging, a sumptuous pancake, plowed clean of debris, we guess, by an overzealous skidder driver looking to chew through some company time. We edge as close as we can without stumbling down the bank. Some of us let out the moans of dogs at the park, trapped behind car windows.

But it's real estate only one person can have. Brian scribbles on a shred of cardboard torn from the corner of a tree box. He folds it up and puts it in his pocket.

Pick a number, he tells us, from one to a thousand.

Where else is livelihood based on game show rules? We huddle, glancing at each other sidelong. We go around in a circle, announcing our numbers. Some pick low; others too high. I am one of those people who never win anything. Not grocery store pull tabs, not door prizes, not scratch-and-win lottery tickets. But today my number comes up.

Shit, say my workmates, drawing the word out into syllables.

I drop my bags and my dry sack, my boots and my drinking water. The rest of the crew members heave their kits over their shoulders, their shovels with the handles worn down by thousands of slides of the palm. They trudge on down the road in hopes of better fortunes. It's a terrible freak pleasure, getting away with cream, since it almost always comes at someone else's expense.

Sean, our most senior vet, has the misfortune of doing the ugly top side, which affords him a view of my bounty. He watches me through the morning, as neighbors do. I watch him, too. I go back and forth, climbing up to the road to refill my bags again while he's trapped on his weedy knoll. At noon he climbs down from his piece to bag up and find some lunch. He stops above me and leans on his shovel.

Hey, guess what? he shouts down to me. I'm writing a book, too! It's called *Run, Charlotte, Run!*

It might be difficult to imagine people fighting over a blasted tract of land, but scarcely a day goes by without some kind of blowup—border disputes and competitive riling and schadenfreude. We're like cavemen with a hunk of trophy meat to be carved up into pieces. We're superstitious, perhaps to hide the fact that our job is mercilessly, randomly fair—or unfair, as the case may be. We have no unions, no benefits, no holidays. When the work runs out we're laid off. Our bosses bid for jobs at silent auctions, and so all our perks come bundled inside the tree price. Everyone gets their time in the weeds.

At the end of a day, cream or crap, we are still the same old blue-collar mortals. I'm a few hundred dollars further away from zero, no more or less happy, with an aching lumbar, throbbing feet, and a pile of empty tree boxes so big I wonder if we plant trees just to compensate for all the cardboard. Brian comes by and snaps a photo of this tower. Then we light it on fire. The cardboard has been waterproofed with wax, which sizzles up like a Roman candle. Sean comes down from the hills to join us. Late in the afternoon, dusk slips over our shoulders. We feel the chill of evaporating sweat. We hold our hands to the flames to get warm. We rotate from front to back, like chickens on a rotisserie, as smoke pours into the sky.

We're offsetting our offsets, we say.

SOME OF us live in the logging barracks down in the village of Holberg. Some of us are marooned on the edge of town in the "motel," though there is no neon sign to indicate that's what it is. The motel is a compound of dwellings with a muddy parking lot where dogs roam, pooping with impunity. Inside these units, we find mouse droppings in all the cupboards, and in the drawers, plates of toxic-looking turquoise pellets. Our bathroom has a tub with a dissolving nylon shower curtain and peach-colored slime all along the hem. Our toilet flushes with a disposable razor tied to a string. But there is TV, always good satellite TV, no matter where in the wilds we find ourselves. We wander around opening and closing doors, turning *Survivor* on and off. What are we doing besides looking for an escape hatch?

The couples live here because it's the only place with double beds. I share a small cluster of rooms with K.T. The walls smell of cigarettes, and the carpet shows the footprints of the previous tenants, but we are delighted by this secret boon, a privacy the residents of E Bunk will never know. We cross the threshold and shut the door, feeling as if we've gotten away with something.

K.T. is built like a basketball player—tall, with long-fingered hands and ropy forearms. He plants trees like Wayne Gretzky plays hockey, with speed and finesse that elude his own explanations.

If I could clone your boyfriend, our boss often says, I'd be a rich and happy man.

K.T.'s appetite for work is matched by an astounding through-put of food. He eats for fuel and not for taste. When he inhales an entire box of whole-wheat spaghetti, I'm reminded of eating's thermogenic purpose. Tomorrow these carbohydrates will be converted into human effort, calories transformed into muscle flexion.

K.T. is a goofball Newfoundlander, and I am often the victim of his foolery and leg pulling. It's a trait his whole family seems to share, expressing their love with gags and ribbing. He's also a fastidious person, with an aversion to disarray, dust, and filth—it's a masochistic miracle that he's chosen the planting life.

When he comes down with a cold or gets injured he's shocked by his own mutineering cells. He's been planting trees for as long as I have. And like me he's seldom worn sunscreen. It shows around our eyes and especially at the back of our necks, where the skin is as tired as an old lady's purse.

In the evenings we attack a fresh batch of chores. We divide and conquer. The boots need oiling, holes need patching, wet clothes need to be hung up to dry. And then we address our bodies, applying salve to the chafe, ice to the elbows, Band-Aids to the hang nails. We tend to ourselves as farmers feed their livestock.

Do you want cheese in your sandwich tomorrow?

I can't face another sandwich.

Yes or no. Just answer the question.

After the chores K.T. and I watch TV. Often enough, it's just the Weather Network, an analgesic for the brainwaves. At nine o'clock K.T. strips down and folds his clothes into neat, retail squares, as salesclerks do in stores. I step out of mine, leaving my pants on the floor in rumpled, inside-out tubes. Our bodies buzz with fatigue. We collapse on a worn mattress, rolling into the trough, where we'll bump spines later in the night. During the tree-planting season K.T. falls asleep faster than anyone I've ever known, often in midsentence. Then we drift apart, our muscles electric and twitchy with the ghost motions of the day.

When we go to work we're like all kinds of modern working couples—pulling for the team but seldom in each other's company. But here we also work shoulder to shoulder, united in a common purpose. Slash romance: part dirt, part soldier love, annealed in weather and necessity. I wear an engagement ring on days off but remove it when it's time to get dirty again. I keep it in a Ziploc bag hidden inside a shoe.

Nobody wears precious things to a cut block. If you lose some small object—a button, a contact lens—you will never see it again. It's like dropping your car keys down a sewer grate or an earring in the ocean. Once you take your eyes from the spot where you lost it, the view ripples over with repetitive shapes that go on in every direction as far as the eye can see.

SIX BILLION trees planted in the province of British Columbia. An unfathomable number, but not quite as mind-boggling as the size of the forest they replace. With these trees you could replant an area roughly the size of Sri Lanka. At the height of the trade there were an estimated 18,500 tree planters in this country, which is about the number of soldiers in the Canadian army. The average career lasts five seasons.

The first tree planters in these woods were unemployed men put to work by the government in Depression-era relief programs. Conscientious objectors planted trees during World War II. They used grub hoes, rendering the work even more ergonomically unfriendly than it is now. They carried seedlings in buckets and burlap shoulder bags, which they put down to rest every time they dug a hole. They planted in crews of a dozen men, working in rows, separated by an arm span or two. Many were Mennonites who'd been shipped far from the Prairies. They were farmers, used to hard physical labor. Work reminded them of home. Their enthusiasm was also a way to transform punishment into a kind of reward. We know this, too. Hard work done reluctantly is more torturous than work done fast and well.

In the sixties the government again made use of the unemployed, along with prison inmates, for its silvicultural labor force. Men worked for fixed wages, planting quotas of just four hundred trees a day—what an average modern planter can pull off in an hour or two. Reforestation began as community service, as rehab for the planters just as much as for the land. There is something of the misfit rebellion that still endures today.

Tree planting, in its modern, high-speed incarnation, has only been around for forty years. Some say it began in the Purcell Mountains. Some say the first professional tree planters were American draft dodgers hiding out on the coast. Maybe nobody can identify the first professional tree planter, but at some point nearly everyone in the business mentions Dirk Brinkman.

In the early seventies, Brinkman was a long-haired tree planter with an entrepreneurial streak who got the idea to bid for his own contracts. At the time most crews still used the old shoulder bags for hauling trees, as well as that medieval implement, the mattock. Brinkman got his hands on specially manufactured seedling carriers—a prototype of the current ergonomic design.

These newfangled satchels sped things up considerably, but more than that, a new kind of mindset took hold. If you could learn to think of manual labor as a sport instead of purgatory, then you could train to become more efficient. You could learn to keep all your parts moving and to perform several motions all at once. When you decreased the number of movements, you shaved seconds. Seconds collected into minutes, and cents cascaded into dollars. Then, as with one of those demonic Sudoku puzzles, the code had been broken. It wasn't long before everyone caught on. Production doubled and then tripled. Dirk Brinkman didn't invent tree planting, but you could say he helped turn it from industrial gardening into a competitive, peak-performance event.

Dirk Brinkman is now the CEO of one of the biggest reforestation companies in the Americas. Even the Brinkman children plant trees. They look as if they were genetically engineered for it, tall and lean and broad shouldered. Brinkman's wife, Joyce Murray, also a former tree planter, is a Member of Parliament. At official ceremonies, when she plants a tree, she might be the only politician who really knows what she's doing.

IN RICH countries and poor countries, tree planters poke at the dirt with hoes and digging sticks and even earth-moving machinery. People plant trees as carbon credit enterprises. On Arbor Day troops of Boy Scouts break out the shovels. City dwellers plant trees in urban parklands to beautify and oxygenate their neighborhoods. When we do it between the stumps on industrial logging sites it's called reforestation. When a woodlot is planted in an old, abandoned field, it's known as afforestation—though in some cases this fallow turf was also once a forest, albeit many generations ago. Then the only difference between these two concepts—between forest renewal and forests anew—is time.

Wherever men make it their business to cut down trees, chances are you'll find people who make a job of putting them back. Tree slingers. Johnny Appleseeds for hire. Often we work in commodity backwaters, beyond public view, toiling away at the broken land. Mostly, we're invisible. Still, we've seen photos of tree planters elsewhere: in Australia, New Zealand, and Costa Rica. They look a lot like us, dirty and tired and occasionally smiling. We even wear the same tools.

In the United States our counterparts are Mexican migrant workers. *Pineros*, they are called. Like us, they're temporary, seasonal, and nonunionized. *Pineros* migrate, too. They begin in the southern states in the fall and then arrive in the Pacific Northwest come spring. They're a long way from home. And just like us, they're pieceworkers. No pennies drop into the piggy bank until the trees go into the ground, no matter the commute or the daily detours or the plethora of prelude chores. But unlike us, they have no insurance, no way into the clinic when they injure themselves, no backstop when they're laid off.

Many *pineros* live below the poverty line, earning less than five thousand dollars a year. Sometimes they work on private timberlands, sometimes in national forests. Mainly they work for contractors, some of whom are shady middlemen. And so *pineros* endure the usual array of occupational abuses. Their paychecks are mysteriously docked or withheld altogether, or their passports are held for ransom. But unlike us they can't complain. They have temporary H-2B visas, but quite a few have no documents of any kind. As many as twenty thousand Mexicans grunt it out in shorn valleys, out of sight and out of mind.

CLEAR-CUTS ARE illogical landscapes, lunar in their barrenness yet bristling with big texture. The bucked limbs, the twisted trunks, and the rotten heartwood. The logs worth less than the cost of the haul to market. Traveling through clear-cuts is an unstable, three-dimensional affair. Imagine a field piled thick with car parts, knitting needles, coat hangers. Imagine climbing through hurricane wreckage. Add slope and cliffs and waterfalls and weather. Our technique for walking is like jujitsu, performed with both the hands and feet. Slash is a forest's postmortem revenge, a sharp-toothed terrestrial sea. It's not our fault, but it might as well be. Every day the land takes a bite out of us.

There is a clear-cut in the Bowron River valley, three hundred miles northeast of Vancouver, that's the size of a small nation. The largest clear-cut in the world—roughly two hundred square miles. When the cut was fresh, it could be seen from

space. In British Columbia we live among clear-cuts like people of the tropics live in the sugarcane. When we fly over our
province we see shaved slopes. When we drive, slash and stumps
are a highway blur through our windshields. Cut blocks, they
are called in the logging trade, like something you could snip at
with scissors.

The block, as we've come to call it. The bucked limbs, the
reject logs, and the shattered scraps, all of it sun worn and gray.
We've seen fallen logs as big as buses, slash piled high as a house.
A sudden flattening of monstrous biomass, like whalebones
spread out on a beach. Up above us, slash teeters from the ledges
of rock bluffs. Down below it drops abruptly away. Rolling, tumbling, pulled by gravity, settling glacially down into itself.

The chainsaws across the valley sound like mad mosquitoes.
We find the loggers' traces, the crumpled cans, the Coke and
the Budweiser, the abandoned jerry cans. We hear machinery
clanking and grinding, logs scraped down the mountainsides
along skylines of wire rope. Loggers cut. We plant. It's a strange
industrial marriage. And yet, when we look at what's gone, it
seems like more wood than the world could possibly use. We
drape ourselves across the stumps as if they were king-sized beds.
Does it get to the loggers? Is it getting to us?

Our jokes are associative, communal creations. We fire our
verbal rockets into the cosmos, quips that travel out, never to
return. We cook up schemes to start a carbon offset business.
We'll sell green credits on the side. We'll plant our trees with
nameplates, the way the International Star Registry sells twin-
kling points in the night sky. Keep on truckin', everyone. Crank
out more Kleenex, more Starbucks cups, more IKEA coffee
tables. By all means, please, mow down the planet. World, we've
got you covered.

IF WE were to close our eyes at the start of a shift and open them at the end, nothing would look the same—not the scenery, not the weather, not even the people, since our crew is always in flux. Someone is always joining or quitting or rotating through, like traveling salesmen, touring circuses, or flight attendants at an airport bar. Sometimes people stay for as little as a single day before migrating to another crew. The most we can remember about them is the brand of their boots or what they ate for lunch; we might not even recall their names. Showing up, then evaporating—as if they'd never come along in the first place.

Must've been a pretty bad day, we joke.

Maguire is the first to quit. He got jumped outside the pub by some local guys, two logger roughnecks with itchy knuckles. He mangled his fist defending himself. Brad and Doug, who witnessed the fight, went to the cops to report what they'd seen. Some officers took Brad's statement on a scrap of crumpled paper that looked as if it had been plucked from the recycling bin.

To keep the crew full, the boss does continuous rounds of hiring. Fresh recruits, sent our way like numbered Ping-Pong balls in a lottery, pneumatically blown up the pipe. Travis arrives one day with a gaunt face and scruff inching down his neck, looking like he hasn't eaten or slept in a month. He wears dreadlocks, the kind that gather unintentionally near the nape of an unkempt neck. His backpack was stolen in town, he tells us, snatched out of the open bed of a truck. He lost an array of valuables, including his wallet and his medication. *Tells* is not precisely right, since the information arrives by chance, as our gossip always does, like old grocery bags blown by the wind. Travis is a recovering addict. And a recently diagnosed schizophrenic. Or so the rumor goes.

In the field Travis beguiles us. We come across his belongings, strewn on the road's chunky shoulder like garage sale
inventory. We look around but can't find him anywhere, as if
he's been absorbed into the land. When we brush up against his
handiwork, it's hidden in the underbrush. We bend to plant and
find his trees at our feet, choked in ferns and brush. They are
unhappy things, only half-planted, protruding from their holes.
We fix them up sometimes, put them straight in the soil. One
or two, until there are too many to repair, and then we turn
around and flee.

One day Brian and I catch sight of Travis at work in the field.
We stand on the road observing from a distance, as spectators
watch athletes warming up around a track. His planting style is
a long, exhausted stumble followed by a furious pounce. Brian
explains that Travis has been going to work on an empty stomach. He says he can't afford groceries.

If we know what it's like to plant trees on an empty stomach,
it only happens by accident. Sometimes we leave our lunches
behind on the countertops. Or our day bags are ransacked by
ravens or bears or planters' pet dogs. Our blood sugar plummets.
By noon we stumble around in a hypoglycemic haze. Our hands
fumble, and we tangle our feet in the smallest branches. Our
limbs feel like they weigh a thousand pounds. We plant trees,
just like Travis does now, with hunger scratching at our bellies.

Travis dips down over the rise. Brian puffs out his cheeks
and lets out a long, weary sigh. He pats himself down, as if
remembering something crucial he left on the other side of the
world. Then he throws himself into his truck and peels away. I
catch sight of an escaped seedling that fell out of Travis's bags.
It hangs from a branch, swaying in the breeze, even now drying
out and dying.

Back in the kitchens of home, it is reported, food is going missing. Not the iPods or the MasterCards or the laptops. Just the edibles and the drinkables, but never so much that anyone notices. A bottle of beer, a glug of milk, a few slices of bread. We might confuse ourselves into believing we'd consumed these things ourselves. Adam and Brian find empty beer cans rolling around in the back of the trucks. Just one or two, every other day, amid the wet chaff that slops around with our planting bags and tree boxes, the flagging tape rejects and the rotten apple cores.

Crew life enforces togetherness. There is no fate suffered by just one person. No way to hide even the simplest emotion. If we are mad or sad or have come unglued, everyone will know it, sometimes before we do. Our cut blocks are graded like final exams. When one person fails in his or her daily work, we all sink a little bit. There is no way to forget your lunch or your water or your extra dry clothes without impinging on someone else's. We're a hundred miles from the nearest hospital. The only ambulance is our ETV, a work-thrashed Ford F-350 with a fiberglass canopy. Our emergency room is a backpack stuffed with first aid supplies and a spine board strapped to the roof rack. If we fall down and crack our backs or get stung by a hornet and swell up like blimps or puncture our veins or get poked in the eyes, we can only hope, when we shout for help, that someone decides to hear us.

Travis develops a bad case of tendinitis in his wrist, which he splints with a tensor bandage and a brace. Because of this vulnerability or perhaps to push it along, we start to call Travis by his last name, which is coincidentally the same as that of a famous Hollywood nutcase. It escapes one set of lips, and then it catches on until we're all doing it. It must have been this way with fire and cavemen, with plagues in the time before penicillin.

You've got to fire that guy, we tell the big boss. Before he runs out of rope.

ROLAND IS the company owner. His Chevy Avalanche is a rolling office, like the bookmobile. We get used to seeing just his upper portions leaning out through the driver's-side window.

No part of Roland is small. Even his salt-and-pepper hair is big. Some of us say he's the tallest, most expansive man we've ever met. He's French Swiss, a Euro Paul Bunyan, in glasses with buffed steel frames and enough Patagonia GORE-TEX to make a pup tent. He used to be a hippie, a dyed-in-the-wool Brinkman blowhard. We have seen old photos of him alongside Dirk, surrounded by a whole crew kitted out in Icelandic sweaters, big beards, and long hair parted straight down the middle. They look exactly like us except for their general level of hirsuteness. The grubby knuckles, the ruddy, just-scrubbed facial sheen. The ridiculous, reflexive smiles. The coils of wire rope in the backdrop, the wood planks, the industrial outdoors that resemble the mud bogs of destitute Appalachia. Back then, Roland told me, they worked in a big co-op. One person stayed home every day to stir the soup and bake bread and sometimes to care for the children. He mentioned a wall chart they kept in a company office diagramming which tree planter had slept with whom. It turned into a spiderweb, too crosshatched to be useful.

Roland lives in the small island community of Alert Bay. He raised his kids on soy milk and organic granola. They are not tree planters, these strapping boys. They are athletes and university students. But we are Roland's children, too. At work, if the weather is awful or if we're having a sad, unproductive shift, Roland carves out room for us and flicks on the seat warmers. We cram in amid bales of toilet paper, Perrier bottles, and *Harper's* magazines. He prods through our lunches with his index finger and high-grades the Chips Ahoy. In return we smear the mud around on his leather seats.

Roland has a heart as soft as a round of brie, but we think he could break a chair in two with his bare hands if we got him angry enough.

WHEN TREE planters get fired there are no termination letters or requests for resignation. We're *axed* or *chopped, booted* or *shit-canned*. Gone down the road, quite literally. On the day of our first official shit-canning, Travis is the last to know.

I'm not on the list, he suggests at our morning meeting.

Adam puts a hand on Travis's shoulder. Today, says Adam, you ride with the boss.

We know precisely what this ride will entail. We've seen it before with many of Roland's unfortunate hires. Roland can't bear to fire anyone. It takes him many days of agonizing and hand-wringing, but in the end Travis's occupational breakup will take about an hour, which is the length of time required to drive from Holberg to the highway, where the Greyhound buses connect. The Avalanche whizzes down the road. Roland and Travis sit side by side with their elbows on the armrest, peering glumly through the windshield, like a dad and his criminal son.

Goodbye, little bastard. Have a nice life.

For the rest of us, that morning, it's back to the salt mines as usual. When we arrive at the block, white sunlight knifes through torn, bulbous clouds—a sign the monsoon is breaking up.

What is that glowing orb thing burning up in the sky?

I don't know, we joke. But, goddamn, it hurts my eyes.

Today the ravens soar by with their heads and tail flaps swiveling, in search of lunches to attack with their cunning beaks.

Ravens and crows, both members of the Corvid family, are the weisenheimers of the bird world. As we work, they sit on stumps heckling us with their caws and catcalls. They hop along the logging roads, strutting around in their lustrous black feathers as if they were little Armani suits. Crows are just like us, at home in both the cities and the woods.

Crows and ravens know how zippers, Tupperware, and Velcro work, as rookie planters often discover the hard way. These birds hang out in complexly hierarchical organizations. They have dialects and gang signs. They mate for life but then cheat on each other. They're burglars and nest raiders. They collect secret caches of flashy, colorful objects that seem to have no function at all. Rumor has it they'll gang up on one of their own kind, if they see the need, and carry out an execution. And then they'll hold a funeral for their departed. A silent vigil before they lift off, all at once, and flap away.

Do you know the difference between a crow and a raven? Sean asks me in the afternoon.

Is this a joke? I reply.

A raven has an extra feather, says Sean, so it's a matter of a pinion.

If tree planters have a mascot, surely it's the crow.

On the ramble home at the end of the day, we turn to a common topic of discussion: all the ways tree planters can die on the job. You can lose your footing and tumble from a cliff. You can impale yourself on a stick. You can be mauled by bears or scalped by a cougar's claws. You can get lost in a hypothermic delirium. Your boat sinks, and you drown on the frigid swim to shore. You can quit, get left behind on a roadside, then vanish in the gnarl of the bush. A tree falls in a windstorm, pinning you to the ground. Or you can get drunk, climb behind the wheel of a truck, and flip yourself into a lake on some urgent, breakneck tear. There is a deadly fungus whose spores puff up from the soil. Bend. Plant. Stand up. Move along.

You can also commit suicide, someone says.

Despite all of this, our job isn't extreme or deadly or heroic. We have no power tools, no heavy machinery. No guns, no explosives, no underwater breathing. Planting trees is merely almost dangerous. Only as precarious as the speed at which we do it, or how many things we try to juggle at once.

THE WORLD record for planting trees is held by a man named Ken Chaplin, who pounded 15,170 red pine seedlings into a creamy Saskatchewan plain in a single summer day. A record achieved with two sets of planting bags, four tree-planting spades, and three pairs of boots. Not to mention about four days' worth of calories, incredible musculoskeletal stamina, and no small amount of mental fortitude. Similar feats are pulled off with surprising regularity in the silvicultural backwoods, without TV cameras, fanfare, or *Guinness Book* adjudicators. Using techniques devised, once upon a time, by Brinkman and his crew of ur-planters.

When one person plants a huge number of trees all by himself, it's an athletic feat. When many people plant trees all together, it's a movement. In July 2009, a group of three hundred Pakistani villagers stitched 541,176 mangrove seedlings into intertidal mud flats at the mouth of the Indus River. They were all volunteers. Their town was once a thriving port city. But now upstream irrigation siphons off much of the river's flow. Without this freshwater discharge the soil suffers from saltwater intrusion, which poisons their once-fertile agricultural lands. Mangrove trees are a hardy species, able to withstand the region's extreme temperatures and high salinity. But the mangrove forests of the delta have all but disappeared. So too has the marine habitat these trees once provided, compromising the fishery on which many of the locals depend.

Tree-planting efforts proceed every day, sometimes with official billing, but mostly with no headlines or photo ops at all. Oftentimes they take place in fragile, compromised environments. Lands with long, high-traffic histories. Generations of plowing, grazing, and by-hand deforestation have exacted a slow toll that nature can no longer pay back. Chances are, the tree planters are locals. In another time they might have been called peasants. They are the fishermen and shepherds whose livelihoods are tied to the environment in the most primary and susceptible of ways. They plant trees because they've been involuntarily retired from their traditional ways of life, by edict or circumstance or both. Sometimes they've been assigned to the task by their governments, put to work in rehabilitative tree-planting programs. They are farmers whose fields have turned to dust.

Some live in hideously degraded conditions. Their hills are denuded, their valleys alternately ravaged by droughts and flooding. When dust storms howl through, the sky turns burnt orange. In the aftermath the villagers find their houses drifted over to the eaves with dirt. They're forced to dig themselves out of their front doors. When it rains mountains disintegrate, deluging the rivers with tons of mud and grit. Year by year lakes fill in with sediment. Deserts expand. Dry dunes swallow up highways and encroach on major cities. It's a constant war for the locals, who must shovel and bulldoze it back.

These scenes might seem biblical, or like glimpses of a dystopian future, but they are a reality in present-day China. After centuries of tree felling and intensive farming, firewood collection and charcoal making, much of China's landscape has been irredeemably altered. Many of the original forests and grasslands are gone, cleared to make way for settlement and agriculture. China is 27 percent desert but possesses only 10 percent of the world's arable land, and with this slender allotment of fertile ground the country must feed more than a billion people.

The largest tree-planting initiative in the world is unfolding in China. The Chinese have planted billions of trees since 1978 in a collection of projects known as the Great Green Wall, an environmental rehab offensive designed to undo centuries of erosive land practices. The work is done largely by an army of subsistence farmers. The Gobi Desert is expanding at a rate of about 950 square miles annually. Sand dunes are but an hour's drive from Beijing, and it's thought they could reach city limits by 2040. The jury is out on whether all this tree planting is having any effect. Skeptics say the problem is too complex and entrenched, the land too parched to support a forest. Only time will tell.

THE FREEZE creeps down the mountainsides. We wake up to it at dawn, blanketing the contours beyond the windows with an eerie, purplish white. When it snows everything grinds to a halt in the woods. Nature pads itself against us. Even the chain saws fall silent.

Some of us attempt the drive to Port Hardy, though the pass is snowbound, the road to civilization deep and unplowed. On the road from Holberg, where the line on the map turns from solid to dotted, there is a cedar snag nailed with thousands of shoes. Boots worn by intrepid hikers on the way to Cape Scott, as if the old soles exhausted themselves on the voyage. As if these visitors had climbed up and over and become different people, grew new footprints on the other side.

It's here that we meet a traveling kitchenware salesman, in the notch of the pass. His name is Gunter. His wheels are caked with snow. We help him dress his tires in chains, which he produces still tagged and boxed from the trunk of his Jetta.

We're tree planters, we tell him.

Thank you for healing the planet, he says.

After that he gives each of us a glinting knife, the kind that never needs sharpening.

Some of us spend the day back in Holberg without even venturing outside. We hole up in front of the TV, roaming the highs and lows of the satellite spectrum. We sprawl over unmade beds. Tree planting is like this, full-throttle production interrupted by jags of furious waiting. No one does it better than us. We push endless variations of fat and sugar into our mouths. We're bored by our own taste buds, and the boredom feeds our hunger.

In the evening our feet deliver us to the pub. The Scarlet Ibis, a cavern of darkened wood and old carpet, the same red shag featured in the motel. Beyond the windows, the end of the inlet, a diminishing, muddy tide. A wood stove that can't keep up with the draft. We spend the afternoon here, tipping back beer, watching clumps of snow drop from the eaves. The owner's name is Pat, a sturdy, jolly woman with a Dorothy Hamill pageboy and a thing for snug-fitting polyester.

The locals trickle in, mostly men in their late forties and fifties with pot bellies and slow, easy demeanors. Union-shop old-timers who take coffee breaks at the control levers of graders, yarders, skidders, backhoes. Old loggers whose chain saws have inflicted a million cuts and back cuts, dug into the bark of countless trees. Like us, they can drink. It's something we have in common. By dinnertime our crew accumulates. We're celebrating. Travis is gone, and in his place more women have joined our ranks. Rose is a child of tree-planter parents. She wears an urban bob with a bleached streak and a Hudson's Bay Company Eskimo parka. Melissa is an Australian with a constant smile, a spray of brown freckles, buxom lips. Heads turned when they arrived. There were sudden bouts of shaving.

We order jugs of generic brew, whatever flows from the taps. K.T. orders a nonalcoholic beer. Our server makes a face and scratches her scalp with her pen. She comes back with a bottle coated with whitish rime.

Just so you know, she tells him. That's not frost on the bottle. It's dust.

Plates of food arrive. French fries, steak sandwiches, lasagna. We hover, fork tines poised. Missing parties who go to smoke outside or disappear to the bathroom sacrifice their dinners to our insatiable mouths. We weave between tables in an air of happy drunkenness. Pat eyes us wearily. She's seen this routine, or versions of it, every night of the week for years and years. She stands behind the bar with her hand waiting for the debit machine to spit out a tongue of paper. She blows a strand of hair out of her eyes.

In the corner sits a mannequin stuffed with old quilt batting and pantyhose for skin. He wears a baseball cap, a flannel shirt, and a pair of bucking pants held up with orange Husqvarna suspenders. His hand stuffed into the handle of a pint mug filled with crumpled brown cellophane. We spend an hour passing him around, snapping photos, holding him in various forms of romantic embrace. We jostle the tables. We spill the beer. We hold our lighter flames to his extremities. The smell of burnt synthetic fiber fills our noses. We're one beat away from dragging him outside and sacrificing him to the gods.

THE GRUNT work penetrates. It gets inside us, one layer at a time, from our epithelial layers to the innermost connective tissue. In the beginning we collected blisters on our hands and feet. They filled with fluid, only to break and rub away. Now we're bruised on the hips from the weight of our bags, hairless on the thighs from the friction. The chapped lips, the broken fingernails. We fray along the edges.

Manual toil is not just a labor of the hand, like knitting or surgery or diamond cutting. The whole body becomes involved, including the mind. If we're lucky we reach a Zen state in which impulses flow between the nerve endings in our fingertips to the brain's motor controls, bypassing our intellect almost totally. Time whooshes by while appearing to stand still, and the mental chatter falls silent. When we stand up straight at the end of the day we're changed in some small way, as if we've walked out of a theater after a marathon movie. We've been somewhere else. A return to the self after an existential pause.

We fall from the trucks at dawn. Nine hours later we crawl back in, stooped like gorillas, feeling as if we've been pummeled by small, firm objects, maybe lemons in a pillowcase. Our hands are scratched and scabbed, our finger pads etched with dirt. Swollen and pulsating, they feel like the hands of cartoon characters when they bash themselves with hammers. A fatigue so thorough it bungles speech, so deep the whole world gleams.

We came chubby and pale at the end of the winter. In just a few short weeks, we shrink down and harden, like boot leather dried too fast. We have calluses on top of calluses, piled up on our palms and soles. We have washboard backs as well as stomachs. Arms ropy, muscled and veined. We consume five thousand calories every day. Food goes down without much chewing—not so much eaten as garburated. At night we nose-dive into sleep with our engines still gunning, to the sound of our own venous hum.

Everything grows fast. Our hair, our fingernails. Blood whizzes through us. When we cut ourselves we gush horrifying amounts of blood, but in the morning we wake to find new skin grown over the wound. At the same time, sleep ages us. We roll out of bed like Tin Men after a rainstorm. Our big toes go numb, become just tingling protrusions, a pull of skin and bone. You've got to give a slice of youthful zeal, kill yourself a little bit each day.

{ 3 }

ROOKIE YEARS

IN OUR FIRST years as tree planters the wooden carnage was shocking. The skin of the earth pulled back, revealing a sad, organic gore. We wanted to cry but couldn't. Said we would quit but didn't. A numbness of attention crept over us, of the sort induced by megamall parking lots. There was nothing to jazz our rods and cones. We were growing up, paying taxes, burning holes in our own pockets. We were learning to see without seeing.

Who talked us into this? Who gave us our first taste of tree planting? A brother, an old roommate, a friend who slept on the couch—it's always someone else's fault. Whoever it was, they hooked us, poured it into us with their stories of pay dirt and adventure. We let it slip down our throats. We drove rust-chewed jalopies west through the flatlands. We practiced with Popsicle sticks in the flower beds of our parents' backyards. We were young and impressionable. We needed maps just to find our way back home.

Now we could plant trees blindfolded in a pair of flip-flops. Lifers, we call ourselves, as junkies talk about one another. Where is the friend, where is the pusher now? He's a real estate agent. Or she's a mom behind the wheel of an suv, with scars on her shins to remind herself how she could bend and yet be strong.

ONCE, BEFORE I had ever planted a single tree, I lived in Toronto, in a student house, a decaying Victorian manor with bad heating and narrow windows that faced in all the sunless directions. I bought a potted fig tree to spruce up my room. Over the winter I watched its foliage yellow and drop off and whisper to the ground. It wasn't so easy to make a green thing grow.

Six or seven people lived here at any given time, not including boyfriends and girlfriends. Aimee was our alpha female. She had big, curly hair. She clomped around in leather boots with wooden heels. She wore scarves that fell to her knees and miniskirts from sutured scraps of leather. I never saw her in athletic shoes of any kind. She introduced me to a lot of printed words. Al Purdy. Gwendolyn MacEwen. Tom Robbins. The Beats. People who ate drugs and lived like hobos and fell wildly in love and lit up the skies with their voyages through the cosmos.

Aimee was a tree planter. When the spring came around she went out to the Ontarian backwoods and sowed seedlings with her hands. I had never heard of tree planting before. I pictured people conveying seedlings in wheelbarrows. Kneeling in the dirt, patting baby plants down with gentle fingers the way gardeners bed cuttings in potting soil.

That seems easy enough, I said.

Planting trees. A job couldn't get more self-explanatory. I was still imagining girls running barefoot through meadows tossing seeds from their aprons.

Aimee told me about the first time she went out on the job. At the end of the day she crawled into her sleeping bag in all her dirty clothes. She slept for eleven hours. Just describing it, she sounded tired. I thought she was going to tell me she slept the whole next day, but she got up to do it all over again. She told me she'd seen grown men cry.

What else? I asked.

She showed me photos. She didn't have a camera, but her tree-planting amigos had sent her snapshots in the mail. I looked through these rumpled photographic specimens. Aimee wearing a head scarf, her wild frizz escaping in the wind. Aimee looking wiry and deranged by fatigue, dirty about the face. Aimee in tank tops, armpit hair poking out at the sides. She wore round, wire-rimmed spectacles, etched with a haze of scratches. I had seen these glasses. She wore them whenever her contact lenses grew gummy with optic proteins. This tree planting had battered the lenses to hell, and she was left seeing the world through a scratchy mist.

The land depicted in the photos looked flat, the ground littered with gray, broken wood that receded forever into the distance. An ugly place, the color of newsprint, but not one that came alive in photos. No matter how many she showed me, I still couldn't see what she meant.

Are these all you have? I asked, craving more.

Aimee's boyfriend's name was Dave. Dave was a tree planter, too. Once in a while he visited from Halifax, where he claimed to be studying design. He showed up across unfathomable stretches of Canadian geography, emerging from the darkness beyond the kitchen window, giving whoever was washing the dishes a fright. He came out of the winter blitz wearing a mere corduroy blazer, a scarf wound several times about the neck. He was a lanky man, of indeterminate ethnicity, his jacket second-hand, the arms too short. He carried a small, battered backpack and a guitar in a worn hardback case, plucked from alleyway trash on the way over. Urban hunter-gathering, he called it.

All winter long our house was full of Aimee's friends. They came with backpacks stuffed tight, suitcases with braided rope for handles, beat-up vans that you could hear coming a block away, mufflers wired to chassis with coat hangers. They came for a day and stayed for a week. They carried brandy and brie. They smelled like smoke and sweat and sandalwood soap, the spice of the wild, wide open world in their hair. They all dressed differently. They wore different smiles. But they were the same somehow under the skin and behind the eyes. They had a con-spiratorial way of glancing at each other, like they were getting away with something. They liked to get drunk and laugh. They tossed their heads back, and I caught sight of their fillings. They spoke the languages of the places they'd traveled to, wherever they'd spent their winters. But they spoke another language as well, a patois of bulletlike verbs and nouns to do with the plant-ing of trees. *Cream. Duff. Slash. Crummy.* When they talked about work, I could barely understand them. They had a way of making English sound grubby and strange.

Tree planters seemed to have some curious thing in com-mon—a furious way of being. I knew this from the way Dave burst into a house, breathlessly, like he'd narrowly escaped exhilarating disaster, tumbled from a fire with his clothes still smoking. He was always moving, bobbing, flowing from one action to the next. He insinuated wind. He never called first, and he never arrived by the front door. And when he left it was as if he'd vanished, picked a moment when you weren't looking so he wouldn't have to say goodbye.

Take me with you, I said to Aimee.

The summer would be upon me soon, and I felt the weight of its emptiness like an anvil on my chest.

It's backbreaking, Aimee warned me.

I was adamant. Your back seems fine to me, I said.

In the eight months we'd lived together, I had never seen her cry. I'd never seen her anxious over exams or upset about a substellar mark. I'd never heard her complain about mess or cold or waiting. I had never heard her utter a jealous word. I'd seen her eat stale crullers and drink bad black coffee. I could stand to have my back broken if this was the way a spine could grow back.

IN PREPARATION for our voyage, Aimee escorted me to a store out in the industrial fringes of the city. It took several buses and a lot of walking to get there. She led me through the aisles, loading foreign silvicultural objects into my arms. What kind of a boss expected you to shell out for equipment you didn't know how to use, with money you hadn't yet earned?

A set of tree-planting bags, in heavy-duty vinyl, for carrying seedlings. A pair of tall pumpkin-colored rubber boots with heavy Vibram tread. She acquired some items, too. Some duct tape, a few pairs of webbies, gloves crosshatched with drizzlings of rubber. She purchased these the way she bought everything, by the indiscriminate handful, paid for with dimes and nickels.

I tried on this equipment right there in the aisle, in case a dry run might change my mind. I clipped my new tree-planting bags around my waist. One pouch on each hip and one in the back, stitched down on a foam waistband with two suspender-like straps. They seemed equine to me, like feed sacks.

I feel like a burro, I told her.

.The shovel was cumbersome, bigger than the sleek trowel I'd envisioned. I lifted it to shoulder height a few times and felt my deltoid burn.

It's heavy, I told her. Heavier than I thought.

Welcome to my world, she said.

WHEN THE time came we fled Toronto on a Greyhound bus, our backpacks in the belly underneath. We arrived at the bus station in Thunder Bay a night and a day later, without ever having escaped the province of Ontario. My ankles were swollen, my eyeballs furry.

Eventually a green pickup truck arrived. The driver was a man named Jack, a short guy with stringy hair and a ski jacket glazed with motor oil. He had black grease all over his hands. He pointed his thumb toward the truck's back end, and we heaved our backpacks into the open box. Propane tanks stood in the back, tied down with red ratchet straps.

We slid onto a bench seat with room for three. I sat in the middle and had to move my thigh aside whenever Jack shifted into third or fourth gear. The truck interior smelled like oil, human and mechanical. We traveled down a deserted two-lane highway out of town and into the industrial wilds. The sky dimmed from navy blue to a black so matte it felt absorbent. Eventually we turned off onto a lumpy road. Yellow grass whiskered up between two ruts, the kind of road that reminded me of teenaged tailgate parties and meadowy make-out destinations. The headlights beamed into a clearing. Then we stopped, and the truck fell into darkness. Jack got out. His door squealed on its hinges.

Welcome to paradise, he chuckled deviously. Then he disappeared into the night.

My eyes probed for edges, signs of life. I made out dots of light in the meadow. They were geodesic dome tents glowing pink and blue and mustard yellow with the flashlights and candles burning inside. I could hear a guitar being plucked and someone singing off-key. We may as well have landed at a lunar outpost. I felt filthy, streaked with travel dust. I'd become filthy just from opening Jack's door handles and wiping my hands down the thighs of my jeans. The soles of my sneakers were caked with mud. My jeans were also muddy at the cuffs and wet to my knees from the grass.

We beetled across the field, laden down with our backpacks. I'd been chilled for hours, and my fingers felt like wood. We came upon a cluster of hulking structures, the size and shape of boxcars. Aimee had a tent. I didn't. We were divided by this fact along with many others that suggested themselves to me now. I thought of Toronto. It seemed as far away and inconsequential as Pluto.

Godspeed, she said.

If it were a substance, the speed of God, I felt like it might come in handy in the future. She slipped away into the meadow. Stars shone like pinpricks in the sky. I was a rookie. Aimee was a veteran. We'd be split up because of this fact, sent to work on different crews. I could feel that the drift had already begun, and so I missed her already.

I picked one of the trailers at random and climbed the steps. It had a door handle like a meat locker's. I crept in, my backpack straps creaking on my shoulders. The room smelled of sleepy breath, old sweat, dried mud, farts escaped into the night. I navigated in quiet crashes.

The sleeping bodies around me were female. I could tell from the sound of their breathing. I felt my way onto the upper tier of a bunk bed. My mother had sent me a sleeping bag from home. I knew when I pulled it from the stuff sack that it was the one that was too short, the one my brother and I used to fight to avoid. I went to bed still wearing my clothes. I slid my legs in, curled into a ball, and stretched the bag tight over one shoulder.

IN THE morning I pushed open the trailer door and stepped outside into an overcast dawn. I wore a pair of army pants, two sweaters, a cotton button-down shirt, and a cheap yellow slicker that I'd picked up at a variety store that—it would soon become apparent—had no business selling outdoor clothing. I wore the orange boots from the tree-planting-supply warehouse, and they announced themselves in a halo of radioactive DayGlo light. The grass crunched with frost. I felt like a traveler fresh off a plane, blown back by alien cold with strange coins glinting in my palm. Where to find the toilets? Where next to shuffle my feet? I joined a stream of people heading toward a complex of interconnected trailers, all tarps and mismatched rooflines, like an industrial shanty. Steaming breath trailed around their heads. I let the smell of cooking lure me, for where there was food I presumed I would find warmth.

I found the cook shack thronging with bodies. Fifty, one hundred, two hundred? Each one of them was dirty—an opaque band at the pant hems and sleeve cuffs that traveled upwards to the torso in diminishing gradations. I could smell fermented sweat. The only people who weren't caked in mud were the cooks, and they were coated in a guano of splatters up and down their aprons. I saw no sign of Aimee.

This was a place of slapdash utility, furnished with long benches and folding tables of the sort found in church basements. This kitchen was a whirring machine, more about feed than food. Chafing dishes were laden with scrambled eggs. Trays of bacon and sausage slid in and out of the ovens. Toast went around in the wire baskets of a grilling machine. Every few seconds another four slices dumped out onto a metal hopper. A girl stood by with a paintbrush dipped in melted margarine and slapped each piece as it fell. Huge ladles protruded from blackened stainless steel vats on the stove, each burner flaming full-bore. And everywhere I looked there were people pushing up with urgent, empty plates.

I decided to first address the problem of the lunch table with its own horde attacking buckets full of cookies. As I wedged my way in, the supervisor approached. He was a compact man with hair like Beethoven. He wore a flannel shirt and quilted vest lined with shearling. He walked around amid all this youth like a middle-aged interloper, like someone's carpenter dad. We had a conversation of one-word sentences.

Morning, he said. Ready?

Sure, I answered.

Good, he said, and I knew that was a lie, too. Good was too easy, the wrong kind of word for this place. Neither one of us was really paying attention. I watched him build a sandwich involving just two ingredients, cheese and bread. I copied what he did, moving down the assembly line. He wore a radio strapped to his chest. It had a flexible rubber antenna tied with a strip of bright pink surveyor's tape. I wondered if it was there to remind him of something.

He pointed to a woman with long gray hair. She wore grungy white coveralls and a pink scarf around her neck.

That's Lynn, he told me. Go with her.

Then he evaporated between the bodies of other late risers, with their Ziploc baggies held open, jockeying at my back for the last of the trail mix. I found myself with a plate of scrambled eggs in my hand, scrounging into an old coffee can for cutlery.

After breakfast I fell in with my rookie compatriots, we of the gleaming new gear. We trudged together with our tree-planting bags clipped to our shovels. We carried our shovels like hobos with handkerchief satchels tied to their sticks. We followed Lynn to a row of white passenger vans. Hers was the oldest, the most beaten and dinged. I could tell she had a soft spot for underdogs and lost causes.

We drove to work, in a convoy of identical vans, each one filled with planters. The forest seemed to go north forever. As if you could start sawing and felling, gnawing at the forests and be busy all the way to the tundra. Busy for a hundred years. Which was, in fact, what was happening.

The guy in the passenger's seat produced a roll of duct tape from the glove box. He began an intricate process of pulling strips from the roll and tearing them off with his teeth. He taped the under and back side of each finger of his left hand. Then again horizontally, in rings between each knuckle. It was a complicated tape job, like those administered to boxers before a fight. When he was done his hand resembled a mechanical claw.

The duct tape rolled backwards into a bramble of waiting hands, and then others began this taping routine as well. It made me nervous. I smelled the cloying aroma of peanut butter and jelly. It was the girl whose name I learned, through aural osmosis, was Sarah. She munched a sandwich, even though we'd just finished breakfast. I knew it had to be a comfort thing, the sugar and the carbohydrates, the familiar soft and sticky texture.

The mood in our van was funereal. As we traveled, the road grew rough and narrow as a wagon trail. The gear on the roof rack ahead bounced each time the tires juddered through ruts.

Each of the vans broke away onto its own branch road until we were on our own. We turned off at our destined fork and entered a wide clearing. It was my first real-live clear-cut, though I'd seen pictures on Wilderness Committee T-shirts and in old issues of *Canadian Geographic*. This clear-cut looked nothing like what I'd imagined. It reminded me of a landfill. The same unremitting texture in all directions—flattened wood and stumps, stumps, stumps. It didn't take my breath away, and it didn't break my heart in quite the way I'd expected. It shocked me only in its scale. As I might be shocked in the teeming streets of India or in the blinding white of Antarctica.

The road wound through the open field. Lynn made stops every hundred feet next to flats of seedlings lined up on the roadside, each the size of a large doormat. The side door rolled open, and my crewmates debarked in ones and twos until only Sarah and I were left. Then Sarah got out, pulling her hood up over her head. After that there was no denying where I stood in the crew hierarchy. We drove to the very end of the road, to the loneliest corner of our working territory. Lynn turned the key in the ignition.

This is your cache, she said. Caches, I presumed, were the roadside spots where the seedlings were stored. I took it as code for *get out*.

Outside the wind blasted through my layers in a woefully chilly way, at the same time frozen and damp. I climbed the ladder up the back of the van to the roof rack and threw my gear down at the road. I smelled the last of the van's heat evaporating from my fibers.

Bag up, Lynn told me. Don't take too many.

I had only one flat at my cache. Two hundred trees per tray. Obviously not much was expected of me. The seedlings reminded me of a small living carpet, like wheatgrass from a health food store, the stuff shorn with scissors and fed down into a grinder spewing liquid chlorophyll drink. I ran my hand across the foliage, which was dark blue-green and pliable. It had a nap, soft or prickly, depending on which way I rubbed the needles. Each seedling grew in a tube of soil, and each tube in a paper honeycomb. I dug out my gloves and put them on. They smelled like new skateboard wheels. I lifted a corner of this living spruce carpet and measured out a portion with my hands.

Half that, said Lynn.

I ripped it in two.

Carefully, she added. She squinted with one eye closed against the wind, and for a second I thought she was winking at me.

I shoved a mat of seedlings down into each of my tree-planting bags, then clipped myself in. A few dry flurries zipped to the ground. I studied the sky for the onset of weather, but Lynn had already started walking. I ran after her with my shovel in one hand and my raincoat flapping in the other. I leaped after her across a ditch of wizened reed husks and followed her into the clear-cut, which seemed undeniably torn once I stepped inside it, not only logged, but mechanically scarified into coiling furrows. I followed her to the shadowed margins where the tall trees met the devastation. Lynn knew what she was doing—I could tell by the way she strolled. It wasn't easy, simple walking but more like trying to move through an extinguished campfire. Lynn waited for me at the edge of the forest, where I could hear the trunks keening in the wind. She reached into my left-hand bag and teased a tree out from my supply. I watched her aim her shovel at the ground and hit a soft spot between two rocks. In a single practiced motion she bent at the waist and pushed her shovel forward. The ground at her feet broke open in a clean rectangle. With her free hand she fed the root plug down along the back of her blade. Then her hand disappeared into the hole.

As cleanly and as quickly as she'd bent forward, she stood up. She kicked the hole shut, violently I thought, with the heel of her boot. The little tree stood out of the ground at attention.

Just like that, she said. Only faster.

That same eye winked. And then she left me alone.

I LOST the afternoon in a wet smear of movement and sensation. At the end of the day I felt as if I'd been blown and beaten by the slaps of a car wash. Back at camp I headed straight for the cook shack and threw down dinner. It was fettuccini Alfredo. I didn't even like fettuccini Alfredo, but it was food, hot and comfortingly starchy. Everybody around me was exhausted and happy not to be outside. I heard laughter for the first time since I'd arrived.

The next day also passed in a dull roar. The sky roiled around with clouds and showers and fleeting streaks of blue. I found it vexing, when pawing around in my bags, to pluck one tree from the rest, since they seemed knitted together by the roots. Sometimes I dropped my shovel and plunged both hands in to rip the trees apart in frustration.

The next day, I planted trees with a headache, since my brain was full of blood from bending over. I yanked at my clothing, which had traveled to one side of my body, for this was ruthlessly crooked labor. I learned it was easy to do something once. The trick was doing it a thousand times.

A week flashed by. Scarcely a morning passed without the van getting stuck in the mud or bogged down in a swampy puddle or hung up by an axle on a stump. Lynn would retrieve the chain saw from the back. We'd get out and gather in a small crowd while Lynn crawled underneath the chassis with the chain saw snarling. We'd wait for the sound of the blade biting into the wood, for the shreds of yellow sawdust to fly. Once Lynn had finished dismembering the stump we'd spend some more time knee-deep in the ditch, rocking and pushing at the bumper. I was almost happy, my boots full of mud, flecked on the eyelids and earlobes. It meant one less hour spent out in the cut block, alone, planting trees.

At quitting time, once we'd assembled in the van, we always took turns calling out the number of trees we'd planted. Humiliating, but at least we could be equally humiliated together. One day, Lynn didn't call Sarah's name, and only then did I notice she hadn't come to work. That's how I discovered what happened to the people who quit. One day, present. Next day, vaporized.

If you wanted to abandon ship, you had to find the supervisor and admit to him your failure. Then you packed your bags and waited for something to break down in camp so that Jack had a reason to go to town. You could wait days walking among people who knew you were weak, who looked your way as if you'd abandoned the cause.

That night, Sarah was an empty mattress in the bunkhouse. The next day she was a space between our shoulders, which eventually our biomass expanded to fill. I allowed myself the dream of quitting once a day, and it usually happened before I'd even slapped my first tree into the ground. In truth it took a lot of effort to quit, just as much as it took to keep going.

THE DAYS warmed, and then the bugs emerged. They rose out of puddles, softly at first, then rising to a great crescendo. At

first, a few circled muzzily around my head. With every day
that passed they grew smarter and faster and more aggressive.
Mosquitoes could penetrate a single layer of clothing with their
diligent, probing beaks, and so the hotter it became, the more
clothes we were forced to wear. Black flies landed and crawled
around on woven fibers, looking for a buttonhole or a zipper left
undone. When they found a gap, they crawled in and buzzed
around inside our clothes, savaging all our tender crooks and
notches.

Olive oil, citronella, lavender, Tiger Balm, Off!, Skin So Soft.
There was no slather, no concoction that would keep them out
for good. We wrapped ourselves in headscarves and balaclavas
fashioned from T-shirts. We duct-taped ourselves into our clothing. But there was no escaping the sound, the maddening drone
of insects whose territory we'd strayed into.

So many ways to fall down. A branch caught you midstride
between calf and shin, like a rod thrown into bicycle spokes.
Stepping over a log, you caught your toe on splintered arms and
woody knots. You stepped without looking and rolled over onto
your ankle. Or your tired quads refused to lift your leg to the
height required. A twig caught the lip of a boot sole. In the midst
of digging, you nailed yourself with your shovel blade in the
knee's patellar soft spot. Stumps lurked in tall grass. They hammered you in the shin as you passed over, where the skin was
thin and massacred from the last time you'd done it.

Horseflies landed, burrowed through my hair and bit into
my scalp with their pincers. I spent many an afternoon slapping
myself across the face. The days ripened, and the skies turned
a merciless blue. I saw my co-workers, who each wore a halo of
black flies. Outside this orbit, horseflies whizzed in bigger loops,

like electrons around a nucleus. I squinted through my own veil of winged creatures. I felt them bounce from my cheeks before they touched down and bit into me, one jolting itch at a time. At the end of the day I touched my temples and found the grit of crystallized sweat and crusts of dried blood.

By late spring quite a few tree planters had quit, but I didn't. I stayed until a billion blood cells had died and been reborn. Until my hands looked like rawhide and my breasts had melted away. By the time it got hot enough to put on a swimsuit, I had fuzzy, scabbed shins and a baked neck. When I glimpsed myself in mirrors I saw a teenage boy in drag.

There was something alluring, addictive even, about the job. I liked the feel of loam between my fingers, loved the look of a freshly planted tree bristling up from tamped soil. Planting trees was a whole, complete task. You could finish what you started in just a few seconds. You could sow a field in a day. It meant being outside, unprotected from the elements, but at least weather affected everyone equally. Best of all, in a cut block you could erase your old self. You could disappear almost completely.

Aimee got a letter from Dave. He'd been working out west. She showed me the photo he'd sent: Dave on the top of a mountain with his hair up in a ponytail, wielding his shovel at the camera as if it were a samurai sword. Snow coated the mountains in the background. She would be on her way out soon to join him. Planters, I was learning, were creatures in perpetual motion, leaping at the next spot of ripe dirt, the next town, the next contract. They could drift apart, cleaved by the very activity that had brought them together in the first place. You could cross paths with someone over and over. Or you could spend a half a lifetime waiting to see your old friends again.

THE WOMEN'S washroom was also the men's, and technically it wasn't a room at all. The showers had tarps for walls, and men and women cleansed themselves side by side, coeducationally, standing on forklift pallets instead of bathmats. There were no shower curtains, only hoses and showerheads, water heated by inline propane pods.

The showers had a vestibule, also strung with tarps. Dirty workers stripped down en masse so that no moment would be wasted. No drop hit the grass without first doing its job on an inch of grimy skin. Here was the human body in all its ungroomed imperfection. Leathery hands and ruddy faces juxtaposed with the virgin territory everywhere else, unexposed places that never saw the light. Angry boils and sprays of hot pink pimples. Tattoos. Bruises on thighs the size and shade of eggplants. Scrapes. Scabs. Dirt under the toenails. I had never seen so many naked bodies with all their flaws and simple imperfections. I didn't know people could abuse their bodies this way, like objects with no nerve endings, like beat-up pairs of shoes. I saw what the word *sinewy* meant.

There were no traffic jams. Every meal was a picnic. In the field there was no queuing for the restroom. We just stopped, pulled down our pants, and let go. And if we forgot to bring toilet paper with us to work, there was no hiding that either. There was always someone at end of the day with a torn shirt sleeve or a missing pant leg. Around here we used the language of unadorned fact. I learned that toilets were not called latrines or outhouses, but shitters. The reason there was never any toilet paper in them was because people stole it, hoarded rolls in the corners of their tents. Although trees were for hugging, not for killing, toilet paper was still a hot commodity. As was anything soft, dry, and still unbelievably white.

I queued up to feed in the cook shack, and I queued up to make myself clean. Until I began to feel squeezed through a machine with gears that slowed but never stopped, that slapped out the ingredients of basic human necessity. I emerged at the end of the conveyor belt, clean, fed, watered and ready for nightly shutdown. As if we, like the trees, were also a kind of product.

At night, before I fell asleep, I could feel things happening, changing under my skin. Cells raced, blood poured around. Even my eyelids felt different. Now when I shut my lids the light didn't penetrate. I put my head down and was tossed overboard straight into dreams. Roots, stones, and naked dirt, streaming before my eyes.

{ 4 }

GREEN FLUORESCENT PROTEIN

CASCADIA IS A place name that's poetically accurate, since during the monsoon, water runs everywhere. In early spring we wake up to ominous TV weather icons, black cartoon clouds throbbing out snowflakes and dotted lines of rain. Days of purple skies, as if the sun just couldn't bring itself to come up. Of double wool and kayaking pullovers and rubber gloves whose fingertips fill with rain. Or, we lift ourselves out of bed to snow-dusted mornings. Frost glitter. Sun flurries and fog rays. The beautiful, confused weather of winter wrestling with spring. As it is in much of Canada, March, on the raincoast, is the month of boomeranging winter.

If you drive an hour west out of Holberg along the rim of Quatsino Sound, eventually you come to the open sea, a landless vista at the edge of the Pacific Rim. When the sky isn't gray, it's a powdery blue. Low rollers dash apart on bergs of black rock and then slide down the pebbled beaches. The ocean looks dark and bottomless. At the start of the season we work these western slopes, where the snow melts first.

If we threw down our shovels and began to walk south, we'd cross mountains and fjords and rivers for a hundred miles and eventually we'd arrive at Clayoquot Sound. A lush valley where several thousand people once rallied to save one of the island's last stands of virgin timber. Greenpeace, the Sierra Club, Midnight Oil, plus a salad of activists, grandmothers, and imported urban ragtags. On the way, we'd come across Red Stripe, a mountain shaved on all sides, from shoreline to peak, by disastrously intensive logging. It now erodes quietly into the ocean. Yet no one has ever waged a war of the woods up here. Perhaps it's too far to drive down rickety roads. Perhaps the trees aren't all that pretty.

"Harvesting," it's called, as if these old trees were cultivars, sown and tended by human hands, just like hybrid corn.

If this particular mountain were a face, some of us would be toiling away on its forehead, where everything has a funny way of traveling up. Sound, wind, birds. Other planters slip over the brow ridge and down the cheeks, and we hear them cursing and taunting each other.

Hey, fucknuts! Too tired to do your own garbage today?

Oh, honey. You gonna to be okay? Want me to come down there and dry your eyes?

Officially, marijuana is banned at work. Unofficially, it's like salt in a kitchen. Someone has lit a joint, and the smoke floats up in notes of skunk and moldy grass clippings. We hear snatches of a male baritone singing "Sweet Transvestite" from *The Rocky Horror Picture Show*. Perhaps we hear others badmouthing us, and we're surprised to find ourselves bruised. It's the work that does it to us. The repetition is like psychic sandpaper. We're too tired to fake the social niceties. We're a little stonewashed around the heart.

On the road below, Adam unloads seedling boxes from the back of the truck and then stops to blow snot out of one nostril. The diesel engine gurgles. Sweat glistens on the top of his head, where a lean, V-shaped tuft of hair grows. He smokes furiously, flipping tree box after tree box down to the ground while issuing tactical directives into his walkie-talkie. Adam was born in Poland. In another century he'd be a Slavic warlord in fur and jackboots, poring over maps in a tent with snow blowing in through the flaps.

Adam peers over the edge of the road to where Carmen works. He calls down to her. She stoops to plant a tree, ignoring him the way people on buses pretend not to hear by armoring themselves with iPods. She stoops and climbs some more.

Carmen, he calls again, cupping his mouth with his hands. You've got to wear your high-viz.

DayGlo orange vests, the kind worn by traffic herders. Requisite bush couture, in case we fall and crack ourselves open, so that a helicopter can find our pieces from the air.

Go fuck yourself, says Carmen. She puts her head down and goes back to work as the single moms do, with an unswerving sense of purpose. Fast and yet slow, at the speed of someone hunting for a set of house keys, something small but vital and lost.

Who knows what this grudge is about? It doesn't seem to need a reason. We discover vendettas the same way we learn all the gossip: breakups, crushes, rumors of hiring and firing. Information circulates like airborne particles, like microbes passed skin to skin. In the end we know so much about one another and yet sometimes nothing at all.

Back at the ranch, Carmen and Neil have been orbiting around one another. Their romance blossoms at night in the kitchen, over puddles of olive oil and husks of garlic peelings. Huddled chats on the steps with cigarettes and cans of Lucky Lager. Love: we creep up to it with our hands outstretched as if to the heat of a wood stove. What we are expands and contracts like a rubber band, crushing us all together.

THREE AND a half billion years ago, the earth was bathed in a briny soup, and the atmosphere was a hot swamp of greenhouse gases. Life was microbial. Then a new bacterium was born. Its guts were speckled with light-absorbing proteins. This cell could perform a chemical magic that none of the other floating squiggles of the prehistoric seas could. It harnessed sun rays. With this energy, it transformed carbon dioxide into sugar and in the process pumped out oxygen. These rudimentary organisms are still around today, in practically every environment where sunlight and water coexist. Cyanobacteria—blue-green algae, the beginning of all things.

Without this evolutionary game changer our world would look completely different. It might now be filled with unrecognizable organisms that thrive on methane or carbon dioxide. Instead, blue-green algae multiplied and colonized and began to transform the atmosphere, molecule by molecule, oxygenating it with their exhalations. Over time these simple photosynthesizers, with their nitrogen-fixing abilities, enriched the seas. They birthed the air we breathe. They are the prototype for vegetation today. When chlorophyll showed up on the scene, plants began their long path toward world domination, since no kingdom covers the land surface of the planet so completely.

Plants began as rafts of single-celled organisms, clinging to one another on the surface of warm prehistoric seas. These cells joined forces and even crawled inside one another, and eventually they crept onto the land. As their numbers grew, they spread out in a thin horizontal layer until crowding began. And then they started piling up, one atop another, like people standing on each others' shoulders.

Instead of self-exterminating, they cooperated. The cells on the top did the photosynthesizing. The cells on the bottom provided architecture and delivered nutrients. So began the division of labor, the root-to-shoot relationship that defines vascular plants as we know them today. They developed paper-thin solar panels, both porous and waterproof, as remarkable an evolutionary invention as the human lung. They could tilt and swivel in relation to the sun. Their leaves could channel rainwater to all the advantageous places. They grew stalks and stems to better hoist themselves toward the light and to lift their heads above competitors. This evolutionary rise is reenacted each spring, in every garden and park and untended, weedy corner. A green swell so ubiquitous we take it for granted.

Trees are the ultimate result of this evolutionary reaching. The colossal trees of the Pacific Northwest have developed huge, supportive trunks and broad canopies that waste scarcely a photon. Contrary to popular belief, the upper branches of a rainforest canopy do not intertwine. They overlap, but seldom do they touch. Individual trees grow carefully around one another, their branch tips separated by mere inches. It's a feat of plant diplomacy millions of years in the making, but nobody really knows precisely how or why this phenomenon, known as crown shyness, occurs.

Conifers, especially, are ancient creatures. Their genetic antecedents arose as long as 300 million years ago. Despite their impressive stature, they're really quite primitive. They never evolved flowers to attract pollinators or fruit to lure animals who might eat and spread their seeds far afield. Although some conifers, like larches, are deciduous, most are evergreen. A conifer has stuck to its evolutionary guns, like a reptile or a fish. Other trees have acorns or chestnuts or winged whirligigs or seeds with rubbery casings, spiny coatings, or dangling seedpods that can be eaten whole or ground up as spice. Conifer seeds come packed inside cones, but they are mostly no bigger than a grain of rice. Each seed is a blueprint for an organism that may grow ten thousand times as large as its natal package. Another irony of nature: big creatures sprung from the tiniest genetic blueprints. Sturgeon can have roe as big as peas. But a human, with all our intricately complicated machinery, comes from a zygote that's invisible to the naked eye.

In a nursery, conifer seeds are poked into soil and germinated, watered, and fertilized and sprayed with trademarked chemicals whose names make them sound like engineered rain: Benlate, Rovral, and Captan, Bravo, Echo, and Ambush. Out in nature it's a different story. A ripe cone spreads its flaps and drops its winged seeds only with the perfect combination of temperature and humidity. Some cones drop and are immediately snatched up by rodents, which machine them with their teeth the way we eat corn on the cob. Most of the seeds surviving these forest critters won't germinate at all. They'll lie dormant, woven into the tapestry of the forest floor, awaiting the right season, sometimes in vain, for a century or more. While they bide their time, they may be incinerated in forest fires. Many have no hope at all, because their landing pads are too wet or too dry, not warm enough, or too heavily ensconced in moss. The ones that do sprout may be stunted because of lack of light or crowding or overhead obstruction or heavy competition for nutrients.

If you dig out ten square feet of dirt from an old-growth forest, you might find embedded within it a thousand seeds. Some of these might belong to trees that have long since died out or species that don't grow anywhere nearby. For a conifer, the odds of survival are exceedingly low. But a tree makes up for it with a carpet-bomb reproductive strategy. A healthy parent can grow thousands of cones, each containing hundreds of seeds. In a bumper year a tree blitzes the ground with potential offspring. A phenomenon called, in the poetry of science, seed rain.

A reproductive method like this is expensively rudimentary, subject to the whims of the wind. It's one of the reasons why the golden age of conifers has already come and gone. But millions of years ago in our planetary past, conifers dominated. The surface of the earth was composed of one megacontinent, Pangaea. Dinosaurs grazed and stomped the land. Many of the creatures that thrived during this long prehistoric phase would not be recognizable today. Clams, squids, and sharks of the 20,000 *Leagues Under the Sea* variety. Amphibians and lizards. And all those creepy-crawlies that look like giant cockroaches crossed with centipedes, whose strange shapes we recognize from fossils.

During the Mesozoic, conifers thrived at every latitude from the equator to the northernmost reaches of the globe. New tree species were born, and they diversified and specialized. Most of these genetic families are extinct. The survivors are among the world's oldest living plants, and many are rare and endangered today. These include the ginkgo tree and sago palms, which are tropical plants that look like a cross between a fern and a palm but are neither. Also the dawn redwood, a relative of the California sequoias, thought to have died out until a small grove was rediscovered in a remote province of China. The fossilized stumps of dawn redwoods have turned up on tundra barrens deep inside the Arctic Circle—a sign of the extensive range that conifers once enjoyed.

With time, conifers met a rising tide of competition from the next generation of evolutionary design—angiosperms, the great planetary flowerers. Angiosperms developed a more sophisticated reproductive apparatus. They grew fruit to attract animal distributors and flowers to lure winged pollinators, and with these mobile partners they edged conifers into extreme environments, higher up the mountainsides and closer to the poles. Today conifers still thrive in these cold marginal zones, while the leafy tropical and temperate angiosperms came to occupy the prime real estate around the belly of the globe.

Pangaea split into two continents, Laurasia to the north and Gondwana to the south. As these two landmasses drifted apart, new species evolved into two parallel lineages. The effects of this genetic quarantine are still visible today in the distribution of modern tree types. Conifers that grow in the southern reaches of Chile, Argentina, and Oceania look nothing at all like those in the Northern Hemisphere, though the species of Russia and Canada are quite similar. Many southern conifers belong to the Araucaria family. An example is the Chilean monkey puzzle tree, whose swooping boughs are said to curve like monkey tails. They have tough, spiky foliage, reminiscent of Stegosaurus plates, perhaps not surprising since these trees are one of the world's oldest species and are considered living fossils.

Today, the conifer forests of the Northern Hemisphere are dominated by trees in the pine family. Those elegant, slender-leaved specimens we've come to associate with Christmas—spruce, fir, hemlock, larch, and pine. Most of these are found in the boreal forest, an expansive sheet of tree cover that runs across the upper strata of North America, Scandinavia, and Russia. Trees from the pine family also find homes in more southerly locales at high elevations, on mountaintops in Yellowstone National Park and in the Appalachians south to Virginia.

There are few living things on Earth as old as the DNA of conifers. Modern evergreens are but vestiges of an ancient heyday, a fact that might contribute to the feeling people get, when they hike through an old-growth forest, that they're experiencing something majestic and timeless. Conifer genes have survived for a few hundred million years, weathering droughts, infestations, mass extinctions, and wildfires, not to mention ice ages. It's as if conifers were made to thrive in extremes. In this sense the coniferous forests of the world are heirloom ecosystems, repositories of survivor DNA.

EVERY DAY brings a new mountain to climb. Today I've been assigned a steep wedge of the cut that extends from the uppermost road all the way up to the timberline, where the stumps are so distant they look like gray stubble. First, I must climb the cut bank, the scar left behind after the road was carved from the slope. Here I can see the layers of the old forest floor in cross section. On the bottom there is bedrock, above that a horizon of gray-brown mineral dirt, and on top, like cake frosting, a layer of living earth, which comes in shades of cabernet, rust, and ocher, depending on what's composting inside. Out of this topsoil hang dead roots, spilling like the cords of a circuit box torn from a wall. I've got to climb up with my fresh load of trees. I find toeholds on outcroppings of broken rock. I grab fistfuls of roots to haul myself up, and I hope they hold, since the dirt is as loose and slippery as pastry flour.

On a cut block the slash intensifies the closer you come to a road. It's the nature of the way logs are removed, dragged from every corner by grapples and pulleys and cable skylines to landings where they are loaded onto trucks. Sometimes the ground is piled so high with overturned stumps and cast-off logs that I feel I'm entering a chasm or a maze or a room full to the rafters with broken furniture. Sometimes I walk on logs stacked three and four deep, so my feet never touch the ground. I've got to pass through these sections first, when my load is the heaviest. I poke a tree in here and there, but mostly I travel through as quickly as I can.

Eventually the slash thins, and I find islands of life once again, moss and ferns peeking out between the logs. By the time I've worked halfway up the slope my quads and calf muscles burn, and I strip off an outer layer of clothing. As I climb it grows colder—the upper soils are chunky with frost for some time after the valley bottoms have warmed. Such small changes create new habitats and subtly varied communities. In this upper stratum the residents have learned to love an extra month in the fog, an extra hour each morning in the lee shade of the mountain.

As I close in on the top I find old snow patches. If the snow is clean I'll dip my hand in and eat some. Rodents tunnel underneath these melting heaps. Some creatures find their niches in the snow itself. With climate change, cold-loving plants inch up the mountainsides, year by year. Or perhaps their seeds will blow northward, finding purchase in previously inhospitable locales. Animals, too, will creep toward the sky and closer to the poles, searching for the climes of home.

Once, this place—like much of the North American west coast—was impressively forested with *Pseudotsuga menziesii*, the great Douglas-fir, which is not a fir at all but a species unto itself. A long-lived, mighty tree named after Archibald Menzies, a botanist on Captain George Vancouver's nautical expeditions who first encountered the tree in Puget Sound. Menzies stepped off a ship in 1791 and found a fir tree so big it would have taken eight people just to encircle it with their arms. In his time Douglas-fir forests grew from the south coast of British Columbia all the way to Mexico. Tree trunks grew with such stoutness that it must have been impossible, quite literally, to see the forest for the trees. It must have appeared that behind every tree there was another one, and another, and that they grew this way, inexhaustibly, forever.

A mature Douglas-fir is a columnar giant. Its trunk looks as if it were made of cement. It has craggy, fireproof bark, which can grow a foot thick or more. An old fir forest looks like pillars supporting the sky. But these soldierly looks conceal vulnerability, for high aloft its soft needles fill the canopy like delicate brushes. Like many conifers Douglas-fir grows but once a year, furiously, for just a few months, pushing out new bracts like fanned fingertips. This fresh growth is so tender it may break off in the first stiff wind. There is an airiness in the upper reaches, a reminder that the tree is ethereal as well as earthbound.

Douglas-firs love sunlight. They like to bury their feet in sand. But they don't like to share their space with other species, preferring to grow among themselves. They are a little bit prissy but also opportunistic. They wait for devastation, wildfire, and windstorms, and then they grow rampantly and all at once. But only for a few hundred years, since their fate is to be replaced by cedar and hemlock, their patient rainforest successors.

A felled Douglas-fir can yield a one-hundred-foot log that is knot free and perfectly straight grained. The wood has a distinctive salmon hue. It doesn't warp, is both strong and beautiful, and is therefore prized for structural and decorative uses. It is an economic champion tree—to some, the most important lumber species in the world. That is why Douglas-fir seedlings are always passing through our hands. We dose the land in the hopes that someday there will be many more. An overdose, some would claim, this preferential selection of one species over another. But maybe our manipulation is an inherently human thing, for people have been shaping nature for all of recorded time. Hybridizing peas. Cultivating lawn grass. Breeding dogs and breaking horses. Bringing wild things indoors and then turning them out domesticated.

The biggest Douglas-fir in the world is 242 feet tall. The Red Creek Tree lives on Vancouver Island, near Port Renfrew, but it is less a freak specimen than a dwarf survivor. In the first half of the twentieth century firs that were four hundred feet tall and a thousand years old could easily be found. Families came to visit and to picnic underneath their magnificent crowns.

THE DNA of trees may be very old, but many of today's forests are relatively new. During the last ice age, plunging temperatures killed off much of the plant life in the Northern Hemisphere. Ecosystems were buried in snow and then plowed under by great accumulations of ice. Glaciers piled up to thicknesses of a mile or more, a mantle so heavy that land surfaces sank below sea level under the weight. As they flowed over the land, these rivers of ice ground down mountains and filled in valleys with scree and sediment. An earth-rending upheaval known as primary succession, wrought by forces on par with volcanic eruptions. And so the largest deforestations the globe has ever experienced were caused not by chain saws but by climate change.

At the height of the Wisconsin glaciation, more than ten thousand years ago, forests retreated into ice-free corners of the North American continent. Plants and animals squeezed into tiny coastal refuges along the Pacific and into unfrozen regions farther south. Ice covered all of Canada, the American Midwest and New England, and even portions of Montana and Washington State. The subglacial fringe, from Pennsylvania to the Pacific Northwest, was tundra and cold steppe. The California coast from San Diego to San Francisco grew a patchwork of cold coniferous woodland. The southeastern corner of the United States, all the way down to the peach- and pecan-growing states, had a landscape similar to that of modern-day Maine.

Once the planet warmed the forests recovered. In the wake of the glaciers, trees edged north from their warmer southern havens. Eventually they recolonized the continent, but they didn't stop changing after that. Forests are ecosystems in perpetual motion, though their shifts, to the human eye, are imperceptibly small. If it were possible to capture these movements in a thousand years of time-lapse photography, we'd see that forests are always adapting—growing and shrinking, mixing in composition, moistening and drying out. They're always changing, because nothing on Earth is constant, not the weather, not the climate, not even magnetic north. The Earth's crust is on the move, always slowly, but sometimes with great upheaval.

In nature there is no such thing as absolute stasis. But if such a state could be said to have existed, a moment of sylvan equipoise, of triumphant postglacial return, it would have occurred between five thousand and eight thousand years ago, when the forests recovered from their frigid setbacks. After the planet had warmed sufficiently, they took on roughly the shape that we recognize today. In this fragile period of maximum expansion, humans had not yet wielded their adzes and axes, not yet begun divesting the world of its forest cloak. If you found yourself at the equator at precisely this moment and began walking north to the Arctic Circle, you would see countless forest landscapes and thousands of kinds of tree.

You might begin this journey in the Amazon rainforest, with its staggering variety of plants and animals. You would walk among endless tropical trees, their flowers heavy with scent. You'd see many kinds of sweet, exotic fruit. You'd see vines and creepers and strangler plants, winding their way up the trunks of tall, smooth trees, parasitizing their superlative architecture. Brazil nut trees and silk cotton trees, murumuru palms and big-leaf mahogany. You'd pass through luxuriant hanging gardens of ferns and orchids and myriad airborne plants dangling their roots in midair. These trees never shed their leaves all at once, since it is balmy all year round. There is no need for winter dormancy. As a result, if you cut down a tree, odds are good it would have no annual rings. In the Amazon you'd sleep among ten thousand tree species. You might never notice the same kind twice.

As you journeyed north you would pass through the tropical rainforests of Central America. And then the temperate montane forests of Mexico. Through the grasslands of Texas into the moist temperate woodlands of the American South. You would travel into a transition zone between warm and cool regions. You'd cross into the varied and beautiful deciduous forests of the United States. They'd contain fewer species than hot, equatorial regions, but you'd still find a cornucopia of types. Oak, elm, beech, and maple. In the autumn you would see the leaves change color, from green to red and yellow, a sign of the remarkable angiosperms at work. They draw out every last bit of chlorophyll and minerals before casting their foliage to the ground. Once the leaves have dropped they begin to break down, providing compost in years to come. And this, too, would have its own aroma.

Around the Canadian border, you would cross the Mason-Dixon line of the tree world, transiting from deciduous to coniferous regions. It is not a line really but a gradient of zonal shifts from broad-leaved to needled forest. You'd see firs. And then a lot of spruce. The great variety of species you experienced in the tropical rainforest reduced to just a handful of hardy, cold-weather types. You'd glimpse quintessentially northern animals: caribou, lynx, bear, moose, and even bison. Chances are you'd spend much of this journey trudging through muskeg, bogs, ponds, and peatlands. For in the north there is water everywhere.

It might begin to snow. As you continued farther north, lakes would ice over. You might notice that black spruce have the meanest, sharpest needles. They've got to be tough to resist freezing. You might also notice that conifer boughs are perfectly designed for the weight of frozen precipitation. They catch snow and shed it strategically close by so that come springtime, there will be snowmelt, perfectly positioned for the roots to drink up. These are harsh environments. Summers provide just a few short months of frost-free nights. For much of the year water is locked up in ice.

As you moved north the temperatures would grow colder and the days shorter still. The trees would shrink, becoming more gnarled and dwarfed until some stood no taller than your shoulders. Eventually you would reach a zone of alder and birch shrub. And then you would come out into the clear of the tundra heath, completing your journey through the three great forest belts on Earth.

You may have noticed, walking through jungles, swamps, and pine barrens, that the basic morphology of trees is everywhere the same. Leaves, branches, trunk, roots. An elegant design that is both simple and mind-bendingly complex. On the one hand, you might feel as if you'd passed through an all-connected thing whose infinite sum was much greater than its parts. A global thatch interrupted by grasslands and deserts and lakes but whose reach was so extensive it could be taken as a defining characteristic of Planet Earth. On the other hand, you might take it for granted, like air or water.

Today, only one-third of this original forest cover still exists. Temperate deciduous forests were cut down long ago. There are only a handful of large, ancient timberlands left in the world— the boreal forests of Canada and Russia. In the tropics three areas remain—the Southeast Asian tropical rainforests of Indonesia, Borneo, and Papua New Guinea. The primary forests of Africa are contained largely within the Congo Basin. Last there are the rainforests of the Amazon, ecosystems so richly life giving they are thought to contain one-tenth of all plant and animal species in the world.

TREES MAY be the most obvious thing about a forest, but they are far outnumbered by other organisms. The coniferous ranges of the Pacific Northwest are home to hundreds of different mosses and lichens. In our soggy world, organisms that thrive on moisture and rot do a brisk business. Toadstools rule. There are over a thousand kinds of fungi in every shape and color you can imagine and many more yet to be classified. Some look like horse's hooves, like albino pinecones or beef tripe, like cocktail umbrellas or undersea coral. Some of them are edible. Wild gourmet mushrooms like chanterelles and pine mushrooms sell for exorbitant amounts per pound. Some mushrooms are hallucinogenic. Poisonous varieties, if ingested, can cause gastrointestinal distress, tingling fingers, unquenchable thirst, floating sensations, delusions of grandeur, and even coma. Some work quickly. They have caused people to fall into chemically induced crazes after just a small nibble. The most deadly kinds cause liver and kidney failure. Some toadstools can kill you slowly, over several days.

Above-ground mushrooms are the fruiting bodies of vast subterranean networks. One such fungus, a honey mushroom, is the biggest organism on Earth. It grows across two thousand acres in the rainforest in Oregon and is thought to be more than 2,400 years old.

Despite their homely, blanched looks, humble fungi are among the most important living things in the forest. They're saprophytes, recyclers of nutrients. But fungi are also the unseen life-support system of the plant world.

The dirt in the forests of the Pacific Northwest is poor in nitrogen, which is a critical nutrient for plants. Tiny, underground fungi sheathe the tree roots. But they lack the ability to photosynthesize. They draw nitrogen from the environment and convert it to a form the tree can digest. In exchange the tree feeds the fungi sugars. Together they grow, turbo-boosted by each other's secretions. It's an evolutionary miracle that the conifers have grown to such soaring heights, and they owe their success to this symbiotic relationship.

Often enough, it is an ephemeral association. The embrace of plant roots and fungi forms and disintegrates every year, like a summer camp romance. In the autumn root and fungi tissues dissolve, in turn plumping the soil with organic matter.

Mycorrhizae, these fungi are called. They were discovered

little more than a century ago and are still not fully understood today. Some kinds of mycorrhizae even penetrate plant roots and proliferate inside. They are so intertwined with the tree that if you look at them under a microscope you can barely see where one organism ends and the other begins. In an established forest, parent trees dose new seedlings with mycorrhizae, in effect sharing their fertilizer. After a wildfire mice eat truffles and spread fungal spores, re-inoculating the land. Without mycorrhizae, many of the world's forests would look totally different—they might be grasslands or clumps of dwarf trees. Nature has a gentle way of pairing giants with miniature beings; for example, whales, the largest mammals on Earth, feed on shrimp the size of pinheads.

Interspecies relationships occur everywhere in nature. They are so ubiquitous that we take them for granted. Flowering plants, their roots locked in the ground, depend on the unfettered mobility of animals for wide dissemination—birds, bees, bats, moths, ants, and butterflies are all flower pollinators. These are very old co-evolutionary marriages, millions of years in the making. Sometimes the relationship is monogamous. Yucca and fig trees and many kinds of orchid have exclusive relationships with just one pollinating creature. One-third of the world's food supply comes into being this way. Without this symbiosis we'd have far fewer things to eat, no apples, plums, or berries. No turnips or pumpkins, no cashews or almonds. We'd have no chocolate or vanilla. No coffee or Coca-Cola. Without pollinated flowers we'd be stuck eating ferns, mushrooms, and algae.

Root-fungi relationships are thought to enhance the growth not only of trees but of most plants everywhere. Some 80 percent of vegetation has relationships with mycorrhizae. Some plants can't live without them. Only a small percentage can survive without any symbiotic association at all—those vegetables that kids like to hate: cabbages, broccoli, and brussels sprouts. Symbiotic relationships are so crucial to life on Earth that some scientists propose, in a theory called symbiogenesis, that interspecies collaboration is a driving force of evolution. According to this idea, the origin of species isn't random mutation or competitive selection but reliance and cooperation.

Lichens are simply fungi that have made friends with algae. In the Pacific Northwest they grow on practically anything that doesn't run or slither or fly—tree bark, rocks, soil, and decaying logs. They dangle from branches like napkins thrown over a waiter's arm. Some are bright orange, whereas others are coal black. Some look like barnacles and others look like lace. One lichen resembles a toad pelt. They can mimic anything at all— cabbages or dust or Silly String or antlers hanging upside down. Most look faintly evil, like ingredients for witch's brew. They have poetic names like pimpled kidney, questionable rock-frog, rag (tattered or laundered), and devil's matchsticks.

Lichens are also extremely sensitive organisms. They are supersponges, absorbing the faintest traces of whatever toxins happen to drift past, from air pollution to radioactivity. Like many forest organisms, they grow with excruciating slowness, a tiny fraction of an inch per year. Methuselah's beard is a rare and beautiful lichen that looks like long lengths of fluffy white string. Before it died out in Europe, people wound it around their Christmas trees as tinsel. In North America it loves to grow in the arms of an old Douglas-fir tree. In fact, it prefers an old-growth forest to the exclusion of any other habitat. Once these forests are gone, scientists believe, so too will be Methuselah's beard.

SOME PEOPLE prefer to plant trees with a partner—for the company, the shared snacks, and the subliminal comfort of knowing they won't be caught alone with a bear or a sprained ankle. Some people say their minds have too much to gnaw on when they work in silence. I met a guy once who said he quit planting trees after two weeks for precisely this reason, the unbearable emptiness of the field.

Some people wear iPods to drown out the solitude, but I don't mind being alone, if only because I can't plant trees and talk at the same time. I expend all my brain power thinking about where I'm going to step next and if I'll waste precious minutes climbing around instead of over. When I arrive, will it make a good spot to put a tree? Most days I carry several species, and every three steps I must choose which one to plant, depending on the composition of the soil. I can tell what the earth has in store by the vegetation that grows on top. My hands know each kind of tree by feel alone.

I've got to memorize where I've been so that I don't hit the same spots twice. This is verboten, along with two dozen other planting taboos like J-roots, leaners, air pockets, trees planted deep and shallow, too close and too far apart. Misdemeanors sniffed out by quality control staff, summer interns, or rookie foresters who troll our fields with plot survey cords and measuring tape and quivers of mechanical pencils. Checkers, they are called, and we like them as much as most people like tax auditors— as a necessary, impersonal evil. Maybe they resent us, too. Often they're paid less than us by a factor of three.

A bundle of trees feels fundamental in my hand, like a loaf of heavy bread. I crack the plastic wrapping and slide out a seedling. It's a Douglas-fir that looks nearly edible, like a shoot of gourmet salad. But a cultivated tree, for all its organic seemliness, is quite an artificial thing. It's grown from seed in nursery greenhouses. The seeds come from orchard trees or genetically superior wild specimens. These are harvested by cone pickers. Who are these people? We're workers at different ends of the assembly line. Our paths never cross.

Today I carry extra pounds of fertilizer, which come packed in paper pouches. Tea bags filled with powdery beads that look like swimming pool chemicals. I prod one into the soil next to every tree. Seedlings often refuse to grow without a shot of artificial nutrients. Native ferns and shrubs, the free-range competition, have an advantage, since they were born in the wild. For a year our trees have been watered and protected and cared for, and they grow lushly, with lots of needles—a biological load they must feed all at once without yet having sprouted new roots. A planted tree is like a transplanted kidney. It must knit itself into its new environment and grow a mycorrhizal sheath. It must learn to drink and eat and get along with its feisty neighbors.

Climbing up, I smell cut wood commingling with dirt and the bitter vegetable fragrance of plants. I pass through aromatic zones that fool my nose. I've worked in cut blocks that smell like dill pickles, like wet cinnamon, like mud baked onto a tailpipe. Sometimes I get phantom whiffs that remind me of other places, that plunge me into memory, that make me feel sad or inexplicably happy or a bit of both at the same time. A clear-cut is a protean place. It is both full and empty, depending on the eye of the beholder. It doesn't smell like any air freshener you can find on a supermarket shelf. No laundry softener or room spray or shampoo wrapped in a leafy, green label with the word *glade* stamped on the packaging.

My favorite part of a clear-cut, if such a thing is possible, is the very top edge, where the stumps meet the old forest. I will have climbed hard to get there, but usually it's as clean as a fairway and is a good place to catch my breath. Inside the pillars of the standing forest, the breeze calms. The air is moist and cool. Many of the trunks are marked with lines of spray paint or ribboned with tape—they've survived by inches, for now. This is the block boundary, where the ecosystem cleaves in two. The ground is still clothed with a thick layer of moss, sometimes several kinds in various colors. Sword ferns sway. The wind rushes through the canopy. This is the voice, according to local indigenous myth, of Dzunukwa, a witch-spirit who eats misbehaved children but whose blessing brings great wealth. Standing in the drip line of these forest grandfathers I often wonder what it must feel like to be a faller. Trees crash down around these men all day, like dinosaurs falling from the sky.

Some people think a clear-cut is dead and ugly, but I don't. To me it is heavy with history and ruination and decay, the way a crumbled Doric column tells of extinct civilizations. Branches with chandeliers of trembling, rust-red needles. The corpses of creatures that once lived a dozen stories in the air litter the ground. I find the wrinkly remains of lungwort, which once hung from upper branches. High-flying tree lettuces that perched in the crooks of the canopy. They look not like organisms that lived on mist and tree bark but like something a scuba diver might have plucked from the depths of the sea. I touch them and they turn to mush or to powder, or they crackle into tiny pieces. Perhaps mine is the thinking of scientists who find rat brains fascinating or surgeons who think of sutures as craftwork. A perception of strange beauty that comes from overexposure and the willful overlooking of the obvious.

At this time of year, before the winter is really gone for good, the slash fields are brittle gray, weathered and skeletal as a bone yard, but only when you look at them from afar. Up close and inside there is always something moving between the broken logs and stumps. The dirt is alive. Before the heat of summer the salamanders, frogs, and earthworms are busy sliding in and out of their holes, as if they were renovating. Slugs the size of bananas leave trails of viscous goop. Every five steps I crash through a spider's handiwork, a sticky veil across my cheeks and eyelashes. Water percolates just beneath the ground surface, like a pulse beating under skin. I open a hole and find water at the bottom. I can even see the current, the slow eddying of this tiny pocket of snowmelt as it dribbles through the soil. I wonder how long it will take for this cupful to reach a creek and eventually pour out to sea.

I find human objects, too. Loggers' axes and wedges and chokermen's cables. Mostly they are things that have broken or been used up and tossed aside. Empty Gatorade bottles and juice boxes. Silvery pouches that once held Hickory Sticks and Planters Peanuts. Gas cans that slowly erode, oxidized and consumed by the outdoors. Paint weathers. Edges dull. Sometimes, when the cut is really old, I can't tell what an object is without picking it up and holding it to the daylight. Sometimes I find some stray bit of cast-off machinery. The forest eats the chain saw instead of the other way around.

There is a peculiar energy to a cut block in spring—a cold, moist sizzle. Although the trees are gone, a galaxy of buds and seeds and eggs and creatures waits underground for the right day to burst forth. They build, cell upon cell, with unseen industriousness. Their progress is as inevitable as the French curls of ocean currents or cumulus clouds tumbling across the sky. Nature marches ineluctably forward. It's why blobs of moss grow on cement and mold blackens bathroom caulking. Why we declare war on the dandelions in our lawns. Outside, beyond our fences and sidewalks and window panes, something is always devouring something else. Some ugly, tough-stalked stinker of a flower struggles up out of rubble. It rises, dies off, is eaten or rots down to make room for something else to grow in its place. That's plant destiny. It's our fate, too.

If you could liquefy this energy and turn it into something drinkable, like a green fluorescent protein, you could bottle it and make a squillion dollars. Verdant pastures might spring from deserts. Grasslands from toxic-waste dumps. Humans who drank it would never get old and never need to sleep. Nobody would lose their hair. We could charge ourselves up with sunlight. We could jump over buildings and fling ourselves from bridges and never suffer any injury at all.

Some people think planting trees is as boring and crazy making as stuffing envelopes or as climbing a StairMaster. I love my job for exactly the opposite reason, because it is so full of *things*. There are so many living creatures to touch and smell and look at in the field that it's often a little intoxicating. A setting so full of all-enveloping sensations that it just sweeps you up and spirits you away, like Vegas does to gamblers or Mount Everest to climbers. It has a way of filling up a life with verbs that push into one another, with no idle space in between. So that you just can't believe all the things you saw or all the living beings that brushed past your skin.

{ 5 }

a FURIOUS WAY *of* BEING

BY THE IDES of March, the weather turns a corner, and spring begins in earnest. We come across uncoiling fiddleheads and nascent buds and, soon enough, pendulous catkins loaded with pollen. The forest wakes up from its long, wet dormancy. The air has a different aroma now, not of compost, but of sticky, fragrant life. Even the conifer needles perk up, as if they've been caffein-ated. Each day grows by four minutes. The skies fill again with birds returned from their travels—tiny brown creatures with big songs, like the thrush, whose calls sound like the tweeting whis-tles of sports coaches. The birds are here to breed. An entire air force of swallows and swifts and snipes; martins, dowitchers, and pewees; nighthawks, flycatchers, sandpipers, and wandering tat-tlers. They'll all fly south before the summer is over. Down the flyways to Central and South America.

Helen moves in with K.T. and me. In the real world she's a painter. She carries her portfolio under the seats in her To-yota van. She never went to art school. Hers are tree-planting landscapes, our rain-drab coastal ranges done in the colors of fondant icing. They make our stomping grounds look like Big Rock Candy Mountain. One of her paintings won a contest at a winery. It appears on a Cabernet Sauvignon label.

Did you win a prize? I ask.

They paid me in wine, she says.

How did it taste?

Like shit, she says with a grin.

Helen has a wavy thatch of graying hair. On the block she looks less like a planter and more like a ski instructor. She wears scarves wrapped up to her chin and a toque with a dangling puff ball. In the evenings we hang our wet clothes side by side and listen to them drip onto newspaper. Helen and I make tea and talk in whispers. We talk about art. We discuss what women discuss when left to their own devices. Family, relationships, love. Neither one of us has kids. Perhaps our job is partly to blame.

At dusk Helen carries two hot water bottles out to her van, where she sleeps.

But there's an empty bed, I protest.

I'm a light sleeper, she's quick to say.

There is something intolerable about a couple when you are single and planting trees.

Every day Helen tells me a new story. She started planting many years ago, when some of the boys on our crew were not yet even in high school. Helen owned a husky dog back then. In those days, the government introduced a wolf cull. One day on a cut block, an overzealous hunter mistook Helen's dog for a wolf and accidentally shot and killed it.

Helen and I are both twins. Our siblings have flip-side lives, forty-hour work weeks and mortgages. My brother lives in Arizona. Her sister lives in Ontario. One night, years ago, she drove home with her twin, who lived in the country. It was late at night, and the black pavement rose up to meet their headlights. A procession of fire trucks blazed past them with red lights whirling. They came over a rise and caught sight of an orange glow flickering just under the trees in the distance.

That's our house on fire, her sister said. According to Helen, this is how trouble comes to find a person. Before it arrives, you catch it glimmering just under the horizon.

Time stretches out so that every day feels like a week. We can scarcely recall what it felt like to be at home. Sometimes Helen lingers at the window, pinching back the brittle curtain.

It rains so much, she says, you could almost forget the sun.

She talks like a poet, like a broken-hearted person.

BY NOW we want to give Adam and Brian one of those celebrity conjugations, like Bradam. Every day they split us into two battalions, like the plastic soldiers in Axis and Allies, a board game they play late at night, standing up, after most of us have gone to bed. During the day, they shift us around on the cut block using military verbs like "deploy" and "extract."

They are a unified front, a platonic work marriage. They deliver us home, and then their night shift begins. The after-dark accounting, mapping, delivering, and plotting, the reconnaissance runs for tomorrow. The spare tire changes and the vehicle repairs. Every night, when they scheme for tomorrow, they face some logistical quandary. They need to move ten tons of seedlings to the top of a mountain, only the road's washed out, the map is wrong, and their headlamps have run out of batteries. And at midnight, the truck's rad hose blows out. Or they meet a locked gate to which no one has a key. Or there is no road. Just a trail, a lake, and a derelict aluminum dinghy left behind by the logging company. They bash their way down the trail only to find this craft floating thirty feet from the beach. Adam charges into the water without stopping to take off his boots. To his knees, his waist, then his chest. Then Brian reaches down into the sandy muck, digs out the rope, and pulls the boat to the shore.

Back at his down-island home Brian has a beautiful Colombian wife and two mocha-colored daughters. His wedding ring is so loose on his finger it looks like it could slip off his hand at any moment. He can fall asleep anytime, anyplace. Brian has no crew favorites and no soft spots. You can't work Brian. He won't budge. You can't wheedle and cajole. If you're a girl you can't even trot out the tears. If you vex him or complicate his day, Brian won't say much. But he'll make sure you see the chaff end of every cut block, until you forget what it's like to have a good day.

Brian has just shaved his head, as he does every year. It gives him the look of a Buddhist penitent, or a jarhead, or maybe a bit of both. Brian talks as fast as an auctioneer. His words try to come out all at once, before they've been strung into sentences. It happens when he's tired or when things go sideways on the block, which they tend to at least once a day.

Adam's knuckles are scabbed. His fingers are shaped like kielbasa. Most of the time he looks indestructible, like Achilles, like someone with ninety-nine lives. Like most supervisors, he used to plant trees himself, as if he'd been born for it, like so many Poles who set their hands to the job, as if the capacity for physical work was genetic. If the average tree planter rams a shovel into dirt 200 times an hour, bends over 1,600 times, lifts more than 2,000 pounds, and walks ten miles per day, the Adams of our world find ways to double the score.

Adam used to go into a cut block as if into battle, crashing through everything that stood in his way. He was the kind of tree planter he likes to refer to as the megaballer, an ultraproduction machine. Megaballers are men, plus a handful of women, who can earn several hundred dollars, one thin coin at a time, every single day. Some get there by verging toward the sloppy; others, toward the obsessive-compulsive. They're driven by earnings but also spurred by more subtle motivations. They are the kind of people who can't walk past a game of basketball without wanting to join in and slam dunk it or see a mountain without wanting to climb it and spear a flag in the summit. They are industrial athletes. In pain, they will tell you, a lot of the time.

Mighty contests transpire on a cut block. When two highballers work side by side, it may not be long before a conflict ensues, even if the battle is silent, imperceptible to all but the opponents. All through the work day they'll pound out a blistering rhythm, casting glances, sprinting back to the tree cache to count the empty boxes. It is a sporting event, like one of those marathon tennis matches that persists for grueling hours until someone grows tired and cracks. Sometimes these alpha struggles break out into actual fights, often over unimaginably trivial things. Once the blood sugar and the endorphins and willpower have worn off, only anger is left. The old, bold motivator. Sometimes we all try to find things to think about just to stir our fury so that we'll have the energy to keep going.

We don't need to be highballers to succumb. For anyone, planting trees can become a monomaniacal chase. We spend our days wearing occupational blinkers, scouring the ground with our eyes for just the right kind of grassy hummock, just the spot of telltale moss. Dirt-lust. A drive to propel ourselves to the next spot and the next and to get the damn tree in the hole.

Every time we hit the spot we experience a tiny burst of elation. Success! It dissipates, and then we must replace it with another shot, the short buzz of a tree sent home.

Clock watchers in office cubicles try to empty their days of minutes. We try to squeeze as many verbs as we can into every ticking second. At the same time, we try to lighten our bags— like foraging but in reverse. Long term, the effect is Pavlovian, a sort of target fixation. As with those skydivers who jump out of planes and forget to pull the cords on their parachutes, so focused are they on hitting the bull's-eye on the ground. Perhaps this is what modern workers feel when they veer into the commuter slipstream, gunning to get somewhere fast.

We come to see objects in strict geometries, the world as a well-spaced forest. At the beach we poke absent-minded rows of dune grass stalks into sand. We plant five imaginary trees around fire hydrants on city sidewalks. We take comfort in gridded plains and closed clusters, as if we were waging war against entropy itself, against offending stray things.

Planting trees, we get this *fever*. A tingling under the skin, an itch in the bones. Bend. Plant. Stand up. Sprint along. When we come over a rise and discover a hidden cream patch, we're overcome by the urge to have all of it, to hoard our secret discovery. We get this feeling deep down, as if it were whispered by our cells. If we don't go out and tap that opportunity right now, if we don't go out and *attack* and *kill it*, someone faster and leaner and hungrier will come along and steal it right out from under us. Some days we plant trees as if our lives depended on it. Some old Darwinian thing.

Soon enough, we'll have plastered these hillsides, emptied this contract of trees. It will be time to move on to the next job and the next town. Wherever we go, there are always more trees to plant, more clear-cuts and more stumps. One day we'll get so efficient and expert we'll be right on the heels of the loggers. Maybe we'll even overtake them. And then finally we can sit down to rest.

No wonder we lose sight of the big picture. We're all trees and no forest. Around here the woods are for export. The logs are boomed up and shipped out to sawmills, cut into structural timbers of every dimension. Or transformed into engineered products that have been laminated and glued and veneered. The wood is split apart into cedar shingles. Or stewed into pulp or rolled into paper. It's shipped to the United States, Japan, Europe, and China. After the biggest harvest ever in 1987 the province of British Columbia supplied the world with enough logs—89 million cubic meters—to fill two million logging trucks, all in a single year.

All over the world, every day of every week, trees are chipped and digested and emitted as paper and cardboard and every kind of tissue product. The pulping liquors are refined into concentrated tree juices for the making of scented oils and lacquers and acetones and turpentine and nail polish and nail polish remover. Tree extracts are poured into shampoo, shaving cream, toothpaste, and all kinds of cosmetics that lather when you rub them against your skin. Wood is spun out into gossamer layers of cellophane and rayon. It's converted to alcohols and plastics, acids and resins. Latex and rubber. Eucalyptus and palm. Tree extracts are squeezed into self-tanning cream and acne gel and anti-aging potions. They're stirred into snack foods like frozen pizzas and microwave popcorn and that most shelf-stable of snack foods, the Twinkie. Wood cellulose is even added as a cheap thickener to mashed potato flakes. Wood is ground down into powder and formed into bowling balls and sporting helmets. Not to mention explosives. With this wood flour and xylose—wood sugar—you could hypothetically bake a tree cake. The world eats up 3.4 billion cubic meters of wood every year. If you converted this volume to utility poles, you could string telephone wire around the equator more than four thousand times. Half of this amount is used for firewood.

As tree planters, we are simple, monotasking professionals, purveyors of visually effective green-up, or VEG, as industry calls it for short. We provide raw materials for people who've not yet been born. By the time these future forests arrive, the world will be packed with 50 percent more people, but we'll be long gone. Even now, every minute of every day, someone wipes lunch from his moustache with a paper napkin, then crumples it and throws it away. Someone else flips through a lingerie catalogue, each page a wafer-fine tree slice in her hands. If you die and become an organ donor, I have heard, the empty place in your body cavity is packed with sawdust before burial. Perhaps this dust also comes from around here, some little part of the forest returning with you to the earth.

PEOPLE HAVE been planting trees for almost as long as they've been cutting them down. The ancient Maya sowed an array of helpful tropical species. The original peoples of North America also planted trees—hickory, chestnut, beech, and oak, all of which produced nuts that could be ground down into meal and flour or steeped in water to make nutritiously oily nut milks. In some parts of the United States, fruit and nut trees grow wild with remarkable plenitude, in concentrations considered too high to be coincidental. They're abandoned orchards, cultivated by ancient residents—a kind of living archaeology.

The same phenomenon occurs in the Amazon rainforest,

even though it was once considered an unpopulated, untouched wilderness. High densities of fruiting trees are believed to be, in part, the handiwork of prehistoric civilizations. Like other Amerindian peoples, Amazonians planted the "three sisters"—corn, beans, and squash—along with cassava, potatoes, and avocadoes. But the soils of the Amazon basin are surprisingly infertile. And so these ancient agriculturalists approached farming in a different way: *if you can't beat the jungle, make more of it.* Instead of relying solely on annual ground crops, they planted trees with vitamin- and calorie-rich fruit. Even today Amazonia is full of mocambo, açaí, and cupuaçu, a fatty fruit that tastes like a pear crossed with a banana. Aguaje, which looks like a pinecone but tastes like a carrot. Peach palm, guaraná, Brazil nuts, and ice cream bean trees. Food, in spots where such perennial crops had been planted, would never be far out of hand. There would always be something hanging ripe overhead. The convenience foods of prehistory.

Tree planting appears in the Bible: cedar, acacia, myrtle, olive; fir and pine and box. Logging and planting—the two have always gone hand in hand, since no one needs to replant a forest if one is left standing. Thankfully, arboriculture is basic and self-evident: dig a hole, insert tree, and cover again with dirt. Human hands seem to know what to do without any diagrams or instructional manuals. Perhaps it has always been done as we do it today. Planters of old, making up for lost treasure.

Wood has been precious forever and ever, a versatile natural substance that requires no tending or weeding or watering. Forests have always just been *there*. Cutting trees is as old as civilization itself. Some of the earliest written accounts of lumbering come to us in the *Epic of Gilgamesh*, one of the world's oldest stories. In this Sumerian poem, Gilgamesh, King of

Uruk, ventures to Cedar Mountain, deep in a remote wilderness, to find lumber. He wants to fortify his empire back at home, to dress up his walls and temples. To gain access to these coveted forests, Gilgamesh must first do battle with a monster-protector who guards the trees from greedy humans. These woods are sacred. The gods live under the shelter of the boughs. Gilgamesh defeats and kills the demon and then goes on the hunt for the tallest tree in the grove. He hacks it down and then all of the others. He builds a raft from the logs and floats them back to Uruk. When he returns he's rewarded with fame and the sensual attentions of a beautiful goddess.

The story has some basis in history, since the cultures of Mesopotamia had big appetites for timber. Wood was their steel and concrete, their crude oil. The complex agrarian societies of Sumer and Babylonia, their cities and infrastructure, were all built from wood. Citizens used it for cooking and heating, for the smelting of metals into tools, weapons, and machinery. For the firing of bricks and ceramics. For construction. But as their populations grew, Mesopotamians exhausted local supplies. They logged the alluvial flats of their homeland and then continued cutting uphill, stripping the lowland slopes for the wood or to make room for development and agriculture. When accessible stores ran out, wood became scarce and valuable. Renters took their doors with them when they moved. Rafters were bequeathed in wills.

Eventually the woodcutters of the Tigris-Euphrates valley fell upon neighboring territories. They traveled many leagues, journeying as far as Arabia and even India to satisfy domestic demands. Their missions were fraught with danger and risk, since foreign lands were often fiercely defended by resident hostiles. The return trips would have proved doubly challenging, since the woodcutters had to drag the logs back through unknown terrain while vulnerable to ambush and attack. And so the lumberjacks of antiquity were not only resource extractors but warlords as well. Their operations doubled as military campaigns. When they returned with their payloads they were embraced as heroes, just as Gilgamesh was when he came home.

But eventually the societies of the Fertile Crescent stumbled and fell. After a few thousand years of aggressive agriculture, the land was worn out and depleted. Cutters had cut, and in their wake, farmers had plundered a rich accumulation of fertile sediments—what nature had taken millennia to bank. They'd logged their highlands and headwaters, causing heavy siltation downstream. Riverbeds clogged. Irrigation systems broke down, and the fields became salinized. Cereal grains refused to grow in the new salty conditions. Food yields dropped. Unable to feed themselves, Mesopotamian city-states became vulnerable to invaders. Today the cradle of civilization lies in Iraq, which when seen from space looks not green or blue but desert-brown. The once-abundant marshlands of the Tigris-Euphrates valley are almost entirely gone; only 10 percent remain.

The sacred trees featured in the *Epic of Gilgamesh* are believed to be the cedars of Lebanon, which once grew with fabled abundance in the region between Beirut and Tripoli. This was the land of the Phoenicians, who owed their wealth and status as a maritime trading society to the forests. Their cedars were a rare source of large-dimension, prime-grade wood, exactly the kind required for shipbuilding. But the Phoenicians hadn't always been a seafaring culture. Around 4,500 BCE they emigrated from eastern deserts to the shores of the Mediterranean Sea. They brought Mesopotamian farming methods with them and put these practices to good use in their new home.

They tilled rampantly along the coastal margin. They cut down and traded away their upland forests to neighboring peoples who lacked trees of their own.

As the population burgeoned the Phoenicians crept up the hillsides in search of more arable land, just as the Sumerians and Babylonians had done before them. But as they discovered, once the trees were gone, the rain washed the soils away. They terraced heavily to compensate for the loss, but in time so much fertile dirt washed out to sea that Phoenicia was forced to import much of its food from colonies at the far reaches of the Mediterranean. The Phoenicians lived this way, weakened and overextended, until their defeat by Alexander the Great in 332 BCE.

The cedar forests of Lebanon were important to many civilizations: Babylonians and Phoenicians, Assyrians and Ottomans. Cedar wood is mentioned seventy-six times in the Bible. The wood was used for the construction of temples and burnt as offerings in religious ceremonies. Egyptians used cedar in their mummification rituals. Castles were built from it. To have this wood inside one's house was a symbol of noble extravagance. The Lebanese flag still bears the silhouette of a cedar tree as its national logo, even though the original forest—two thousand square miles of it—has dwindled down to a handful of reserves surrounded by dry, deforested hills.

Logging has always gone hand in hand with civilization. It's a part of who we are, how we've carved a home for ourselves in the world. But historically, the cost has been more than just the loss of scenery. Some scholars have argued that it is the razing of the forests, followed by long agrarian abuse, that has contributed to the collapse of many a now-defunct civilization. Especially in the Mediterranean, where the people once depended on trees to hold moisture, to keep the creeks and rivers running throughout the year. And when the trees go, the earth—the very foundational dirt—follows shortly thereafter.

According to the stories of classical Rome, the Mediterranean basin was once thoroughly forested with pine, oak, cedar, fir, and juniper. Both the Greeks and the Romans lived among the trees and appreciated their thousand uses. But when they prepared for war, entire forests were sacrificed for the construction of triremes—those Hellenistic warships with wooden hulls, masts, and oars—at the peak rate of four or five boats per day. The original timberlands of Europe and Asia Minor may have been thousands of years old, but the life span of a Roman ship was a mere decade. No matter the outcome of battles, the fate of wooden warships was always the same. They burned, were left to rot, or ended up at the bottom of the sea.

Rome fought wars over timber, and whole populations were defeated and subjugated in order that the empire might secure valuable natural resources. Wood was one of the reasons the Roman Empire became so huge. Once colonial territories had been cleared, new land became available for agriculture to feed growing urban populations. The Romans were responsible for much of the deforestation of Europe, and this is also one of their legacies, along with crumbling aqueducts and ruins. Not until the collapse of the empire did some of the woodlands in the outer reaches of the Roman territories begin to make a comeback after an absence of a few hundred years. Just in time for the assaults of the Middle Ages, when the population of Europe quadrupled and its citizens stripped the countryside of half of its remaining tree cover.

The search for untapped forests is one of the reasons people have been attacking and sacking and invading and crusading, as far as we know, since the beginning of recorded time. If history is any indication, we've never been particularly nice to our woodlands. Over and over again, independently and through time, it's as if people and forests were destined to exist in inverse proportion. We revere trees, adore their shade, their wood, and even the rustling, keening sounds they make in the wind. But we also can't bear to leave them standing. Deforestation has been the price we've paid for warmth, light, and shelter since Prometheus stole fire from the gods. And for millions of dark nights and cold winters it's seemed like a worthwhile price to pay for survival.

Wood burns easily and produces heat. It also floats. It's either soft or hard, depending on what you need it for. It is an insulator and warms to the touch. And when we cease to find it useful, it vanishes, recycling back down into the earth. A tree's greatest strength is its tough, woody stem, which lifts its foliage skyward. But this is also a weakness, for with rigidity comes stasis. A tree can't run away. Indeed it puts up no defense at all to our saws and axes. You can't build a wall around a forest, hide it from poachers, or lock it away in a vault.

Perhaps our fatal flaw is inquisitiveness. We don't know how to let an opportunity go by. If an object exists in this world, it can't stay intact, unexamined, unused. We're biological capitalists. If it lives we've got to make the best of it. We've got to hunt, cook, and taste it. Whatever it is, we've got to harness and ride it, pluck it and transform it, shave it down and build it up. We just have to glue, mold, freeze, and melt it into something else that hardly resembles that thing in its virgin state. We've got to get our hands on every last scrap and transform it into something useful, even if we have a million of those things already. We've got to cut it down and wring it out until the final ounce is gone.

ONCE CHRISTOPHER COLUMBUS had reached the Americas, the powers of Europe turned their attention to the western edge of the world. Flags were planted and entire territories claimed for the thrones of Europe and the church. Not much was known about the Native people. Or even the land beyond the beaches, which stretched for thousands of miles farther than ever imagined.

Within a hundred years of first contact Europeans began to arrive on New World shores and to populate the continent anew. First the explorers and then the missionaries, the pioneers, and the pilgrims. They imported a totally new mode of treading the earth, a radical departure from the ways of life that had existed there for thousands of years before. Old World immigrants carried seeds and plant cuttings. They brought domesticated animals. Metallurgy and gunpowder. With these technologies and introduced species they imported the means to clear and build, to trample, plow, cut, and churn.

For Europeans the dominion of humans on Earth was deeply ingrained in Christianity. In the entropy of the wilderness they saw original sin. According to this worldview they were predestined not just to arrive in the New World but to turn it up and strip it down before reforming it totally. This way of thinking has persisted right into modern forestry. For what is a clear-cut if not a fresh start? An opportunity to make a brand-new forest that is neither chaotic nor wastefully decadent. All the trees of a plantation are the same age and size—a convenient, improved design.

America's first colonists endured rustic living conditions, disease, and sometimes even starvation. But quite a few discovered not a cold, tangled wilderness or hostile terrain but a well-spaced forest, a sun-dappled, airy woodland. In many spots on

the eastern seaboard new arrivals disembarked into grassy meadows, as if they'd been ready-made by nature for both pasture and
plow. These forests were open and fertile—symbolic, it must
have seemed, of the New World itself.

Soon enough immigrants began to arrive from all stations
and walks of life. Puritans and yeomen, indentured laborers and
wealthy citizens with a hankering for land. As they spread out
they encountered uninhabited Native villages, as if everyone
had picked up and fled. They found the overgrown remains of
agricultural fields that still showed signs of furrowing. This must
have seemed fortuitous, if not divinely manifested—to arrive,
after such a long and uncertain journey across the Atlantic, to
find all the heavy lifting had already been done.

These amenable landscapes had little to do with the continent's natural disposition. They were modified environments,
created by Native societies over many generations before the
influx of Europeans. Indeed, aboriginal people all over the
Americas had made extensive renovations to their territories.
What they lacked in steel and beasts of burden they made up
for with flames. From Amazonia to Canada, fire was both axe
and scythe. They burned their lands at regular short- and long-
term intervals. Fire kept the forests in check. It opened clearings
so that crops could be planted. Freshly burnt meadows sprouted
back with tender grasses—fodder for deer and other game, which
greatly enhanced hunters' luck. Shrubs also proliferated, and
these provided berries and medicinal herbs.

And so the New World was not an insect-infested, ungroomed wilderness so much as an outdoor living room, a
partially domesticated space. The local inhabitants weren't
hunter-gathering savages, picking randomly for forage, eating
whatever got in the way of their arrows. Neither did they live

in a pagan idyll, perfectly in tune with nature. They were just as willing to bend the land to their will as the Europeans were, though they did it in different ways. Regular broadcast burning improved their food stores and reduced workloads. It allowed them to build complex, well-populated societies. These cultures planted trees. They logged. They collected firewood, sometimes aggressively. Occasionally they even exploited their environment to the point of collapse.

But almost as soon as the Old World met the New, a Pandora's box of diseases began to wreak its devastations across both North and South America. Little more than a century and a half after the arrival of Columbus both continents were all but emptied of their original inhabitants. Up to 90 percent of indigenous populations had been decimated by deadly plagues—especially influenza, smallpox, and measles—to which the locals had no immunity. New immigrants weren't the conquerors of an undiscovered country so much as its secondary inhabitants. Inheritors of a geography that had been shaped and mellowed long before their arrival. If the land looked wild at all, it was because the fire keepers had reduced in numbers to the point of near extinction. In their absence, the woods regenerated. The trees reclaimed the grasslands, and North America became more forested than it had been for ages.

By the seventeenth century, the new Americans had made serious inroads into New England's fine oak stands. Oak was cut for barrels, containers of choice for many an exported commodity. It was used for ships' masts and hulls, lumber and charcoal. New England hardwoods were sent back to Europe by the shipload to feed the needs of a motherland that had long ago exhausted her domestic stocks. Plantation farming in the

South also demanded clearing huge parcels of wooded land. But despite the many practical uses of wood, most of the primary forests of the colonies went up in smoke. To keep warm in the winter, a family could burn up to thirty cords of firewood in one year, all of it sent up the stovepipe or the chimney. By the time the colonies declared independence from the British, the forests of the eastern seaboard had been utterly transformed.

By 1850, the population of the United States had increased tenfold. Once the first American states had been settled, frontiersmen and women moved into the territories in search of open terrain. A man could claim title by clearing a patch of forest and throwing up a log cabin, that quintessentially North American pioneer dwelling. Settlers pushed into the Midwest, cutting as they went. The forested frontier receded. As eastern forests became depleted, the sawmill towns of New England dried up and disappeared or were supplanted by the factories of the industrial age.

But the Great Lakes states had white pine, and lots of it. As American cities began a phase of furious development, new logging towns sprang up in the Midwest to fuel all the building, smelting, and shipping. Soon enough, these new and growing towns required transportation links and hubs. Next came the age of the iron horse. Railroads consumed obscene amounts of wood, even before the steel had been melted, poured, and cast. By 1880 there were 100,000 miles of track in the United States. Each mile rested atop more than two thousand wooden ties.

Logging passed from the hands of individual woodsmen into corporate boardrooms. The timber business always seemed to require a fresh new site, a virgin source, which it consumed before moving on to the next locale. In time, America's white pine forests thinned, too. Logger barons shifted their gaze to untapped forests in the West. Great Lakes towns were left in environmental and economic ruin as the lumbering wave passed through like a locust plague in slow motion. It was an industry that seemed to contain the seeds of its own betrayal. The bust implicit in the boom.

By 1900 half the original forests in the United States were gone. Industrial logging finally arrived in the Pacific Northwest. Just in time, at the start of the Great Depression, for the invention of the world's first mass-produced chain saw.

WE'RE UNDER the gun, production-wise, says Adam at the morning meeting. So it's going to be an extra long shift.

Everyone groans. For some reason we are always *under the gun* or *behind the eight ball*, though it is tough to imagine planting trees at gunpoint or even to explain why reforestation need be frantic when in fact it is a gentle occupation. The seedlings have nothing to do once they've been stuck in the ground but grow for a whole human lifetime.

And, he adds, I want you guys to tell me when I'm driving like an asshole.

Adam usually gets us to work and home again as if it's an emergency. He attacks the task like a drag racer, pupils zipping back and forth across the road from object to object, stone to corner to puddle. He points his forehead over the wheel, eating the road with his eyes. Only two weeks remain on this contract in Holberg, and after that we will begin anew in a fresh locale.

We hardly ever tell him to slow down. We can't get home fast enough, even though it's not *home*, not really, not in any committed sense of the word. It's the place where we gather our food and dirty laundry. The place where we lather and feed and smoke up and then crash into bed like tired waves gliding their way to the shore. Rarely do we tell Adam to ease off on the gas. But there are times when we think, *I'll just shut my eyes.*

One afternoon, Helen rides in the passenger's seat—as she often does, since they have a nice way about them, Adam and Helen. They share the fond, silly banter of grown-ups who are romantically immune and therefore safe in each other's company. Three guys ride in the back seat: Pierre, Kyle, and the new kid with poet glasses who earned the nickname Quick Dry after wearing summer trousers and an acrylic sweater to a freak spring snowstorm. Their luggage sits heaped in the truck box, and it jostles in time with the chassis.

The sun dips. The view out the window is beige rock and rushing cut block. Then forest, cut block, and forest again, like curtains parting, one after another. Every time they turn their ears to the windows, a different earthly music drones by. The open air of the clear-cut, the low shush of tree trunks thrumming past. They careen from the cut block back to the village of Holberg. A sunset, so rare in winter, turns the sky from cool pink to molten yellow. The outdoors looks transformed on warm afternoons like this, a reminder that the sun is shifting its attentions between hemispheres.

Adam and crew have worked late, and the sunset beams at a near-horizontal slant. Their truck tears around a corner, ripping a line of dust through the afternoon calm. The tires bump and shudder over corrugated ruts. They lift over a rise. As they round the bend the cab is set ablaze with oblique golden light. The windshield is filmed with layers of rain and road dust that no one has bothered to clean. Adam squints into it. Helen shields her eyes with the back of her hand. The sun blinds them all for a floating second, so they can't tell where they are, as if dangled in time and space.

The truck plunges abruptly into shadow. From bright blitz to sudden dark relief, all the crannies and intricate contours of the landscape resume all at once. Adam stomps on the brakes. A streak of roadside grass. The truck whistles by one of those quarries at the side of the road that engineers use for road building. A rock face blown out of the ground with dynamite, a deep pond filled with stagnant rainwater that could be shallow or bottomless or rimmed by jellied clouds of tadpole eggs.

When the tires leave the gravel, all the truck's passengers lift from the seats, momentarily cut free from pull of the earth. They can't see the water, but perhaps they smell it underneath them, feel moist air touch their skin. The engine whines. Clothing lifts away from limbs. Body hair stands straight. There is the tug of centrifugal force on the skin. The sudden clenching of muscle. And that peculiar cool detachment of those who've succumbed to fate and small errors.

Adam hits the buttons on the armrest with his fist, and all the windows in the truck hum down. The cab billows with the strange wind of a roller coaster, blowing everyone's hair around in confused gusts. Later, it will occur to Helen: *He thought to do that.* As if he'd done all of this before, crashed a truck into a pond only to discover that the openings fail once the electronics have submerged. Or as if he'd read it in a survival manual.

The truck corkscrews. The surface of the quarry whizzes past Helen's window in a brown, liquid sheet. The truck meets the surface upside down, skidding down with gravity onto the water's surface. The nose of the truck meets the earth with a muffled bang. Adam tumbles. Helen's seatbelt snatches her back, and the boys in the back bang up against the roof. The truck tips sideways, pinning Helen at the deepest part of the slant. And then the water rushes in, icy cold and dark as iced tea.

Helen jabs the release tab of her seatbelt buckle, but she's hanging upside down, and her weight prevents its release. Cedar tannins, a whiff of fermented scum. It gets into her hair first, a phantom touch, as if she were dipping her curls ends first into a bucket. Water rushes against her scalp, frigid and lung shocking. It swirls up past her eyes and then her nose. In the seconds before it envelopes her mouth and chin, she thinks to take a bite of air. Adam tumbles against her. She feels the dense weight of him crash against her side, and then he is gone, climbed up and out into the light.

Helen wrestles with the seatbelt. Her lungs pull tight. The buckle refuses to budge, and there is the irony of it—the very device that was meant to keep her safe. Airless panic glimmers to the top. Helen thinks: *I guess this must be it.*

Adam braces himself against the steering wheel and the armrest between the two front seats. He digs into the water, reaching in up to his armpits. He finds Helen's seatbelt. He goes at it until it relents, but not without biting off the nail of his index finger. He gets a grip on Helen's jacket and pulls her into the air. She surfaces with her hair slimed over her forehead, black grit peppering her lips and cheeks. She coughs up a mouthful of ditch water. The truck's cab is full with water and upside down and sideways—a familiar space turned surreal, like a funhouse crazy kitchen.

Adam lifts Helen out of the cab, and together they struggle up the sludgy bank. The boys in the back stand in a bubble of air, up to their chests in water. They try the door but find it jammed. There is ditch grass beyond the window and mud smeared down the glass. And all their belongings will be wet and ruined. The cameras and headphones and all manner of digital cut-block devices.

Cover your eyes, Adam shouts.

They crouch away from the window, and then Adam kicks in the glass.

Soon there is aftermath. Brian's crew arrives in their truck to find upturned wheels and half a crew in a daze, as people are in the minutes that trail behind accidents. K.T. is among Brian's people. He clambers over the bank and heads straight for Helen, who's knee-deep in the ditch, soaked and shivering. K.T. asks if she's all right. She wipes her hands down her cheeks. Her earrings are tiny silver dragonflies, and they tremble beneath her earlobes.

In the end no one is seriously hurt, not on the outside anyway. But tomorrow there will be a long tangle of forensic bureaucracy. Forms to fill out and photos to be taken and adjusters to be called and environmental assessments to be done to see if diesel has leaked from the fuel tanks. But for now the air is tinged with adrenaline and relief and just the smallest hint of jubilation. Because of this accident, it's a pretty good bet tomorrow will be declared a day off.

IN THE weeks that follow, Helen won't be the same. Nobody, not even Brian, wants to discuss the *incident in the ditch*, as she comes to call it. The worst part, she says, is that no one can look her in the eye. It vanishes from conversation and then from our collective consciousness, as if it had never happened at all. As if we had no way to deal with Helen's near-miss but to disappear it from the record.

Helen is an artist. She believes in beauty. She's the only one among us with any faith in seatbelts. She almost drowned in a puddle, armed with nothing but a souped-up gardening trowel and a plastic safety whistle. Once we finish the job in Holberg, Helen will pack up her scarves and her tea bags and her cans of organic coconut milk, making sure not to leave behind a single clothespin. She'll peel out so fast I'll spot the skid marks her tires made in the gravel.

See you in a few days, she'll sing.

I think I'll never see her again. She'll send me an e-mail long after the fact, omitting a telephone number.

The truck was a write-off. Adam walks around with a white sausage of gauze taped around his index finger. He says he felt nothing at first, when he lost his fingernail to Helen's seatbelt buckle, before his finger began to pump out blood. Only afterward, in the way that pain comes to pool on the surface—slowly, once the healing has begun. For days after the crash, he'll jam his finger in ratchet straps or mash it by accident under tree boxes. Every time he feels that awful crush, I hope he thinks of Helen.

{ 6 }

the TOWN *that* LOGGING MADE

BY APRIL FOOL'S DAY it's time to move on. All those Holberg trees tucked into soil, left to begin their long lives. We flee in a convoy of diesel trucks, vintage Toyota Forerunners, and grungy sedans. We head to our next bonanza, on the opposite coast of the island, the sheltered side where all the people live. Here towns are linked by the Island Highway, which runs a straight shot down to Nanaimo, the nearest big town. If we wanted, we could hit a casino in a dangerous three hours and change.

Cell phone signals. Wireless Internet. We blaze into Port McNeill like loggers on an off-shift tear. We come upon the irresistible allure of neon and signage and spending, the aroma of deep fryer grease. News, connection with the real world. We take our appearance for granted. Our weather burns, our wind-tanned faces. The corded forearms and the pants tied up around our narrowed hips with climbing rope or boot lace. The clear irises, the furrowed squints of people who spend all their time outdoors without benefit of sunglasses. Town people, we are sorry to say, look like boiled perogies by comparison. Clean, indoor folks with trimmed fingernails and marshmallow complexions. Even so, our men gawk at all the local girls, who sashay up and down the hill in tank tops, some pushing strollers, with words like *Juicy* printed across the bums of their sweatpants.

The citizens of McNeill stare at us, too. We have stained teeth and crazy haircuts done drunk with electric clippers. We scuff down the sidewalks in dirty jeans and alpaca toques, our shirts untucked and the laces of our hiking boots trailing behind us like afterthoughts. We look hungrily deranged, like crazy gypsies descended from the mountains to pick through the dumpsters for chicken bones. *Oh*, we see their mental wheels grinding, *it's them again*.

You can buy all kinds of things in Port McNeill. There are two strip malls featuring knitting and craft stores, an art gallery with paintings of killer whales pirouetting out of the water. These clichés derive from the Robson Bight orca sanctuary, located just south of here, a place where pods of whales come to exfoliate on barnacled rocks in summer. In the geographic center of Port McNeill, we find the provincial liquor outlet. A strangely gigantic supermarket with flags flapping from tall poles. A big empty parking lot spiked with tall klieg lights that illuminate half of town.

Here you can meet all your rainbow-kite and wind-chime needs. You can order breakfast and lunch all at once in the form of a logger burger: two beef patties crowned with processed cheese, bacon, and a fried egg. If you can think of a drug—leafy or crystallized or liquefied—chances are you can find it here. You can snort and shoot and guzzle to your heart's content, we've been told, at parties that last for days. But if you want to recycle, you've got to deliver your cans and bottles yourself to a depot a few miles out of town.

PORT MCNEILL was born as a tent camp on the beach in the 1930s. Small-time operators worked a radius around town, a chunk of land that would eventually become Block 4, Tree Farm Licence 39, an old hemlock and cedar forest spread over valley flats and rugged mountains, much of it logged off today. In the early years, men dragged timber from the woods along corduroy roads lubed with fish grease, and later, along boardwalks built from planed logs. They drove trucks with solid rubber tires. Before internal combustion, they grunted monster trees out of the bush using steam donkeys—cast-iron cabooses, all boiler and winch, an example of which is now a town monument parked in the grass down near the marina. Back then it could take two men all day to fall a tree. Many of them died trying.

Driving into Port McNeill, we descend a hill sloping down to sea level. The town appears at the crest of the bowl, sheltered from the ocean tumult by a thumb of peninsula upon which nobody seems to live. Three thousand people reside here, and nearly everyone makes a living, directly or indirectly, from the logging business. They live in modest dwellings, mostly—mobile homes and two-toned ranchers. The lawns are no-frills, mowed in tidy stripes. Few gardens, few birdhouses. Flower pots made of old tires turned inside out. The people with the waterfront property aren't loggers, as many working stiffs will tell you, but the proprietors of spin-off ventures. Doctors and dentists, the owners of the helicopters that swoop around the forests carrying fallers, foresters, us. But even then, at a glance, nobody's getting filthy rich.

But what do we know? We're drive-thru citizens.

British Columbia was built from commodities, and resource towns dot the province from top to bottom. We've done our time in quite a few of them. They have names that start with the words *Fort, Port,* and *Prince.* They feel, temporarily, like home. Towns with a single economic tap. The primary employer is a big corporation with regional operations and division offices staffed by middle management. The real chiefs work elsewhere, in different cities, and sometimes other countries. These are people who have never been loggers, who are often enough executive transplants, judges, and accountants, men trained as corporate generals.

The local employees—the millworkers and fallers and heavy-equipment operators—are mostly men, since there are few jobs for women. Many are the sons of loggers. They have as little use for Brooks Brothers and Cole Haan as do the gauchos of Argentina. They live in houses arrayed in grids and culs-de-sac, thrown up in the style of boom eras gone by. Their streets are picturesquely named after trees that get fed through the saws and the chippers—that is, when the mills are actually running, since logging operations are profoundly vulnerable, as they have always been, to the caprices of the market. With every downturn, there are layoffs and slowdowns and shutdowns. Some men work but a few weeks per year.

OUR NEW home is a flat-roofed hotel complex with a diner, a pub, a beer-and-wine store, a dining room, and one subterranean banquet hall. The Haida-Way, it's called, though it lies two hundred nautical miles south of Haida Gwaii, the ancestral islands of the Haida. These are the traditional territories of the Kwakiutl, or Kwakwaka'wakw, as they prefer. The Kwakwaka'wakw once wore broad rain hats and robes woven from cedar bark. Despite their modern predicaments they were, and still are, a wealthy, dignified people.

For mariners these waters are precariously nutty with islands, cluttered underwater with shoals and rocky reefs. Islands look like mainland. Passages lead to dead ends. Sometimes the air hangs so heavy with fog that clouds, sky, and water appear to merge into one gauzy plain.

The ocean has always been a great provider. Clams, oysters, crabs. Even now the locals have ways to prepare a fish that would stagger an Iron Chef. Some remember how to cook a whale. There is scarcely a celebration or a feast that doesn't include salmon—pickled, candied, smoked, canned, or barbecued, to name a few modes of preparation. They still catch oolichan, a type of smelt, which they bury and allow to rot for several days before boiling it all down to a fishy grease. It is the New World version of extra-virgin olive oil, and it tastes, I've been told, sublime on a baked potato.

The hotel proprietors aren't Kwakiutl or Haida but Greek, and they own one of the briskest businesses in town. The hotel's accommodations are divided into two tiers. An inn for tourists and respectable travelers, and a cinderblock annex shoved up against a hillside like a hobbit bunker. It's home to itinerant workers who arrive late in the afternoons driving pickup trucks emblazoned with company insignia. Nonunion guys with blackened hands and faces crumpled in greasy exhaustion. They wear Viberg boots, jeans, and Stanfield's logger henleys stitched from heavy gray wool. Like us, they're contractors and subcontractors—men far away from home.

Our crew has lodged here each spring for years. We open

the door on sagging beds covered with floral polyester bed-spreads. Lamps that look like huge avocados cast the low-watt lumens of a candle, not ever quite bright enough to read by. In the kitchenettes there are bottles of dish detergent whose level never exceeds one finger's width. K.T. and I arrive early to avoid getting stuck with one of the rooms at the end of the building, which have tin boxes for showers instead of bathtubs. That feature "compact kitchens" with fridge, stove, and sink merged into one curiously unhelpful appliance. We haul in our plastic bins and our SealLine sacks, and we breathe in the stale air of our new abode. Housekeeping, warned of our arrival, has whisked the towels away. They've exchanged the standard creamy plush for thin terry rags in a shade of brown so dark you could oil your boots with them and no one would know the difference.

One layer of single glazing separates us in our bedroom sanctum from outdoor, public activity. When we watch TV we lay our heads on pillows just a few feet from the bumpers of cars in the parking lot. Our room affords a view of the beer-and-wine store, where there is always steady traffic. A different car parks every five minutes. Someone unfolds from behind the wheel, pushes in through the doors, then re-emerges with a case of Lucky Lager or Canadian. Trucks driven by slow-ambling men. Sometimes a taxi cab with the front and back seats full of people. Leathery women wearing feathered mullets and stonewashed jeans, long cigarettes in hand. Sometimes in the mornings people sit in their cars with their eyes closed and the seats tilted back, waiting for the doors to open.

WE LIE in bed on a Friday night. Tomorrow we work, beginning our shift just as everyone else is letting off serious work-week steam. We poke earplugs into our heads. Next door, we can hear the *thumpa-thumpa-thumpa* from the pub, which on the weekends transforms into a nightclub complete with karaoke and whirling dots of light. After ten, the parking lot gets messy with sound. Heels click along pavement. Howls and mewls and squealing tires. The barking volley of romantic squabbles taken out into the night.

These rooms hold years of our archaeological traces. We've smuggled our dogs in, though none are allowed, and they've busied themselves while we're at work by gnawing at the legs of the furniture. When I roll the drawers open, all the knives are burnt black at the tips. We've spilled every kind of solid and every kind of fluid. We've emptied ourselves of mad youth in these rooms, of impulses bawdy and tawdry.

It must be some kind of inevitable payback that tomorrow we will have to be up at dawn. Country music blares from an open car window. When the pub closes, the revelry collects and transports itself into the room above us. We call the front desk to complain but get no answer. We dial some numbers upstairs. No answer there either, though we hear the telephone ringing overhead amid the clinking of glass and the cackles of heavy smokers.

The next morning we drag ourselves out of bed, and we're surprised to hear the upstairs partiers hoisting themselves as well. We recognize the purposeful stomping of those making ready for work.

WE MUSTER for our prework briefing in the underground ballroom. We sit around tables pushed together in the shape of a horseshoe. At the front of the room we note an array of AV machinery: an overhead projector, a screen—the implements of corporate tutelage. The panel lights above us flicker and fluoresce. People eat wedding cake down here and dance for the first time as married couples.

At the head table Roland prepares to address us. He rubs his hands together as if washing with phantom soap, a thing he does when he's nervous, when he's worried we'll fuck up in front of the client. The client in this case is just one person, a plain-faced woman at the end of the table. Her name is Janice. She is a small person in a collared shirt, a puffy down vest and a pair of cargo pants. She wears her hair in a tight ponytail, drawing attention to a high forehead and severely doctored eyebrows. She's young. At some fledgling stage, we guess, between forestry graduate and certified professional.

Next to Roland sits a burly, flannel-shirted stranger with ruddy cheeks and flyaway white hair. Roland introduces him as Ron, a forestry consultant. We're not precisely sure why Ron has been sent in our direction or who pays his invoice, only that he looks expensively knowledgeable. He is a tall man wearing worn jeans and rolled-up sleeves, with a sonorous voice that sets us instantly at ease. Ron moves authoritatively to the wall and flicks at the lights.

Once upon a time, he begins, we tried to plant trees like dirt farmers.

But a mountainside is not a tilled field, and a tree is not a cornstalk. A forest floor is something different, a living, breathing carpet of rootlets and microbes, worms and fungi, not to mention a dozen kinds of underground plankton. You can't really tell where the living things end and the sediments begin. Many of these life-forms have only just been discovered, even though they exist right beneath our feet. Creatures that look, under a microscope, like little monsters. Spiders with lobster pincers. Ants with warty antennae and forked tails. Hermit crabs with bulbous noses and shaggy streamers trailing from their legs.

Ron relates to us the biography of a tree, flashing cosine growth curves and cross-sections of plant guts at the wall. Each spring, before a tree can grow leaves, it must put down roots, gathering strength for the summer's photosynthetic burst. Our trees are born in nurseries, sown in Styrofoam boxes, sprayed for a year with watering hoses, daubed with fungicides, and then frozen like Popsicles for the winter. They are thawed in the spring, sometimes by accident and sometimes too late, then transported hundreds of bumpy miles. A dozen droughts and shocks before they arrive in our bullying hands.

We've planted trees in every kind of dirt, every way our foresters dreamed up, using techniques that Ron might cringe to imagine. We scraped away the rich topsoil with our shovels to get to the gray dust underneath. We crammed trees into oil-stained sands and wood chips—ground that scarcely resembled earth anymore once it had been flattened and rolled over a hundred times by machinery. We planted trees in soil that had been ripped and mounded, disc-trenched and shark-fin barreled. We planted trees tight together and far apart. We carried genetically engineered specimens with weird, curly branches. Fads washed over us. We planted trees dipped in reconstituted pigs' blood. We tented trees with plastic boxes and foam nets. We draped the ground with napkin-sized bibs to beat down the brush. We planted with dibbles or with odd Finnish contraptions that looked like spud guns. We used seed dispensers that clicked out one tiny seed at a time and then hatted them with plastic cones. Foresters would try everything and anything just to make a brand-new forest. But we keep these thoughts to ourselves.

Ron reminds us of the simple temperaments of trees. Fir like
sun and sand. Cedar like shade and moist, plum-dark humus.
All of these things we know, have felt them in the grooves of
our fingers, but somehow, in all these years, we've rarely heard
them spoken aloud. We're quiet in our shock. We think of all of
our forester-overseers who've made stabs at doing it right, but we
can count them on one hand. In our trade there's nearly no one
who'll stand up for the forests until he's fired or retired.

What is the single most important thing out in the field? Ron
asks us.

We snort and guffaw, toss around a handful of cynical jokes.

It's the little trees, says Ron factually. You should be nice to
them. You should treat them like infant organisms.

We endure another moment of shifting silence. We fidget in
the dark. In the moment after Ron finishes and Roland moves
toward the wall, there must be quite a few among us considering
the terrible karmic crimes entailed by piecework. That squidgy
shame of people who work in high-volume situations. Those
hatchery people who stir yellow chicks around on conveyor belts.
Farmers of veal and lamb. People who deal in baby creatures. So
much to overlook.

When Ron is done, we clap. Before we can finish our
applause Janice stands up.

I agree with everything Ron says, she tells us. Except for one
thing. I think the most important thing in the field is *you guys*.

We glance at each other sidelong. Oh, the push and the pull
between *Homo sapiens* and forests, between loggers and envi-
ronmentalists. Everybody knows the most important thing isn't
trees or people or even marmots, murrelets, or spotted owls.
If any of those things were true, none of us would be sitting

here right now. We'd all be elsewhere making a living, mixing cement or licking envelopes or sitting on tall poolside chairs supervising children while they swim.

Janice is the company's silvicultural administrator. For the next month she'll be our quality control officer, our supraboss.

I've never planted trees, says Janice. But I've read a lot of books.

We knock knees under the table. Janice has studied the studies and we have planted the plants, but never the twain shall meet. She flips through a slew of transparencies shot through with bullets and lists and acronyms. She brings us up to speed on company SOPs. She lists the various types of PPE we'll be utilizing in the field. At the end of the day, she tells us, safety is her company's number-one priority. It's because logging has always been dangerous, fatiguing, high-production work. Even today in logging camps the walls are papered with hazard warnings and fatality alerts. They feature grim line drawings illustrating the particulars of every accident. All the crushings, amputations, fires, explosions, and collapses. The hand-drawn victims are usually faceless, but they are always wearing hard hats.

Hard hats, says Janice, are mandatory for everyone at her company, and so will they be for us. This is a stipulation we hate, since there is not much risk in a clear-cut that something will drop from the sky. We're to bring safety glasses, in the event of an eye-poking situation. High-visibility vests and whistles. She deploys these objects like a flight attendant wielding a seatbelt buckle. Compress bandages, which look like maxi pads stitched to tensor bandages, in case we jab ourselves in the jugular.

Fin makes a ring with his arms and puts his head down on the table inside it.

What the fuck is an SOP? Doug whispers.

No clue, I say.

Some of us stray to the bathroom at the back of the room. Some pour coffee into Styrofoam cups and squeak plastic stir sticks around on the bottom. We move on in our briefing to the matter of ISO certification, which from Janice's tone means a lot to somebody, somewhere far from here, high up in the glassy cliff of an office tower. None of us can say what these international standards mean or how they affect us, even while our education is in progress. A bunch of words sprinkled over us like magic dust. We think it has something to do with Due Diligence, which as far as we know means going through the motions of giving a shit while you're doing something terrible to the environment.

NOW WHEN we commute to work, we take an aluminum-hulled water taxi from the town docks. We leave at dawn when the sky looks like boiled newspaper. A fresh breeze off the strait slaps the halyards against the boat masts. The marina is alive with sounds big and small, metal tinkling and clanging and chiming.

Our boatswain's name is Tyson. He has freckles and buzzed, cowlicked hair. He wears sneakers and baggy jeans creeping down on his boxer shorts and a chain that runs from belt loop to pocket. He waits for us on the dock with a mooring line in one hand and a brown bag lunch in the other. We know enough about Tyson to imagine his mother packing it for him. He grew up on boats. His father, Bill, has piloted us to work dozens of times. Their family owns the local whale-watching vessel. Still it's no small thing to entrust your marine commute to a guy who looks like his other vehicle is a skateboard. What choice is there anyway? Perhaps we are just hopelessly terrestrial, more at peace with dirt than with water.

We gurgle out of the marina, and then Tyson points us eastward. To the north, Vancouver Island peels away from the mainland. The ocean widens into Queen Charlotte Strait and the Inside Passage, the seafaring route that winds its way through a protected, snow-capped archipelago, northward to Alaska. Industry is everywhere. On any given day we see tugboats towing log booms and barges carrying wood chips and sawdust. We pass the circular buoys of fish farms and their netted corrals of jumping salmon.

We skim along as if on the surface of a plasmatic skin. Flocks of cormorants putter across the surface and dive under the prow of our boat. Islets dot the water. Trees crowd their shores. The only naked real estate is outcroppings of rock, lapped by the rising tide. No square inch of eligible dirt has escaped the reach of conifer seeds. On lucky days we'll see orcas and minke whales or whiskered sea lions lazing on knobs of rock, warming their brown blubber in the hazy sun. Harbor seals hitch rides on deadheads. Even the shoals are crazy with life, dotted all over with gulls. There is nowhere to glance without catching sight of some creature swimming or sleeping or trotting or flying over all of this salty, snotty fecundity.

On the other side of the channel, the mainland is like a tight hide stretched over the earth, torn at the edges, the ocean seeping into the rips. Here, water and land interpenetrate in a maze of channels and passages, bays and lagoons. The currents churn through rocky narrows, fast as rivers in flood. We find our way down the neck of one of these inlets. The land on either side rises from green folds to dramatic mountains inland. The water calms. It looks like rippled glass.

Eventually we tuck around a breakwater made of logs chained together and push up to a dock, a floating wooden pad nailed with old tires. A ramp to the shore consists of two runs of planking wide enough to accommodate the wheels of a pickup truck. An upturned sea star lies flat on the planks, as if it had flung itself from the water in protest against something deep down and unseen.

We alight on a landing of tumbledown hangars that were once used for the repair of backhoes, skidders, and heavy yarding machinery. Rounds of wood are arranged as chairs around wire rope spools where loggers once settled in to wait for boats and flights out. Derelict trucks slowly oxidize, digested by the temperate jungle.

Our boss keeps a couple of dented trucks for today's purpose, vehicles that seldom see pavement or highways. And here they are waiting for us, deposited overnight by the transport barge that plies these waters, delivering industrial cargo. Our truck beds are laden with stacks of tree boxes, which are in turn covered by white Silvicool tarps. When we spot these bumps from afar they look like distant mounds of snow. That's how we know the ride is over.

We slide onto damp truck seats and haul out, deeper still into the bush, along a set of potholed gravel ruts that once was a smooth, wide logging road. The air is saturated and clammy from yesterday's rain. Scraps of fog drift around, and the treetops comb the clouds like carding brushes dragged through scraps of wool. What isn't logged is scrappy, remaindered forest. We pass swamps that look like mossy savannahs, sprouted with sphagnum moss, Labrador tea, and lonely bog pine.

Mostly we see hemlock trees, since these coastal forests are built largely from that species. The indomitable, much-maligned hemlock. Common as lawn grass, the most unexceptional tree in the glade. Its name brings to mind

Socrates's poison cup, though the graceful *Tsuga heterophylla* is unrelated to the toxic herb. It is a shade-loving, valley-bottom specimen. It has a droopy leader and a tipsy aspect, like a tree in a Dr. Seuss illustration. If you've been walking in the woods of the Pacific Northwest and you have needles in your shoes or down the back of your shirt collar, chances are they came from a hemlock. It has so many flat, short needles it can practically grow in the dark.

Hemlock, in the logging trade, is a junk tree. A lowly species, humbly priced, hardly worth the cost of dragging it from the bush. It suffers from the curse of omnipresence, since it's always the tree standing in the way of the other, more valuable species. And so it meets its fate. Although it's difficult to say just what is wrong with hemlock, other than its badmouthed brand. The wood is strong and straight and even-grained. And yet, historically, it's been no good for much except the chippers and digesters of pulp mills. Forty years from now, when there are 9 billion of us on Earth, maybe we'll wonder why we were so picky.

Today I ride with Adam. At every fork in the road he stomps on the brake to consult his wrinkled map. He scans the trees for old placards marking the block numbers. There are none, or they've been eaten by explosions of bush and vines and moss. We lean toward the glass, scoping for signs of the day's financial opportunities. We do it out of habit, this daily read of the land, like skimming the morning paper.

Saplings whip the undercarriage. The road grows choked with plants until we're driving at the speed of an oxcart. Finally we nose into a wall of vegetation. Adam turns the map upside down and then right side up again. He studies it, pinching his bottom lip. The land beyond the windshield defies

cartographical simplification. No edges are crisp; all the boundaries are blurred by things growing and transforming in time.
Alders whisker up from the ditch. Leafy runners creep down
the road like the veins of alien vegetable invaders. Our hearts
fall, along with hopes we didn't even know we had. We are no
match for this kind of wilderness, with its abandoned, shambling fertility.

Adam, says Pierre. This can't be it. I think it looks planted
already.

We're here, Adam decides. Then he turns around and eyes
up the faces in the back seat. He looks us over one by one. I try
to avoid his gaze, but then he catches my eye and flashes a grin.
The one with the dimples, the expression he always uses when
he wants me to do something fruitlessly awful but necessary.

WHEN THE time comes, I don't so much climb down as tumble
in, penetrating the vegetation the way people wade into swamps,
arms held above the shoulders. Rainwater clings to the branches,
and within seconds my sleeves and pant legs are drenched with
it. I pick my way over and under a perimeter of strewn logs on
the slough at the roadside. Beyond that I'm met by a steep downhill slope burred with salal and huckleberry and last year's brittle
fireweed stalks. They snap against my thighs like dried linguine
noodles. The air smells of celery. I can't hear a single chain saw,
no clanking machinery, no squeaking brakes, no distant hum
of logging trucks. It's a particular kind of stillness once the cutting's been done—a silence like waterlogged wool.

There are scarcely any traces of human existence, save the
regrowing hills, some of which were carved up long ago, the
wood used for things of terrific historical urgency, wooden airplanes and railroad ties and newsprint, which have long since

passed from usefulness into the landfill. I scan the view, hoping for some sign of modernity, a flash of metal or a straight line or a splotch of artificial color. But there's nothing, not even one thin power line.

Even a razed forest tries to resume where it left off. This land, if left to its own devices, will grow back in a chaotic jumble of leafy herbs and ferns and tough woody shrubs. The scrub may be replaced, after many decades, by deciduous species—red alder or big leaf maple—which shed their foliage over dozens of autumns, nourishing the soil. If conditions are right after a century or so, conifers will creep in along the fringes. Douglas-fir will outpace the leafy trees, growing and intertwining and thickening the canopy until it closes over completely. Several hundred years may pass. Eventually cedar and hemlock push up between the firs until, a thousand years after the forest fell, it arrives back at the place where it began.

An old forest is a protected environment, as constant as a rare book library. The trees themselves may be the most awe-inspiring feature, but their trunks, roots, and branchy latticework serve as ladders and thoroughfares and dwelling places for countless organisms—birds, mammals, and insects, mosses and ferns and fungi. The canopy is a big green umbrella, providing precise combinations of moisture, shade, and heat at every altitude from deep dirt to branch tip. Whole megalopolises of wild things call this home. They intermingle and depend on one another for food and protection, population control and decomposition. From eyeless soil dwellers to birds who balance their eggs in high, mossy crooks to furred critters who live so high in the canopy that they may never in their lifetimes touch terra firma. A forest is trees, but it is also everything that lives on and inside and underneath the trees. A clear-cut tears many of these relationships asunder, for a few centuries anyway. It creates biological confusion, a jumble of drastic suddenness for which the residents are unprepared. A clear-cut is like sending a Jamaican out into a snowstorm wearing flip-flops and shorts. Logging, like the devastations of a fierce wildfire, hurls a forest backwards in ecological time.

Even now, this place drinks the hours. I glance down at my watch; the whole morning has passed in what feels like minutes. I lose my footing and slide five steps downhill. When I want to descend it works the opposite way, and I'm snagged like a plastic bag on a branch. The moment I move more than a few unimpeded steps I'm waylaid by physical annoyance, whipped in the eye or poked in the gut or slapped in the face by branches. I swing my shovel like a machete, even though I know it's a useless waste of energy. If I can't find a way to flow with these hostile textures instead of against them, my frustration comes back to me in kind.

It must have felt something like this when the first Spaniards and Englishmen floated up to these shores. Many would have considered the entire continent a geographic headache, an obstacle to get around on the way to Asian spice lands. A man could walk in any direction and face chiseled peaks, swamps, ravines, and frothy, bone-chilling rivers. It must have been frightening and miserable and enraging knowing once a summit was climbed there'd be another one right behind it. If you broke a leg or came to blows with a bear or succumbed to a fever or hypothermia or hunger in this seemingly foodless, evergreen jungle there would be no one around to help you. You could shout all you wanted and nobody would hear, except the ravens, peering down from their treetop lookouts.

AT NOON I grumble back up to the road, soaked to the skin and on the hunt for someone to complain to, but back at the tree cache there's no one. I shove a brownie in my mouth. Sly crunches up over the rise with sweat trickling down his temples.

Tabarnac, he says. I quit.

Then he folds down onto his knees like a camel. We take our time bagging up again, since there isn't much to be gained by hurrying. We talk about all the other jobs we might possibly get if we could only escape this one. We could be letter carriers. Landscape artists. We could be bricklayers or graphic designers. Sly says he'll go back to Quebec at the end of the season. He's got a girlfriend waiting, or half-waiting, which is all you can do when your lover works in the bush three thousand miles away.

I've seen Sly every day since we began, and the contours of his face are as familiar to me as a sibling's. He has one of those bodies whose fat stores burn up early in the season, and now his face recedes into its own concavities, all brow, nose, and chin. Sly and I wonder aloud at our high calorie-to-dollar ratios. We wonder why we keep coming back year after year. Perhaps it's the allure of dirt, a kind of industrial gardening addiction. Perhaps it's Stockholm syndrome, contracted, as it is in cults, from hunger and deprivation. When we want to quit, there is nowhere to go. No way to flee without a boat or a floatplane or a helicopter.

And so we fill our bags up again.

Our pay trickles down from a logging company. A business nested inside larger conglomerates, management firms with names you might mistake for investment brokerages or real estate consortia. It's not so far from the truth. High above us are parent corporations with fingers in many pies, from logging to property development to breweries. Janice's employer—and ours, too—is on the verge of a buy-out. This merger follows fast on the heels of the last one. Back in town, the company signs are still wet from the old paint job. They used to carry the logo of Weyerhaeuser, the American forestry giant, and before that, the Canadian logging juggernaut MacMillan Bloedel. Before Janice was silviculture manager there was Steve, and before Steve there was Kevin. All of them shipped out to other jobs and divisions.

But we're still here.

Before we arrive at the ragged scene the long, lumbering train rolls through. "Logging" encompasses all the attendant processes: the plotting and surveying, the cruising and road blasting, the sawing and bucking and log trawling, and then the long haul to market. But even before the logging plans are devised blueprints are concocted for the management of future forests. Before these silvicultural prescriptions can materialize there must be inventories. The government determines the total trees in the forest, a number derived from aerial photography, remote sensing data, satellite imagery, and surveys.

How amazing and baffling and difficult this feat must be, the counting of all the trees in all the woods, since forests, in Canada, stretch over 1.5 million square miles from coast to coast and cover nearly half the country. The woods change every minute of every day, growing and shrinking, thriving and dying continually. If such a task were conducted by hand and on foot, it would keep an army of surveyors busy for several lifetimes, and once they were done, they'd need to begin all over again. How to measure all the life in the wild? It's like trying to figure out how many snowflakes lie frozen inside the Arctic Circle.

Once a forest inventory is created, the government decides how many trees logging companies can cut. They do this by determining how much wood all the forests have produced— how much the trees have grown—in any given year. A pie chart is drawn and wedges are cut. This is the wood available to be harvested. Naturally, "available" is a hotly contested word with a dozen elastic meanings, depending on how you look at trees and whether you are an environmentalist or a capitalist, an ecologist or a registered professional forester. Perhaps the trees are in your backyard. Perhaps it's your job to saw them down.

The forest is measured not in trees or bugs or salmon-bearing streams but in cubic meters. Or board-feet, one of which is a plank of wood just big enough for a grown man to stand on. The Annual Allowable Cut, or AAC, as it's known, is the maximum harvest that can be hauled from the woods by logging companies. This is an amount doled out every year, like an allowance or a trust fund deposit, but it is not a fixed number. Logging firms can float it up by investing in good silvicultural deeds like planting trees. And so tree planting is a promissory note to the woods. Because we plant trees, logging companies can cut more today. And that is the irony of us.

Like most of the forests in Canada, this is Crown land, the property of the people, who pulled it out like a rug from other people some centuries ago. Cutting rights are leased to logging firms in exchange for rent paid to the government. Stumpage, it's called. And this number, too, swings around every year, depending on which way the economic winds are blowing. When times are bad in the lumber trade, rent is hardly anything at all—a stimulus to forestall layoffs and mill closures. But competitors from other countries think that makes Canadian forest products too cheap. And so there are trade disputes and duties and tariffs slapped one atop the other. Followed by long negotiations and many-paged legal documents and treaties to fix the disagreements.

The logging business is so tangled and complex, so busting with legalese and formulas and acronyms, what normal citizen could be expected to comprehend it all? We can hardly be blamed for asking obvious questions. Just eight generations ago this land was pristinely stacked with virgin old-growth. Where did all that wood go? And why is everyone now so broke?

JANICE SHOWS up in the afternoon, as if materialized out of cloud vapor. I presume she has arrived by company crew boat or some more expedited form of transport. I watch her clamber down over the rise. Janice is an awkward climber. She maneuvers across the hillside with all four limbs, with a crablike technique that is part walking, part crawling. She wears a hard hat with a chain saw visor and ear muffs, though it's difficult to imagine her wielding such a tool. She wears a surveyor's vest weighted with field accessories. I crouch in the slash, dig out my hard hat from my empty back bag. The hatband is wet and smelly, and when I squeak it on the seepage runs down my face like dirty tears. There is no way to hide in a clear-cut. You can only feign ignorance.

Janice crabs her way up. I keep moving. Nobody goes to the trouble of climbing a slash pile just to give you good news. Eventually she arrives at my side.

I want you to respect the naturals, she says.

But there aren't any.

You'll just have to look harder.

Even when they look like that? I ask, running my shovel blade over a sad-looking hemlock with just a spray of yellow needles clinging to its utmost branches.

Even when they look like that, says Janice.

Janice disappears over the hilltop in search of someone else to attack with her plot cord, that long pink cable she uses to conduct her quality control samples. I pull out another tree, one of a batch that has seemingly come out from a clearance sale, from a corporate nursery whose workers employ, in their hasty packaging, a loose and lazy wrap. By the time I get it into my palm, half the dirt falls away from the roots. I finish the job, whacking this infant organism against my thigh. Soil fans into the air with shimmery bits of vermiculite. I dig a little grave and shove the broken stem down, burying the evidence of my deed.

In the afternoon Adam stops to see me. He stands on a stump and looks down on me as I trip from one tree to the next. He wears a cranky, pinched expression. Janice has been giving him hell.

How's it going? he wants to know.

You have eyes, I say.

I don't like planting trees in front of Adam. He keeps a silent tally of the trees I plant and the seconds I waste under his gaze. He watches me bang in seven trees. He lights a cigarette. That's how I know he plans to stay awhile.

I just saw a couple of cougars, he says.

He met them on the road as he swerved around a corner. Golden and muscular, they tensed when he met them, though surely not from surprise. It used to be we saw only parts of these wild felines, a tawny flank or a tail flashing as they leapt out of sight into the bush's high nooks and branches. Now they hang around like big housecats guarding lawns, with swishing tails, brazenly staring us down.

It happens all the time, these animal encounters, now that wild and suburban territories interpenetrate. No grizzly bears live on Vancouver Island, and yet, not so long ago, a young boar paddled over from the mainland. Was he swimming toward opportunity or fleeing the hazards of his rangeland? He was never tagged or studied, because when he reached the far shore, a local shot him. In north-island villages cougars have been known to attack people in backyards and on the sidewalks. They stalk the tiny and the vulnerable: children, pets, and livestock. Cougars are excellent predators. They're also expert disappearers. I have never seen a cougar, though I'm sure a cougar has seen me. Naturally, such an elusive animal is very hard to account for.

WE FLING strips of flagging tape to mark our trees, and the wind whips them away, wafting our red, blue, and yellow shreds high into the air. We have a view of the water from our hillsides. The inlet comes alive with ripples, then riffling whitecaps, until it's blowing so hard we can hear our nostrils whistle. Some of us are caught out in it, wearing only polypropylene undershirts. We shiver just looking down at the water, since later we'll have to cross it.

Brian comes by. He shouts to us from the window of his truck that we'll be knocking off an hour late. With the blustery weather all the floatplanes in the area have been grounded. Tyson, in our boat, had to make another lap into Port McNeill and back again, on account of some contractors down the inlet who got stranded.

There is no accounting for the ocean, as any fisherman can attest. You can predict the weather but not the precise shapes of the sea. There are too many variables: tides, currents, waves, and wind. Some people think nothing of venturing out into its convulsions in a kayak, a rowboat, or a dinghy. I was raised inland, and to me, the movements of the ocean are ceaselessly awesome.

Tides seem so normal and yet so nearly cataclysmic, great deluges of water coursing into one another, bathing the world. The sea unsettles me. I often feel a tightness in my chest just gazing out at its shimmering surface, which masks such abysmal depths. Sometimes, even a thousand feet above sea level, looking down at its infinite blue, I have to glance away.

At the end of the day I climb into the truck. I'm met with a blowing heater and the sodden limbs of my workmates. I guess from their postures that we're all exhausted. We'll suffer the long commute but not willingly. I feel that strange sensation on my cheeks, a ghostly residual prickling after a day spent blasted by the elements. It's pushing 6 PM. The sky looks swollen, about to split. Janice rides with us, an extra body pressed into the back seat, her shoulders shoved up into our armpits. She'll have to boat home with us now that all the company transport has fled the inlet—at a sensible time, before the weather swept in. For a moment I feel bad for her, as if her presence among us says something about her place in the division-office pecking order. It can't be easy to be a small woman in a workplace like hers. A woman, period. For the first time it occurs to me that she's probably a lot tougher than she looks.

At the dock, the wind sounds like surf, blowing ball caps from our heads, plastic IGA bags from the truck boxes. Our tinny crew boat bobs and slaps at the dock, its engine burping smoky bubbles. Tyson sits at the wheel with his hand at the radio knobs. He listens to the marine weather report, that robotic male drone that skippers tune to before they ship out. He flicks it off as we board, watching each of us duck in through the rear hatch. He laughs grimly, like someone about to be joined in his misfortunes.

It's blowing twenty-three knots, he tells us all. But, don't worry, I'm good to twenty-five.

With two weather fronts colliding, the sky is a chowder of wild colors both dusky and bright. A mere Force 6 on the Beaufort scale, precisely halfway between dead calm and a hurricane. A small-craft warning is in effect, which around here is as useful as a UV advisory in Death Valley. The clouds are blown to shreds. Clots and clumps whiz along. The sun descends, poking shards of orange light at the ocean.

We crowd onto the vinyl benches. Some of us scarf down sandwiches while we still can, day ripened and soggy, dribbling flecks of tuna down our wet clothes. Some of us, considering seasickness, opt to stay hungry. We skitter around with the laminated nautical charts in the seat pockets. We turn up our iPods and push the toques down on our foreheads. Rose swings aboard with an unlit cigarette in hand. She wears sunglasses with oversized lenses, like a hungover celebrity. She sits down on the deck, on a hump of backpacks. Then digs for her lighter, which is one thing she never loses. She grew up on a float home, as a child swam every day of the year, and even now is never, ever cold.

Tyson shakes his head. Tell Rose to come inside, he says. He has sudden authority for someone so young.

We bang on the glass and wave Rose inside. She tucks the cigarette behind her ear and comes in, and then the door is slammed tight. That's the last of the open air we'll breathe until we get to the other side. We have goose bumps, our bodies cooling. Our clothes are still wet, clinging to our thighs. We are with the ocean as we are with the weather. We just don't know how we'll react until we're out in it.

Get ready, Tyson turns to tell us. It's going to get bouncy.

Bouncy. I consider this word and imagine things silly and fun, like those castles kids bash around in at birthday parties.

Do you puke on boats? Brian asks K.T. Just wondering, he adds, before I sit down next to you.

We pull away from the dock. Tyson throttles up with his knee propped on the seat cushion. We skim down the inlet, drawn out into the storm by the pull of the tide. Beyond the mouth of the inlet Queen Charlotte Strait widens before us, transformed since morning into a long shiver of waves. Home is just a darkened smudge in the distance. Vancouver Island, so big and yet so far away. We have an hour ahead of us, perhaps two. Some of us, sitting in front near the windows fold their arms across their guts. We're a tight squeeze with Janice among us, though in some ways it's better this way—a rough crossing, all wedged in together.

Have you ever read that book, K.T. asks me, *A Perfect Storm?*

It's what he always asks when we get ourselves into this situation.

The ocean is decisively foul, the tide running against the wind. It rumples and rolls, as if it were trying to tear itself apart from the inside out. A fisherman friend once told me that if you fall overboard at this time of year, you have just twenty-two minutes of consciousness. To be rescued or to get yourself to shore, if there is a shore close enough to swim to. If you can be found before you succumb to hypothermia. Indeed, in this big wild, if you can be found at all.

We take the straight shot across, where there are no islands, no lee to buffer the winds. We get hit broadside by waves, and as we push out into the strait they swell and crest, collapsing down onto themselves. When we roll down into the troughs there is nothing but water, as if we've landed on the surface of an oceanic planet with not a scrap of landfall in sight. From Tyson's contortions we gauge it's less piloting a boat than riding waves, each pushing and tugging from three directions at once at the boat's moaning propellers. We're alternately swamped and then teetering, all the water dropped out from beneath us.

The water is the color of graphite. The wind licks the foam from the waves and whips it into the air. The wipers can't keep up with the slosh of water. Tyson keeps wiping our steam from his view. Sheets of water pour across the bows. We sit two to a bench, pressing against one another. As the boat rolls and pitches the people in the outside fall out of their seats. They do this a few times, and then they just stand up in the aisle, hanging onto the seats, moving their bodies like people do on surfboards. There is a mug on the floor with a broken handle. It scuttles, but nobody bends to pick it up. We zip our jackets, push fists down into the tubes of fleece sleeves.

I sit aft, wedged against the windows. There's only a quarter inch of tempered glass between me and sea. When waves clobber the boat, a pattern begins to form, a swamping followed by a roll so that I'm pinned to the hull by the weight of the boys, looking out the windows as if through the pane of a glass-bottom boat. Looking down into it I can see inside the waves. I think I might even see fish.

Some people are afraid of snakes or elevators or open spaces or even butterflies. I'm not too worried about sharks, slimy things, blood, home invasion, or even being left all alone. But I'm quite terrified of the ocean. Not of boats precisely, but of the substance itself, its ruthless, indifferent enormity. When people fear heights they say the worst of it isn't vertigo but the unfathomable urge to leap, to give oneself over to it. When I'm aboard a boat in a storm I feel a horrifying desire to claw my way out and dive overboard, to fling myself like a sacrifice into its murk.

There is a cluster of islands that marks the halfway point in the center of the strait. We pass by them every day. It's a relief but also a sickening milestone, since we still have another half to go. I grip the seat cushions, hanging on to the vinyl piping with my fingernails. My nerves are as tight as piano strings, every pore hair open, every cilium bristling at attention. Even my eyeballs feel tight. I often tell myself I should live more intensely, but I think I would crumble if I had to feel this much every day.

Barges sink. Boats capsize. Floatplanes go down in the fog, and helicopters crash into mountainsides. People die out here all the time. They die the way people do on highways—a tragedy that lasts but a little while until it blows over, and then it's business as usual. The victims are at work, mostly. A cheap kind of death, as occupational fatalities often are.

Then the sun goes down, the sky fading from indigo to black. And then there is nothing to see in any direction. It might be an improvement, this blindness, no view of the next approaching wave. No pinpoints of light on the horizon, just the slosh of dark water against the window glass. The rhythmic whine of the engines, struggling to stay on top of the waves. Still there is the smell among us of work and sweat and adrenaline.

Tyson's driving is a full-body workout. He stands for the entire crossing, steadying himself with lower body wedged between the seat and the wheel. Through his T-shirt I can see his back muscles working. He's got the lumbar curve of someone young, who's not yet abused his spine with years of labor and bad posture.

Finally we creep around the northern tip of Malcolm Island, where there is a lighthouse. A single optimistic dot of light. We turn south, upwind into the sea, the hull alternately cresting then pounding the waves. This takes another hour. No one is wearing a lifejacket.

Nobody relaxes until we chug past the breakwater, and even slipping into the calm of the marina we have nothing to say. It's nearly nine, and our clothes have crisped on their own by the heat of our bodies. We slouch up the ramp in our sneakers with all our luggage, our bags and straps drooping from our shoulders, wet with salt water. The wind howls. In the orange streetlight of the parking lot, Roland awaits us, wiping his moustache and hand washing with his invisible soap. Already our thoughts have gone home ahead of us. We'll have to eat, go to bed, and get up again in the morning.

I jitter up the ramp. All the smokers light up. Janice climbs the dock ramp behind me.

She says, My company would never have done that.

The straight shot across in open water, she means. Undoubtedly her company would have found a safer, longer route. But we aren't of the company, only next to it. And even though people are the most important thing there is, there will be no safety briefings, no near-miss reports, none that we'll hear about anyway. But certainly there will be more man-days, more cost cutting and maximized efficiencies, and more new forests spread as thinly as possible across the claim. Janice's voice cracks when she talks. She's as tired as we are. And tomorrow, back at the office, she'll have her own brand of surviving to do.

RAIN OR shine, no matter the storms, the show goes on. We motor from Port McNeill over to the mainland or to lonely unpopulated islands that seem to exist solely for the benefit of chain saws. Sometimes there is no dock, just floating booms leashed to the land by huge planed tree trunks, jutting steeply down to a lip of shore. Caulk boots, for obvious perforating reasons, are forbidden on board the crew boats. We disembark onto these floating booms to shoe up. We wobble in an unsteady row, balanced on sloshing logs, since there is no way to climb up to dry land without benefit of boot spikes.

Sometimes, when the water is deep enough, the boats nose up to bouldery landings. We shinny out onto the prow and alight on knuckles of rock. We step down onto beaches spongy with bladder wrack, mud and pebbles sucking at our sneakers. Kelp like slimy green lasagna noodles. And beyond this, there is usually some final, humbling leg to do on foot. A bushwhack through a fringe of glamour trees at the shoreline, then a heated slog up through an old, overgrown cut block. Perhaps these are failed plantations that await eventual restocking. Perhaps some of us planted here years ago.

Hey, dude, aren't these your shitball trees?

As we puff it upslope in single file, we curse at each other's backs.

This place is a fucking gong show.

We *know*. So shut your cakehole already.

The woods, once skeletal and wintry brown, are now adorned with greenery. In the belated moneymaking portion of the day we part a sea of leaves, blades, and stalks and tunnel through. We plant trees in root-choked mounds. We find horned slugs as big as bratwurst. We open holes with our spades and murder earthworms by the pound, slicing their wriggling bodies. We come across the creatures of the springtime, narrow snakes and centipedes and beetles with hard, black bodies. Skunk cabbage sprouts up out of mucky soil in yellow phallic blooms. We plant a tree, and it disappears into this shag of wild, fermenting carpet. Free to grow is what they call a new forest once it's surpassed the competing brush—returned to the wild like a borrowed pair of shoes.

On the long commutes home, quiet sets in. People drift off in unlikely positions, the hum of the engine droning us to sleep. We make the kind of talk that comes only once we've run out of pleasantries. We eavesdrop.

When she left, someone murmurs, I didn't give a shit.

We reread the newspaper until it's in tatters, traveled all the way—a day late—from Vancouver. Bread-making conglomerates perfect a recipe for a brown loaf that has the mouth-feel of white Wonder. The UN cuts food rations to the Sudan in half, blaming donor fatigue. Six million people living on a thousand calories a day. That's a pint of Chunky Monkey ice cream, which any one of us could put back in eight minutes, left alone with a tub and a spoon.

Brad tells a story about accidentally paying four hundred dollars for karaoke while teaching English in Korea. He has a degree in sociology, a discipline he refers to as "the painful study of the obvious."

I used to use my right hand, says Fin. But then I broke my wrist. And so I switched to the left. And then when I broke my other arm, I went back to the right. And, boy, I'll tell you, it was just like coming home.

Home. It occurs to us as if for the first time, haloed in warmth and cleanliness. Our own beds. The twitter of the phone when it rings. Our girlfriends and boyfriends and spouses who say the whole world should recycle paper just so that we'll run out of work, get laid off, and be forced to come home. And the children, who are sometimes so young they can't yet say how they feel. And the parents, who also lack the words. Bend, plant, stand up, move on. Brain above the heart, brain below the heart. And so on. We've just begun to get homesick, even if we've got no fixed address. For now we look at scraps of rainforest scenery whizzing by. Some venture out on the back deck just to be alone, blowing themselves to bits.

THERE ARE no statutory holidays in Planterland, no Labor Day weekends or Thanksgivings. But just in time for Easter, it snows. We spend four days idling around the motel rooms, hurrying up and waiting for the work to rematerialize, speed-dialing the boss, as if he might have an answer for the melting of snow or the angle of the sun.

Our bodies are crumpled, but our minds are wide awake. We're cranky, hungry for something to swallow, feeling an itch beyond the fingertips. Underneath our boredom lurks an idle despair. The thing you feel when your car breaks down on a woe-begotten highway littered with Blizzard cups, Dorito bags, and used condoms.

K.T. and I can't stuff ourselves full enough. Tater Tots, hollandaise sauce, cream puffs, Oreo cookies, pizza pops and cheese-bread fingers, beer, bags of chips. "Turkey dinner" sandwiches from the grocery deli counter stuffed with cranberry sauce and mashed potatoes. We drink coffee dressed with coils of whipped cream, and then we suck back the nitrous oxide from the canister. It's as if we're larding ourselves up for some future austerity.

At night, we party. Our celebrations feel like a letting-go of the days' constrictions, as if we've taken our brains out of their holsters. Perhaps we're just trying to forget.

We begin with Rose, who is the unofficial epicenter of every party. It starts as it usually does, with just the girls hiding out from the men. Her room is a perfumey, smoky swamp. On the floor rests a Rubbermaid bin full of her wardrobe. She packs it around like an exotic dancer or a traveling stage actress. For lack of uncluttered surfaces to sit on, I collapse into Rose's cloth-ing tub, amid the animal prints and the tongues of georgette. A sheer garment hangs over the TV. Glossy magazines kick about on the floor, *Us* and *Vanity Fair*. Rose went to art school, and in her off-hours she gets deep into projects. She says she spilled india ink on the carpet, and since Monday she's been trying to scrub it out. The blotch has spread into an inky explosion, a fatal blotch in the middle of the floor.

There are two beds, both rumpled. We talk about astrology. There's a prescription bottle on the bedside table. *One a day*, it reads. Rose shows me a photo of her as a baby taken inside a tepee. Her mother has dark hair in braids. Rose's middle name is Blueflower. She flashes her driver's license to prove it.

Rachel, our freshest arrival, comes to join us. She admits she's never planted on the raincoast before. She's a small woman, so petite she looks like someone who forgets to eat, like hypothermia waiting to happen. We listen to Rachel's music col-lection. To Ladytron and Blonde Redhead on an iPod plugged into portable speakers. We drink wine out of liter flagons, out of water glasses that get rinsed, never washed, by the chamber-maids. They work a room as we do a clear-cut—left to right, top to bottom, then get the hell out to the next one.

Rose's room fills up with people. Melissa enters, wearing polyester pinstriped pants, snow boots, and a hat with furry flaps. She takes off the hat and shakes out her hair to show us how it has knitted itself into dreadlocks.

Get the scissors! we cry.

After a while we can't keep the boys out. They're bored, rang-ing around outside the door. We hear knocks, and when we don't answer they hurdle the balcony railings and slap their hands on the sliding door. Soon, we're all squeezed in together. We sit in rows on the beds as if in some odd form of church where, for benediction, you get a shot of Fireball or Cuervo Gold.

In previous seasons there has been naked wiggling on pool tables. There have been illicit white powders, snorted from the tops of restroom hand dryers. Unfathomable seductions in hand-icapped bathrooms. Liaisons with local girls in mobile homes on the fringes of town. Shots of vodka tossed back like white fire against the tonsils. There has been drunken, crooning karaoke and bouts of sloppy dancing. There have been fisticuffs, doors kicked open. Stabbings by transvestites. There have been con-ceptions. Betrayals and infidelities. Breakups and tragedy and tears.

Now we jump between the beds and drop cigarette ash on the bed spreads. We've been unleashed into thirty-six hours of freedom, the furthest we'll get from next week's round of slog-ging. We fall into off-duty withdrawal after long days jacked up on endorphins. If there is an intoxicating substance we will drink it. If we have the keys we will drive it. If there were but one tree left on the planet we'd hunt it down with our bumpers at maximum velocity and wrap ourselves around the trunk. We're the guilty survivors. Not of the disaster, but next to it. The peo-ple to the left of the environmental crime.

When in Rome.

Tomorrow is Easter Sunday, the day of resurrection, and all over town there will be plenty of hangovers. Our chambermaid will drop by with an armload of fresh, dirt-brown towels. She's built like a coat hanger, with dentures, a smoky rasp, and a nur-turing spirit that is indefatigable, even with us.

The Easter Bunny forgot me, she will confess.

In this town there is something wistful and heavy in the air. It makes you a little heartsick every time you draw a breath. The log dump bullies the waterfront, its landing stained rust-orange from the mashed bark of rainforest trees. There are a string of jetties and marina floats and a BC Ferries terminal that services the tiny island communities of Sointula and Alert Bay. And beyond this, a stretch of rocky shore where blue herons stand around looking out to sea like old men in trench coats. Swirling crowds of bald eagles, in numbers you can't even count, talk to each other in screeching trills. The weather is mostly gray and windy.

This is the hometown of NHL player Willie Mitchell. The people are friendly, and they converse with the easy demeanor of folks on "island time." When the local soccer teams win, everyone honks, as with a motorcade on the way to a wedding. Germans pit-stop in rented RVs, northbound to the Prince Rupert ferry. Ecotourists on kayak tours, whale watchers. Oprah Winfrey and Bill Gates, the salesgirls often mention, have stopped off in their superyachts to admire the rough, aching beauty. On certain days of the week you can see cruise ships sail by, three or four in a row. You can stand on the shore and watch these monster boats churn. Princess, Norwegian, and Holland America steam by, and then they are gone, Alaska-bound, leaving nothing to mark their passage but a gritty plume of exhaust.

{ 7 }

at the END *of the* REACH

THE MONTH OF May, in the coastal rainforest, is a time of lushness and warmth before the heat of summer sets in. I trade my synthetic thermals for men's cotton business shirts. K.T. breaks out his wide-brim hat. The clear-cuts are sultry with humidity. The afternoons are mad with robins and chickadee song and woodpeckers hammering the hell out of snags. The conifers let go their pollen, and it drifts above the treetops in clouds of Martian green. In the evenings we hear the haunting call of the Swainson's thrush—an upward spiral of beckoning notes that echo out in an old forest like the sound of a sad flute in a cathedral.

We leave Port McNeill behind. We travel south, across the Strait of Georgia to the mainland. Three road trips and two ferries later we arrive at the Sunshine Coast, though "sunshine" is a relative term in the rainforest. This is a peninsula of voluptuous land, separated from the rest of British Columbia by a pocket of ocean called Sechelt Inlet. We must take a boat to get here, though it lies on the mainland, since mountains divide it from the province's highway system. Some of us recall the scenery from *The Beachcombers*, a show about log salvage operators, which was filmed here in the seventies and eighties and still holds the record for the longest-lived drama on Canadian TV.

We roll aboard our new home, a ninety-eight-foot offshore landing craft called the *Lasqueti Daughters*, a barge with a hull the shade of carbon paper. Its three white decks stack upon one another at the stern in diminishing layers, like the tiers of a wedding cake. The foredeck is an open cargo area surfaced with rough planking, a prow that ratchets down onto the shore like a jaw. We walk aboard, shouldering a month's worth of luggage, and let the boat swallow us.

We're yapped at by a little snaggle-toothed dog who looks like he's wearing a sable coat with a copious ruff. The *Daughters* is loaded with people and duffel bags and plastic tubs. Then three battered, mud-smeared trucks wedge in, as if with a shoehorn, leaving just enough room between their side mirrors to fit a folded newspaper. With so little space to spare, if we want to walk from bow to stern we've got to climb over the trucks: up bumpers, boxes, and cabs and down over hoods. But mostly we are crammed with white tree boxes, piled everywhere, ten feet high. We have to shimmy sideways between the waxy, white rows as if pushing ourselves through a tight maze carved out of snow.

It is a miracle the boat floats. Overstuffed hockey bags. Cartons of cigarettes. Ziploc bags full of B.C.'s other cash crop — fuzzy buds, crystallized with resin. Digital music collections. Laptops. DVDs. Flats of beer. Spare shovels. Books. Magazines. Musical instruments. New spring wardrobes of quick-dry pants and pastel cotton shirts plucked indiscriminately from thrift store racks. We have this feeling, upon leaving the shore, that we should pad ourselves for some unknown adventure, whatever the voyage has in store.

Sly and K.T. play chess on a table of tree boxes, on chairs fashioned from tree boxes. Melissa and Oakley recline across cardboard corners in the sun, beeping out photos with their cameras. Others take naps on the truck hoods, sacked out against the windshields or on the roofs of the upper decks. We relax as tree planters do—horizontally, wholly. The ocean is the sharp indigo of new denim. A floatplane comes whining and wavering out of the ether. We're overcome with foolish, vernal optimism. There's new money in the air.

We're fresh from the rare glory of three days off in a row. Most of us burned a straight line home and fell into bed. We blinked our eyes, and now we're back again. Our citified smells drift in the breeze. Bounce sheets, cosmetic potions, the perfumed emollients in the shower racks of home. Our men have shaved and gotten haircuts. They flash untanned strips of skin at the neck and ear. We're lingeringly happy, for the most part. A little frazzled, too. Especially those of us who've spent the weekend with children hanging around our necks.

Those of us who look the most relaxed are the ones who don't ever go home. Melissa's family owns an inn in Tasmania. Doug spends his winters in India. They're always crossing oceans, but when they plant trees, home is wherever they happen to be. Doug wears sunglasses and his beret, like someone embarked on a luxury cruise. Melissa still scuffs around in her winter boots. When your true belongings live on the other side of the world you've got to make do with one wardrobe. Carmen has put in an offer on a house. She chews her fingernails and bobs her foot, fretting about the mortgage paperwork, which will now be left unattended. Adam's mood has also changed during his time off. Home tires him out and ramps him up in equal measure. Now he runs around shirtless, heaving spare tires and fuel drums, though the weather is just a few degrees too cold.

Logging operations now reach far beyond the limits of any village. The harvesting was done, sometimes years ago, from logging camps that have long since pulled their nails and folded down their walls. Or from floating barge camps that featured vending machines and wall-to-wall carpeting and even helipads. They've been tugged away to other locales. Or the cutting was done in inaccessible mountain nooks, the logs slung out by air cranes. And so, all up and down the coast, tree planters live on boats, since there are no motels and no campsites, sometimes scarcely a landing on which to park a truck.

There are no telephones or mail of either the electronic or the enveloped variety. Only the boat's VHF radio and the boss's satellite phone, which costs a buck a minute, whether the call is urgent or frivolous. We're less than one hundred miles north of Vancouver, but it might as well be light-years. We're incommunicado, which is as much an anxiety as it is a great relief.

THE LASQUETI DAUGHTERS pushes away from the shore like an ark in reverse, a boat built for the export of all the weird, misfit specimens. Land and sea peel apart. We bob in a gentle swell, cracking beer tabs though it is barely noon. At the peninsula's northern edge, we pass the small hamlet of Egmont. We cruise by the waterfront real estate, modest cottages perched above lumps of purple rock. Marinas full of green-bearded watercraft. Many of Egmont's residents live on the east-facing slope, with a view of the inlet's far shore. Some years ago this panorama sold to a consortium of NHL players, a logging contractor, and a

California tycoon in the biggest land deal the area has ever seen. An eight-square-mile block—most of a mountain. The world would want to know, said the hockey players, about the incredible wildlife, about the secret, rugged beauty. All this place needed, they promised, was a time-share resort with a pool, spa, and five-star hotel. It never happened. They logged it instead, from the top all the way down to the bottom.

We steam past this clear-cut now, marveling at the thoroughness.

Looks creamy, we all agree.

Who planted it?

Not us, we lament.

Next, the conquest for bunk space. We're greeted in our expeditions by our skipper, Peter, who has tufted white hair, a stubbled face, and moist blue eyes. He speaks with a rusty English accent. He wears an untucked flannel shirt with the cuffs undone, corduroy trousers, and oxfords with professorial soles.

If I were you, he says to me, I'd take that one right there. He points to a window on the upper decks.

The *Daughters* is a woodwork maze of varnished passageways, nooks, and compartments. In the central part of the main deck is the galley, the kind of kitchen you might find at the back of a vegetarian café. Shelves and compartments full of coffee mugs, serving platters, and ecstatically painted bowls. A collection of high-end commercial appliances. Utensils hang from the walls and the ceiling. In the middle of it all, Keira, the cook, wears a pair of industrial ear muffs against the noise of the diesel engine, its cylinders hammering beneath our feet. She's processing cheese with one of those deli appliances that could slice your entire palm in a moment's inattention.

On the upper decks we invade the sleeping berths. There are

four doubles and one dormitory we've already started calling the bachelor suite. We have coupled remarkably well, despite all our differences. Brad and Melissa have fallen in together and claim one of the doubles. Carmen and Neil share a berth as well. Rose has made a boyfriend out of Fin. He wanders the decks shouting her name, like Stanley from *A Streetcar Named Desire*. K.T. and I haul our belongings to the cabin Peter recommended. He's right. It's nice. It won't be long before Adam and Brian sniff out our find and try to wrest it from our grip. We sit down on our backpacks to wait.

Peter sleeps in the wheelhouse on a king-sized mattress. Keira has a cabin so small it seems to exist only between the walls. To reach it, she climbs a companionway from the kitchen up into the ceiling. Later, I learn that Keira is the daughter of tree planters. She has taped to one of the cupboards a yellowing photo of her and Carmen playing as little girls in a muddy camp amid a jumble of spare tires. We talk about this photo and then catch sight, through the galley windows, of a yellow stream of urine released from the upper decks. Keira sighs and shakes her head. The bathroom is just aft of the galley. Its door yawns open and shut with the bobbing of the boat. It will swing on its hinges a thousand times before this job is done. Two showers, a sink, and a single toilet that for the next month all twenty of us will share.

AS WE round the point, Egmont slips from view. We pass through a spot where the waters of the open strait commingle with outflows of Sechelt and Jervis Inlets, like three open mouths breathing into one another.

Jervis Inlet lies before us like a backdrop from *Lord of the Rings*, one of those ominous entrances with forested mountains and granite cliffs rising abruptly from each shore. It looks more like a wide river than the ocean. Snow-dusted peaks with trees sprouting up from rocky perches. Green streaks of meadow where avalanches have mown down the woodsy growth, year after year. It's the kind of place where no people live, not really. Where, if you glance in the right direction, you could fool yourself into thinking nothing has changed in a thousand years.

Jervis runs fifty-five miles from head to mouth, a zigzag of water with three elbows and three deep, narrow reaches dredged by prehistoric glaciers. Like many coastal fjords, its stone walls rise vertically from the water, obliterating the notion of a shore. The water is so deep that boats often do not have enough anchor chain to secure them to the sea bottom. Instead of anchoring their ships, European explorers tethered them to the enormous tree trunks that once lined the shore. The inlet gives no hint of tapering until an abrupt kink at the very end reveals no treasures, no paradise, no elusive trade route, just a cul-de-sac of sedgy mudflats. Here George Vancouver arrived with high hopes of discovering the Northwest Passage only to turn back in dismay. *All our hopes vanished,* he wrote.

It was once a busy territory, home to the people of the Sechelt Nation before disease cut the population down to a smattering. There is still a camp located at the old Deserted Bay village site, owned by the band. They rent it to people like us. There's also a religious summer retreat perched on rocks deeper down the inlet, where it's possible to be waved at by Christian girls in bikinis if you pass by in a boat at the right time of year. Situated at the lip of Princess Louisa Inlet, it was once an upscale resort, the Malibu Club, visited by Hollywood royalty not long after World War II. Otherwise, Jervis is a wild place, awesome in its ragged beauty to the point of feeling hostile. No one goes unless they have something specific to accomplish.

A place of secrets.

Last year, our forester pointed at some cliffs at the far end of the reach.

I don't want *anybody* to go past that point, he said.

Why not? we asked.

He spat a stream of tobacco-brown juice at the ground and ignored the question. Just don't go past those bluffs, he repeated.

The wildest part is deep down at the back of the inlet. That's where all the rain comes from, where all the fog seems to settle. A corner of the world so wild and huge, so hauntingly bereft of human presence, that to go there is to feel unwelcome. Just a few years ago, this boat took another crew down Jervis Inlet. At the farthest reach, while they were at anchor, a tree planter hijacked a skiff in the middle of the night, made his way to dry land, and hanged himself on the shore. There are few tree planters on the coast who haven't heard this story or some version of it. Who haven't heard the *Lasqueti Daughters* talked about as if it were a ferry plying the waters of the River Styx.

THE JOURNEY continues through the night. It's tough to sleep with the engine groaning away. We pretend to ourselves in our bunks that we're just about to drift off. And then, finally, we're startled awake from thin dreams with the night at its predawn darkest. We hear the grinding clank of the anchor and then silence. We wake again inside our mummy bags—it feels like minutes later—to the smell of wet bacon.

The early risers hoist themselves up, slide into sea-damp clothes, and descend the companionway to the galley, where Peter has assembled our breakfast. It's 5:45 AM. He has the rumpled look of a man who's been standing up all night, squinting into black sheets of ocean. Arrayed on the counter is a heartening spread, glistening with grease. Scrambled eggs and sausage in quantities sufficient to feed our small army. This man has seen how tree planters eat and has dealt with crews who burn fat as well as fossil fuels. Hot lipids look good to us. Calories smoked in our metabolic furnaces like rice paper in a flame.

I am not a morning person. Yet I've learned it's better to get up early to avoid the pandemonium of reaching hands, the urgent press as the clock ticks us toward departure. Outside on the deck I find a lunch table laden with fresh bread, platters of cold cuts, cheese and tomato slices arrayed in fans. It's a foggy morning. A sunrise chews at the sky's murk. Doug, in his beret, sits at a galley table with an old *National Geographic* spread before him, one with a feature on seahorses. Tomorrow it will be an issue about timber wolves, and the day after that, back to the seahorses. Nick hovers at the coffee urns with a mug hooked on his thumb. Steam dribbles from the coffee maker. Peter saws bread with a large serrated knife. The sound is woolly and comforting. We don't talk. It's the last quiet we'll hear until we are alone with our work, which has its own intolerable roar.

WE ARE to begin at the inlet's middle reach and work our way deeper into the land as the days progress. First stop, a long jetty built from crushed, gray boulders, a road surface cobbled on top of this, smoothed with the finer granulations. An empty log boom attached to its flanks like a huge wooden hoop. Peter steers the boat to the end of this jetty and drops the lip of the barge down on the edge. The trucks groan to life and roll off. We follow on foot with our baggage slung over our shoulders. We look like a troupe of ragtag mercenaries tumbling onto a beach in search of a war.

A chill blows down from the high, snowy slopes. We can see

our breath, though we're deep into spring, as if we've slipped backwards into winter. We arrive at a heart-shaped landing fringed with alders and maples, shaded with unfurling greenery. From here we rattle out to the cut blocks, three trucks in a line down a lumpy road, like a procession of slow-moving elephants. The woods are smeared with dew.

Our land for the day unfolds as we round the corners—a long, steep swathe banked against a mountainside. It's a big cut, a fresh one. The land is the color of toast. Half of us are destined for the gentle lowlands. The other half for the rough end higher up, where white rocks sit like huge knobs of salt, the boulders of a talus slide where the mountain crumbled out from underneath itself many centuries ago.

Might as well bust out the shin pads, says Neil. I already know where I'm going.

Got that right, says Brian at the wheel with an over-the-shoulder smirk.

We roll down our windows to get a better look, and the cab fills with the smell of resin. Orange stumps dot the field. At the edges of the cut stands a wall of Douglas-fir trees, each as uniformly aged and shaped as the next. Their trunks look like telephone poles, some collapsed against the neighboring forest, blown back in winter storms. Tree flesh, cracked and mashed, lies splintered as far as the eye can see. A second-growth forest, or at least it used to be.

What's the price? we ask.

The price is the price, says Brian.

We blame it on Roland, as usual.

Trucks grind up the hill. At the top, we alight. We find the evidence of the original harvest, the old stumps rotting down into chunky mounds. Old cedar stumps, it doesn't escape us, surrounded by the fresh remains of a different kind of forest—an arid, new plantation.

ADAM GIVES us our plan for the day. K.T. and I will share our land. It's a rare thing, and a little bit melancholy, since we work at separate speeds, never crossing paths all day. The most I'll see of him, besides his lines of trees, is the dirty shirt he shucks off at lunchtime and leaves hung on a branch to dry.

Split it down the middle, Adam tells us now.

K.T. doesn't waste a moment shoving his feet into his boots. He sets out in just a thin thermal shirt, despite the cool of the morning, a sign he plans to fire up the jets. I try to keep up with him—there'll be no way to catch him later—but my laces won't feed fast enough into the grommets. My hands have lost all their finesse. He loads his bags and clips in. He slips over the brown slough of the road. I hear the clink of his shovel as he sets himself to work. He makes the task of planting trees look effortless, like bending to tie a shoe. I slide down the road slough after him and cut my shovel into a clutter of rock. In time, the orange square of K.T.'s shirt slips off into the distance and finally out of sight.

Halfway into my morning, a sneaky rain floats down in a mist so fine it feels dry, like snow. It begins so airily I don't even notice until my hair is dripping. It soaks me through to my innermost layers, as if the weather had picked my pockets.

Adam pit-stops to dump off more trees. He calls down from the road. How is it down there?

Bony, I shout.

You don't need a PhD to note the difference between a virgin forest and a recycled one. The ground here is stones embedded in sand, covered over with crusts of sun-dried moss. Digging

into it with my shovel is like working a spoon down into a jar-
ful of teeth. I scrape handfuls of dirt together and shove them
around the stems. Deep rainforest replaced with low-fat soil, a
trompe l'oeil. A forest-looking forest.

FOURTEEN THOUSAND years ago, this land was buried in Pleis-
tocene ice. The ecosystems underneath flattened, scree-strewn,
beaten down under the weight of glaciers. A few millennia later
the ice receded, and life crept back in from the fringes. Lodge-
pole pine edged north from California. A few thousand years
after that, as the climate cooled and moistened, Douglas-fir
and Sitka spruce took over. And then, about the time humans
took up agriculture, the monsoons came to visit the Pacific
Northwest.

The rainforest titans began their creeping ascendancy, hemlock and cedar sprouting up in the mist, a patient, prodigious
succession. The forest floor thickened into a living, breathing sponge, endometrial in its plush complexity. A broad quilt
webbed with fungi and bacteria, fed by the composting tissues
of plants and animals. Even now, old-growth soil is ancient
and alchemical. A world beneath our feet that's oceanic in its
unknown fecundity. Crustaceans live in it. Out of this dark fun-
dament, life is born of inert matter, from rocks and clay and
sand. Trees germinate here: light-drinking organisms that suck
molecules from the air and transform them into a wondrous
polymer, which is both strong and flexible. And when they are
done living they disassemble and return to the earth. Dust to
dust. We've touched this stuff, dug it up, rubbed it between our
fingers. A cabernet-toned humus so plentiful you could dig for
an hour without seeing anything that resembles a mineral, no
trace of gravel or grit.

Dirt. At home we try to scrub it and bleach it and vacuum it up. We try to deny it with our various under-sink surfactants. But in a place such as this, dirt is a precious, underrated thing. A tree planter's bread and butter crumbs. It's also nourishment, substrate, and habitat. Just one layer of biologically active soil, as thin as a sheet of newsprint or as deep as a few feet thick, on which all living things, sooner or later, depend. Plants sprout from this dirt and are eaten in turn by all the other creatures of the food web. This soil relies on its own living architecture to hold it in place, just as mammals need their bones. Around here it blankets steep ground and is lashed by winter rains. It has been subject to the punishments of heavy machinery—scraping and compaction and erosion.

After a cutover, all the layers of the forest are hacked away: the canopy, the understory trees, the woody shrubs and the soft-stemmed weeds and ferns. The sky comes crashing down to the ground. This is an incredible amount of material—for every square foot of forest floor, many times that in leaf cover. The web of branches that once caught fog and rain is bucked up into brittle flotsam. The soil, once bathed in understory gloom, is undressed, blasted by the sudden, brash light of the sun. All the dusky, micro-tilling fauna are exposed to baking heat and plunging frosts, where once they were protected by the canopy.

Earthworms swim around underground passing grit through their inner tracts, breaking down pebbles into loamy castings. Worms and mites, ants and springtails and nematodes and microbes. They do the work of chewing and churning, bringing minerals to the surface and moving organics downwards. Their secretions dissolve rock. Over time these tiny beings *make* the dirt. Without the miniature life of the forest floor, the living matrix begins to unravel. Water must find new ways to flow through the ground, since there are no roots to drink it up and slow its progress downhill. Occasionally the running rain will sweep everything along in its path, all the way down to bedrock. Sometimes we plant these mudslides, too, nailing them with fast-growing alder.

It takes at least four hundred years to regrow an old forest naturally, but the kind of time required to make soil is millennial and geologic. You can't build a forest floor in a nursery or manufacture topsoil in a mill. The dirt is the dirt, and that's all there will ever be for as long as it takes for the woods to grow it back. The forests of the world may sequester carbon—1,146 billion tons of it—but two-thirds of this is stored not in the trees but underground, in soil and peat.

If soil has a fate, it is to travel to the sea, where it will sediment and harden and rise up in some distant future with the force of tectonic buckling. Perhaps millions of years after mountains are made, these rocks will grind down again. From stone to sand, from river to sea. In a treeless place, with the rain and the slopes, this process is quick-cycled, the dirt slipped down the creeks like a disintegrating sweater put through the wash. The third-hand forest, when it grows, will be leaner than the one it replaces. And the next one more brittle still. Logging even has a name for these diminishing returns. *Falldown.*

Our workplace is a crash site. Two forces in juxtaposition. One is old and slow, accumulating biomass. It wants nothing more than to build. The other is fast and rapacious—our appetites, seemingly without end. Most days we're too busy making money to see it this way, but sometimes we look up from the rubble and the wood chips. We feel the breeze cool the sweat in our eyebrows. We gaze down at the ocean, where this same earthly breath ripples the water. Tide running one direction, wind running the other, like the quivering fur of an animal rubbed the wrong way. We feel a mild ache in our chests. A brush with a thing that's been lost forever. Or maybe we feel nothing at all.

WE'RE NOT puffing along like a steam train anymore but conserving fuel until the end. We've still got weeks to go. Our feet and hands are swollen. We have been this tired before, though we scarcely remember when. It must have been last year. We look out through a haze of fatigue. It tinges each breath, flattens the taste of food. Even our hair is limp. But our tiredness is the chronic kind, the sort that makes us jittery and hyper. At night we suffer from a strange insomnia. We drank all our beer within our first week, and now we've run short on ways to anesthetize ourselves. We stay up past bedtime in the galley, playing cards and listening to satellite radio. Or we lie in our sleeping bags eavesdropping on laughter, the clinking of mugs—the sound of clandestine stashes, of port and St. Remy. The talk, the jokes, the gossip sizzles in our ears. Sleep, by comparison so brief and monotonous, whisks the day away as if it never happened.

We may be sick of looking at the same old faces and forgetting what week it is and grinding through our daily prostrations. Despite all of this we bask in a peculiar contentment—for no reason we can think of except that we're warm, fed, and dry. Stripped of choices, we're ship-bound, with nowhere to be but snugged in among our occupational siblings. It's the annoyed delight of people marooned in a snowstorm or a power outage. Nothing to do but light candles, play crib, eat chocolate chips and drink wine for dinner.

In the little cabin I share with K.T., the floor is the size of a queen bed. The ceiling is constructed of beautiful varnished wood. Each panel is a solid sheet nearly five feet wide, without a single knot or flaw. It's not the kind of wood you see very often anymore. When I lie in bed I consider the size of the trees and also the men who felled them. Luxury wood. The wood of the rich and famous.

K.T. and I have a square window, a ceiling sloped down toward the decks and the bow. All the lines encourage our gaze out to the gray sweep of the ocean. We've spent two weeks aboard the *Daughters*, the tree boxes dwindled down on the decks like melting snowdrifts. Mess moves in to replace them: a couple of forty-five-gallon fuel drums. Blown-out tires. Strewn articles of clothing. A blue windbreaker. Tree-planting bags clipped through the handles of shovels. A fluorescent prawn trap buoy, a coil of green hose. The sun dips, and we're plunged into a lavender dusk feathered with cirrus clouds.

K.T. says, I'll give you ten bucks if you massage my forearm.

Your money, I remind him, is worthless here.

K.T. and I have two narrow bunks built into our walls, one stacked atop the other like bookshelves. We lie in our separate berths, talking to each other from above and below like Akbar & Jeff, those cartoon twins in fezzes. We smell the dishwater in the sink downstairs. A mouse has been scrabbling. It chews and scrapes in the deepest part of the night. We hear it but never catch it. In our cabin there are signs of leakage from above, brownish streams down the walls.

The bachelor suite is separated from us by a Plexiglas port-hole, a square of cardboard for a curtain. We eavesdrop on the inmates, a phalanx of single men who sleep cheek by jowl. Pierre, Sly, Oakley, Jake, Doug, Nick. So used to being around each other they fall asleep farting and talking about girls. Tonight Jake shows around a photo of his mother.

Your mom is hot, says Pierre.

There is a brief discussion about who has dibs on this romantic pursuit, once the contract is through and we return to civilization. This is not a rational conversation. It belongs to the wild, jungly, right-now—to an outdoors without an indoors, to life smeared around, mashing one discrete thing into another. To cabin fever, which is really just claustrophobia pushed out into a vast, wide open.

We listen to Jake talk about the fictional vicissitudes of Ian McEwan's *Atonement*. We never pegged Elfie for the bookish type, mostly because his every second word is either loud or profane or both. Such are the surprises of working life, where our talents are mostly hidden. We listen to the rustling nylon of sleeping bags. The scrape of pages turning.

Is Pierre fucking ready to roll the fuck over and turn off the light?

I don't know, dude. Fucking ask him yourself.

Fuck, sighs Pierre, clicking them into darkness.

There is no privacy. No unshared indulgence. No TV or Internet. No traffic or sirens or take-out food. No anonymous comfort of strangers. No silence. And yet we've never felt less alone.

Keira finishes her prep for tomorrow and then climbs up into the ceiling to bed. The sun descends and the fog slinks down the mountains until just a wafer of clear air hovers on the still and mercurial water. Gulls mope on the old log booms. We hear snoring through the walls. Keira rubs her feet together in her tiny sleeping berth. K.T. dangles his hand over the side of his bunk. We touch fingertips for goodnight. I hear dripping and then the flap of unseen wings. And then finally the day lies down.

WE MOTOR deeper down the inlet. The *Daughters* moors at a shambling dock made of tilting floats nailed with roof shingles. As we pull up Keira checks out the window, all the while slicing and chopping. At the very last second she dashes out onto the deck and climbs the gunnels with a fat, blue mooring line in her fist.

On shore, we find a cluster of rambling structures. An old camp situated on a gravelly landing amid tangles of salmonberry bush, alder, and cottonwood switches pushing in at the edges of a disused gravel parking lot. A cabin painted the governmental peanut brown used on buildings throughout national parks of Canada. A few dented Atco trailers parked behind.

Two men live here, engineers who drill and feed explosives down into rock. They blow up the land's inconveniences so that the roads can go in. They come out to greet us wearing down vests and Stanfield sweaters with holey elbows and the nutty, jubilant look of people who've spent too long alone in each other's company. Their boat bobs at the dock, a small white motorboat, its freeboard hairy with algae. Behind this outpost there is a notch in the land, a drainage along which the logging road runs. Behind that lies a high slab of snow-covered rock, like a mauve-toned cake domed with white frosting. Inexplicably, we find a weather-beaten stuffed animal tied to the branches of a bush. A teddy bear strangled with flagging tape. A sign or a warning—there's no way to tell.

In a few days civilian interlopers arrive in the camp. A group of five men, dressed in camo, jetted down the inlet in an aluminum boat with a roll bar and twin turbo engines. The following morning they rise at the same time we do and zoom off down the inlet, their vessel laden with Pelican cases and coolers and an ATV. Toward whatever kind of guerrilla mission they've come to accomplish.

Even at sea we must have days of rest, a pause for our tattered bodies. On the night off, Adam and I wander up to the ramshackle trailers with the hope of scoring time with a washing machine. We find three of these visitors on the dusty landing, standing around in a circle with beer cans in their fists. We introduce ourselves to a guy named Dale, who says he's come all the way from Michigan. He's a retirement-aged man wearing aviator glasses and dentures a shade too white. Dale waves toward his friend, who lifts his chin to us. The friend stands at a propane stove on a tripod, attending to some meat sizzling dryly in a lidless pressure cooker. He stirs with a fork. The tines scratch the bottom.

Dale has soft, white hands. Like his buddy, he's still wearing a camouflage turtleneck, matching pants, and an anorak printed with foliage. The pattern reminds me of seventies upholstery. He tells us he shot a bear yesterday, and he can't stop smiling.

A guy in a ball cap, logger sweater, and jeans materializes between our elbows. His name is Brent, and he's a hunting guide, hired by these men to lead them to quarry. He is tall and trim with a neat goatee. He has clear blue eyes that are at the same time deeply bloodshot.

Brent shows me the dead bear—a slab of purple meat covered with a bearskin—bungeed to the rack of their ATV. The guts they left on site. The head looks like something half-alive, something between a rug and a sleeping creature. I look into its open eyes. It's got a battle scar that gives the lower lid a sad, drooping look. The meat, Brent says, is going to be sausage. I run my hands through the fur.

Brent tells us that bears around here have pelts softer than anywhere else he's seen. He wonders aloud if it's because of their rich diet. As my fingers comb the bearskin, he probes me carefully in the eyes.

It was an old bear, he murmurs.

To prove this he opens the bear's jaw and flashes some ground-down bicuspids. The bear's mouth is bloody. He steps away and comes back with a roll of paper towels.

It's good to cull the old ones, he assures me, wiping his fingers one by one. They kill a few cubs every spring.

The hunters discuss their quotas—one bear per person. They talk about technique and ammunition. One member of their team, their younger companion, hasn't managed to bag anything yet.

He's still out there, they laugh, tossing glances toward the ocean and the sunset. Trying to score.

Don't go anywhere, Dale urges. He disappears behind the trailers and returns with a shingle-sized scrap of steel. There is a divot in it. The steel is at least an inch thick. Yesterday he took a shot at it from twenty paces, and the bullet almost penetrated. Dale begins to tell us about his gun, which, from the complexity of his description, sounds like an assassin's instrument. It is constructed of titanium with a custom scope. Crossing the border, he tells us, he opened the hard case, and half the station's agents came around the desk to ogle it. He shows us one of his spent shells. It's as long as a middle finger. Adam's eyebrows rise. Knowing Adam I'm sure he's estimating the price tag on this trophy hunt. Yet these hunters are drinking the worst beer in the whole country, Molson Canadian, and perhaps this, too, is meant to be part of the rustic adventure experience. I wonder if we can wrest some of it from their clutches. As soon as I've glanced at their beverages, they shove two ice-cold cans into our hands. It's the first beer we've tasted in at least a few weeks that hasn't been lukewarm. It goes down quick and frosty.

Brent hosts high-ticket hunting treks all year round. Bears in the Canadian summer. Cougars in the Russian winter. You track them up the trails through the snow, he says. And then they set the dogs loose.

Brent, I guess, is as shrewd a businessman as he is a bushman. This place is for him, as it is for us, a living. At the moment he's primed to catch the truth before it slips from our mouths: it's not really hunting. We see scat heaped in disconcertingly large piles. We spot ursine shapes from the rails of the *Daughters*, grazing the shores at low tide. We see them from the truck windows. When they run from our bumpers their fur quivers, rippling with blubber and muscle underneath. We bumble into bears when we're wearing neon orange vests and singing at the top our lungs. We run into bears, and we don't even want to. We're practically tripping over them.

Have you guys seen any bears up there? Dale asks, opening his palm to the deep end of the inlet.

No, Adam says without hesitation. Not a single one.

Our beers are empty. My arms are filled with clothes hot from the dryer. It's time to go.

Come back, they beckon. Bring all your girlfriends. We'll build a big old fire.

ONCE UPON a time, our primate forebears lived not only among the trees but in them. Eventually they swung down from the boughs and became ground dwellers, living in the treed fringes for shelter and protection. Back then we were hunter-gatherers, a sustenance phase that dominated our prehistory for more than a million years. Hominids didn't need to disturb the forests to forage, though sometimes they burned clearings to encourage the flourishing of favored foods. Mostly they kept on the move, exhausting local stores of game before picking up their walking sticks. About 250,000 years ago, we were only one million humans living in roving clusters. Our footprints were not great, and nature absorbed our traces.

A mere eight thousand years ago, we discovered gardening. We settled down and became home-dwelling denizens of villages and city-states, passionate about our homelands and territorial about our *terroirs*. With the shift from hunting to agriculture, people moved away from the forest, since crops require sunlight, irrigation, and the borrowed fertility of alluvial plains. With husbandry came pastures. And then came the cutting of forests, since both crops and trees demanded dirt so wholly there was little room for sharing. Our minds began to change about the woodlands.

Beyond the protection of city walls, the forest concealed dangers—wild animals, darkness, and disorientation. In our fables and folktales the wilderness is an unfriendly realm, a place of deep, existential terrors. It's where crazy people go to wander alone. Where the guilty end up when they've been cast away from the tribe. In Greek and Roman myth it is the site of dissolution and metamorphosis, where humans transform into hybrid abominations—the human horse, the pungent goatman. In the mythic wilds we encounter chaos and decay. And lust. There isn't a vestal virgin who enters the woods alone and comes out with her white robes clean. The wilderness is where you sleepwalk, where you stray, where you lose yourself in unconscious Neanderthal taboo.

The forest breeds aggressive florae as well. In our fairy tales beanstalks rise monstrously from cursed seeds. Whole cities grow over with thorns and thickets. There is something malevolent in the vegetative entropy that lurks at our civic fringes, in the weeds that creep along the far side of the moat. It is as if the wilderness seeks to reclaim what we've hammered and carved from its heart. And so we must remain forever vigilant with our brooms, torches, and scythes. All over the world, animistic monsters of the wild symbolize the threat of this backslide. The yeti of the Himalaya, the Sasquatch, bigfoot, and the abominable snowman. The ignoble savage who'd once been human before being snatched back by the jaws of evolutionary time.

It's a remarkable contrast, in our paved and climate-controlled world, that creatures can still be deadly. Great white sharks and komodo dragons, box jellyfish and saltwater crocodiles. Another beast that still lurks in this liminal twilight is *Ursus arctos horribilis*. The grizzly bear. Perhaps grizzlies still inspire fear because of the way we come across them in the wild—often enough, by accident. A twig snaps. Something ominously large crashes unseen through the underbrush. Or a grizzly appears in silence, a lumbering shadow in our peripheral vision. We glimpse a long sweep of brown fur. The silvery shoulders and wet lips. And if we are close enough, two beady, unfathomable eyes. The mind can't quite believe what the senses register until all the parts coalesce into one creature: *Bear*.

Sometimes we arrive at work to find grizzly bears hanging out at our tree caches, snuffling among our boxes, occasionally thrashing the cardboard to bits. We catch them sauntering down the roads, since the flat gravel surface provides easy conveyance for them, too. We have seen some of the biggest bears of our lives at the back end of Jervis Inlet. We startle them with our engines, and they run ahead of our grilles. They are as wide as refrigerators and as tall as our truck hoods, all muscle and shuddering pelt. They run at a brisk lope but can easily keep up with a vehicle.

To see one from the cab of a moving truck is one thing. To encounter one when we are on foot and alone, without weapons or armor or even pepper spray—that's quite another story. Whenever I wander into a bear's company, I can't help but stop breathing. It must be the paralysis of squirrels when they smell a wolf. A kick from the ancient brain.

North American bears come in a range of colors from black to brown to cinnamon to vanilla. The white-coated Kermode is a genetically recessive black bear that roams isolated parts of northern British Columbia. Grizzlies are bigger than black bears and less common. At birth a grizzly can weigh as little as a loaf of bread. Full grown, it can be as heavy as a Harley Davidson motorcycle and run at speeds approaching thirty-five miles per hour. These bears are the largest terrestrial carnivore on the continent. In the world, they are second only to the polar bear.

They may be legendarily toothy beasts, but grizzlies eat mostly plants. In the spring they consume leafy greens and skunk cabbage. In the fall they gorge on berries. In Western Canada they congregate to claw spawning salmon right out of streams. The fish carcasses they leave behind on the forest floor are a source of fertilizer, imported all the way from the sea. Occasionally a grizzly will take down an elk or a deer. They will eat carrion or steal another animal's kill. They're opportunistic feeders. Traditionally bears have found garbage dumps quite appealing.

Grizzlies are mostly solo animals, and their distribution on the ground is often thin. Males can occupy a territory of up to seven hundred square miles in order to fulfill their significant caloric requirements or to home in on females during mating season. Like many animals whose numbers are dwindling—martens, red squirrels, and caribou included—grizzlies are sensitive to wildfires and clear-cut logging, all those encroachments that shrink their habitat. Like so many reclusive creatures, they like deep wilderness, space, and quiet. They like an old, mature forest to stomp around in.

Grizzly bears may dabble with humans, but they prefer to live deep in the wild, far beyond highways and settled outskirts. When their travel corridors are cut or roaded or interrupted by cut blocks or golf courses, they retreat. Their numbers shrink whenever they are marooned in ecoreserves or in parks with impermeable boundaries. They need space the way birds need all of the air. Grizzlies move with the seasons, across big sweeps of land as well as up and down the mountainsides. Their territory once extended through the western American states into Mexico and spread as far east as the prairies. Now they are found only in pockets of the contiguous United States, in Alaska, and in Canada's westernmost provinces.

Although it may seem as if grizzly attacks are on the rise, mostly it's the headlines that grab our fascination. Grizzly bears seldom go looking for a fight. They don't need to. They're the kings of the forest. They will charge and maul if they are defending their food or young or if they are taken by surprise. They steer clear of any place that smells like humans, for pretty good reasons. In 1805 Lewis and Clark shot at grizzlies before they had even seen one up close—also, perhaps, for good reason—before western biologists even knew what grizzlies were. If a bear tussles with a person, its fate is sealed. It may win the battle, but tomorrow it will be hunted.

EVENTUALLY WE work our way to the back of the inlet, the mudflats where nobody likes to go. Back here, pregnant cumulus clouds dump rain as if it were Miracle-Gro. The valleys are always socked in with fog. Decadent vegetation gushes up from every available crevice. Club mosses that look like furry vines. Slimy liverworts. Ferns sprout from the smallest pockets of dirt, crooks high up in the trees and cracks in boulders. The ditch ponds are skimmed with rainbows of algae. Bear dung lies all over the roads, as if the bears were trying to tell us something.

We drive away from the beach, across a mucky landing. The trucks spin and fishtail just to escape it. We climb from sea level out onto the spidering roads. This place is a whispering remnant. The logging was done years ago, and the camp has now been dismantled. No skidders or yarders or barreling haul trucks, just the strange quiet of fallow land redoubling and gathering strength.

We park on a switchback. Our crew stands around in the fog, stomping our feet down into boots. We await the thump of blades, the helicopter from the base in Sechelt. Some big noise to scare the bears away on the ridges beyond the trees, to cut up the clammy roar of this place, which K.T. likes to say is the sound of getting lost.

Adam comes at me and K.T., his hands cluttered with objects.

You two, he says.

He gives me an ink-scratched map, a golf pencil, and a radio in a chest holster. Plus a plot cord, which means K.T. and I won't see anyone until the helicopter swoops down to collect us at the end of the day.

This is your mission, Adam adds, should you choose to accept it.

We have a choice? K.T. asks.

Not really, says Adam.

K.T. and I have been to work in helicopters a hundred times, and it never loses its thrill. Sometimes we lift off and set down on helipads crafted by loggers, their stringers made from planed hemlock logs. Often there are no landing pads. Then the machines hover down onto big stumps or abandoned trunks. We push our gear out the open door, then step out gingerly onto the skids. We're blasted by rotor wash. We throw ourselves down into the salal and the woody shrubs, hoping for something other than a hidden stump to cushion our landings. Sometimes our pickups are no less exciting. Our pilots can't find us in the mist. Or they can't find anywhere to set down that isn't too steep or jumbled up with slash, no slope with enough clearance for their long rotor blades. JetRangers. A-Stars. Hughes 500s. For the most part we are assigned excellent pilots. Some are ex-military. They're undaunted by wind or fog or tight, obstructed openings in the trees. They have to be this way. The logging pushes higher toward the mountain peaks, deeper into the bush, beyond the reach of any road.

When the time comes, K.T. and I load our baggage into the helicopter's cargo boot. We climb in. The chopper lifts off. Once we're in the air we see nothing but the inside of a cloud, gauzy light beaming from all directions. Thin streams of water bead down the plastic dome of the canopy. It's a short flip. We're in the air less than five minutes before we begin to descend. The outlines of a cut block coalesce through the mist. We see a light green bowl of land, surrounded by spiky green treetops. An old cut, a plantation started years ago by another crew but never finished.

The helicopter sets its skids down on an old road. Adam has told me it washed out in a mudslide somewhere down the line. We get out and give our thumbs up, and the helicopter flies away.

We breathe in jet fuel fumes. And when those drift off we can still see our breath, as if the machine's blades thrashed all the warmth from the air.

Our supply of seedlings came in a netted sling earlier in the shift, the same way babies are delivered by storks. K.T. and I stand with our heads bent together peering at our map, the paper dotted with raindrops blown down from the trees. What appeared to be just a tiny creek on paper is actually a gushing waterfall. Its flow crashes down like a crowd stomping its feet. Low-lying clouds waft and curdle. We can throw a stick farther than we can see.

We make a plan to penetrate the outermost fingers of the clear-cut and work our way back to the center. First, we cut through a riparian strip, a margin of trees left behind along the creek. We wade through in our caulk boots, soaking ourselves to the knees before we've even begun. Our feet find purchase between the stones. The water flows a frothy white, at once heavy and effervescent. If we fall in so early in the day, we'll have to work in a fury to stay warm.

On the other side we arrive in a tiny pocket of clear-cut, fringed with tall trees. The fog thickens. I get a feeling, a hunch at once familiar and peculiar. A prickling at the back of my neck. My ears are full with thundering water, and the air is like vaporized milk. We are two senses short. This land is what people like to call *big country*. So huge I wonder how two living creatures might ever cross paths. Still, a shiver passes over my scalp. I get the feeling we're not alone.

So does K.T.

Let's stick together, he says.

We go to work, down a steep neck of the cut. We plant trees in long lines, horizontally with the contours of the land. We work like knitters at the same sweater, bumping up to each other and then turning away. When we meet in the middle, we share flecks of conversation before drifting out of earshot.

There's a *cougar* over there, says K.T. with suspicious nonchalance, nodding toward the trees.

Really? I gasp.

Yeah, he tells me, she had frosted hair and acid-wash jeans. She wouldn't let me go until I gave her what she wanted.

Funny, I say. Really hilarious.

He likes to find ways to make people laugh, me especially. If I don't crack easily, he'll work relentlessly at splitting my sides. Does it not show mettle? A sense of humor in a place like this? Might it not be the measure of a cut-block companion, a lifelong partner in crime? We inch up the hillside together. We both wear Pioneer raincoats, exactly the same kind, like matching tourists. My radio, in its harness, crackles and burbles with the chatter of distant crewmates.

Once we've finished, we cross back over the creek to refill our bags. The mist blows through in patches, skimming our faces, as we march down the road, like millions of tiny cold bubbles. K.T. walks ahead of me with a purposeful stomp. When his heels lift, I see the caulks flash on his boot soles. They're worn flat and polished, since he hasn't gotten around to changing them. It can only mean he's tired of planting trees.

We pass through a strange smell, a musky blend of wet dog and old garbage. We slow down. K.T. rounds the hillside. He freezes into a full-body flinch. He holds his hand out to stop me in my tracks.

Cubs, he says.

K.T. starts into a crouched, backwards walk. And because he retreats, I do, too, without asking questions. We reverse like two people trying hard not to break into a run. We return to the creek, scanning for signs of motion. K.T. reports what he witnessed. Three cubs, this year's brood, no bigger than basketball sneakers. They have black-brown fur, so young they wobble more than walk. He admits he didn't see the mother bear. Without a doubt, she's close by. A black bear, he guesses, from the look of the cubs.

We wait for another few minutes for the mother to show her signs, but no one comes, not even the wandering babies. We decide she must be busy ripping into our packed lunches. We decide to climb down into the cut block, to put the log jumble at the roadside between us and trouble. We pick our way down through the slash and then into the standing timber that borders the stream. The ground is cleaner here, and if need be we'll have a better chance at running, even though we know we'll never outpace a bear. They're old trees, massive trunks moaning and swaying above us in the wind—useless for climbing, since the nearest branches are a hundred feet up.

Bears can smell rotting meat from miles away. They can sniff a human's footfalls hours after the trail has been hiked. There's so much air churning around today, surely the mother bear has picked up our scent. Surely the waft of our lunches attracted her in the first place. We hunker down to wait. K.T. and I stare up at the road for so long I get a crick in my neck. In our idleness we glance around at the clear-cut that surrounds us.

Wow, says K.T. It's really creamy down here.

A conundrum presents itself. We have more trees to plant, more household wage to collect, but we can't do much with a bear in the way. But that doesn't stop our daily itch, our possessiveness of the land. There's opportunity in risk. It's why fishermen head out into storms for one last turn with the nets.

It's why we'll overstay our welcome in a bear's backyard, after it's warned and huffed and even charged us.

Do you think she's gone now? I ask.

We could check, says K.T.

In the midst of our discussion, we catch sight of the sow, who has climbed a promontory of slash. A tall brown bear with shoulder humps and an enormous black snout. A grizzly.

Guess those weren't black bear cubs, says K.T.

On regular days, not much of anything happens. But when the plot starts to move, it avalanches. Now my blood zings with adrenaline. A knob of fright pushes up in my throat. The sensation is not entirely unpleasant. In all my time planting trees, I've seen only one other grizzly, and it sprinted away as soon I came close. But never a family. I know I'll be sorry if I don't get to see the cubs. A part of me, anyhow.

This bear's fur is the color of butterscotch. She breathes steam and shakes like a dog from head to rump. The droplets fly in a silvery corona. If it weren't for the roar of the creek I'm sure we'd hear her sniffing. With her puffy face and low, pinched brow it seems as if she's wearing a facial expression I can only describe as weary vigilance, the look of single motherhood in the animal kingdom.

She definitely knows we're here, says K.T.

Bear alert, I say into my radio.

Adam comes on the radio. Can you work around it? he asks.

It's a grizzly, I reply. Three little. One very big.

We're coming, says Adam.

Our helicopter pilot drops into the conversation. Tell me what the fog is doing, he wants to know.

I'm unsure how to answer, because every few seconds it lifts and lowers, like diaphanous stage curtains.

It's variable, I say.

K.T. and I devise a hasty contingency plan. If the helicopter can't make it in we'll walk down to the valley along the creek. We'll hope we don't run into geographic dead ends, cliffs, or raging river torrents.

The mother bear climbs down from her perch and disappears. After the radio chatter falls away all we can do is wait for the helicopter to arrive. We listen to the breeze comb what's left of the trees. Canopy rain spatters down on our cheeks. We feel a little helpless.

The mother bear reappears at the edge of the road. This time, she's closer. Her nose works the air. She's "looking" for us. The breath falls to the pit of my lungs, and everything around us, all the wet branches and glossy leaves, recede into a grainy middle distance. They look both extra vivid and not quite real, as if we were watching a documentary film.

I hear the beating of distant helicopter blades and feel a wash of ambivalent relief, because now we have a new problem.

I hope the pilot sends her running in the right direction, says K.T.

We are in the trees at nine o'clock, I say into my radio.

The sound of the helicopter emerges from somewhere deep in the valley, echoing in the trees of the upper forest. The noise grows stronger until it pounds over our heads, whisking the air around. The machine descends through the clouds. I catch sight of the black registration letters on its underbelly. The pilot has removed the cockpit door, as they often do in the fog. He leans out into the open air to get a clearer view and hovers down over the middle of the cut block.

I see it, the pilot says through the radio.

After that, I lose the thin dribble of the pilot's voice. There is simply too much thrashing, metal and echoes and slices of cut-up atmosphere. We hear the engine come down a few notes and know it's time to move. K.T. and I climb up to the road meet it.

A helicopter, with its turbo-powered strength and guillotine-sharp rotors can be an intimidating hunk of machinery, even for a human. In an attempt to frighten her away, the pilot buzzes the grizzly, lowering to just a few feet above her head. The cubs scuttle. Their mother rears on her hind legs and gives the air beneath the helicopter a swipe with her claws. Then she drops to the ground and heaves herself away.

Once she's left the scene the pilot settles the helicopter onto the road. We jog to meet it. On our way we stop to snatch up our bags. They've been gashed open, ransacked, and left to fill up with drizzle. We duck into the helicopter and clip into our seatbelts. As we lift, we see this grizzly family in the midst of their escape. The cubs dart between their mother's legs and hide beneath her torso. They run like this, sheltered by the bulk of her body. She's a thin bear, we see from the air, her fat stores whittled down from hibernation, pregnancy, and lactation. She climbs up and away between the stumps, fleeing with her brood between the tender stems of a juvenile plantation.

The helicopter rises to altitude. It peels away from the mountainside in a stomach-tugging nosedive. K.T. and I huddle in the back seat. With the open door, we're blasted by the wind, wet, and cold. The pilot makes chatter through the headphones, and I answer his questions in a post-adrenal daze. We pass through veils of rain. When we emerge on the other side I see nappy treetops. The clear-cuts like jigsaw puzzle pieces, the little green lakes in the distance. All of it so repetitiously tiny, so inconsequential from above.

In a few minutes, we set down on a road I've never visited before, a valley bottom with greened stump fields rising on either side. We alight with our tattered luggage, and then the helicopter swoops away to attend to other members of our crew. The air is warmer here. We catch sight of one of our trucks parked in the distance. We see the same old accoutrements of the job, stacked tree boxes, our crewmates working, oblivious to the events of our day. We kick around in the gravel, waiting for Adam to arrive. I feel odd, not quite inside myself, my brain not yet caught up with the sudden safety of this new locale. I'm really hungry.

We dig through our packs to assess the losses. The outer layers of scrim-reinforced vinyl have been shredded into strips. Each ribbon measures the width between the mother bear's claws. The contents are rain soaked. From all our belongings, we salvage two dry shirts. Our lunches have been devoured, the containers cracked and crushed, the teeth marks still visible in the plastic. At the bottom of his bag K.T. finds one intact sandwich. He opens the box, and the air between us fills with the yeasty whiff of fresh bread. He ponders the sandwich momentarily and then tears it in half. He sizes up each of the pieces in his hands and takes the smaller one for himself. We push bread into our mouths. We stand like this on an open road, a hundred miles from our home in Vancouver, looking into each other's face. We chew without talking.

Last year we read a story in the news about a bear attack on two hikers. They were a married couple. The bear lunged first for the wife, knocking her to the ground with a single blow of its paw. It chomped down on her shoulder and dragged her into the bush. The husband ran away. To find help, he claimed afterward. But we knew the truth of it. He ran in blind terror to save himself. It wasn't his fault. Life and death and wild animals. You never know what kind of person you'll be.

Would you have run? I asked.

Never, said K.T.

When else might we ask such strange and illuminating questions were it not for planting trees?

It's just cheese and lettuce, says K.T. now.

It always is, I reply.

The sandwich. So bland and loathed every other day of the week. But today, because it's all we have, it tastes like the best thing I have ever eaten. It tastes like the perfect food, comforting and substantial. It reminds me why the loaf is the most ceremonial of human staples, made to be broken and shared.

K.T. and I watch three of our crewmates toil away in the distance. They work abreast, tumbling over a rise, cascading down toward the road. They're running out of land, shouting at each other while they battle it out for the narrowing remains. A diesel truck rumbles toward us. It's the battered red truck, whose coils we've got to heat three times before it will start in the mornings. Soon we'll be back out in the field.

The sun beams humidly behind a gruel of clouds. Blood beats in our ears. Our salivary glands gush. We hear our breath whistle through our inner passageways. My heart still gallops in my chest, pulsing blood up through my neck. I seldom pay attention to this tireless organ. But still, it will thump away without pause or fail—if I am lucky—for the better part of a century. Life rushes up in its mortal constituent parts. A he. A she. A sandwich torn in two.

{ 8 }

EXTREMOPHILES

IN JUNE THE vegetation is drunk on long days of warmth and sunshine. Herbs grow leggy and insistent; fireweed and horsetails push up past our waists and sometimes even our heads. What a northern summer lacks in length, the plants make up for in gusto, turning out their green finery all at once. The alders and cottonwoods have popped their leaves like millions of tiny solar sails. The conifers bolt out bright new growth. All is rustling. The very air feels crowded. Soon it will be solstice, the day eighteen hours long. The globe will tip on its hinges, and then we'll begin the slow tilt back to winter's somber lull.

Spring eases into summer, but it's not all glory. June is also a showery month. The sort of jaunty drizzles Pierre likes to call English rain. With this combination of heat and water, the bugs emerge, not in a rising wave but in a sudden blitzkrieg. No one aboard the *Daughters* is prepared except Brian. He totes a bottle of full-proof DEET like a sheik with the world's last barrel of oil.

We steam north up the coast, tracing the mainland until we've reached the latitude of Port McNeill once again, nearly looped back to where we started. One last tour remains, at the site of an old logging camp deep in Seymour Inlet, yet another of those aquatic inroads into the mainland. This one, we know from experience, is even less traveled than Jervis.

We arrive at Woods Lagoon, where everything has changed and yet remains exactly the same. Beyond the rise of the shore lies a bald, sandy patch the size of a hockey rink where the camp used to sit. All that's left are a few behemoth hemlock logs bordering the creek. They serve the same function as concrete medians in parking garages—to stop people from reversing, in this case down into the stream. A few pickup trucks linger here, left behind for contractors with ends to tie up at distant fringes of the claim. The camp has been dismantled, piece by piece, and shipped away. Roland says it's because of mold problems in the camp's walls, and perhaps that's even true. But as far as we can tell, most logging operations pull out in the end for the same reason people push away from tables once they've had their way with the food.

The *Lasqueti Daughters* moors at a partially submerged dock. To disembark, first we must step down onto a loose scrap of waterlogged plywood that gives us just a couple of dry footsteps before it sinks underwater. Up the hill we see the cavernous hangar where mechanics used to perform surgery on motors and drive shafts. Rusty pulley blocks and wire rope spools lie around, nibbled at by encroaching grass. At the highest point we find an old hunk of unidentifiable machinery with a masonry brick positioned on top. If we brave the camp bear, who still patrols these parts, if we climb up the hill and then atop this old contraption, and if we stand still on the brick facing the right direction, our cell phones bleep to life with a single wobbly bar of reception.

Now that the camp has been abandoned the only other vessel in the water is a barge, harnessed to the shore with lines of the heft and seriousness used to tether tankers to docks. A Rubik's Cube of Atco trailers stacked upon trailers, interconnected with steel catwalks. Flights of steps, reminiscent of cheese graters, that ring out when you climb them. Long banks of fluorescent lights. Black rubber runners in the hallways hide perforations in the linoleum where working men have walked illicitly in their caulk boots. Oily tunnels down to the generator, which bangs away into the clear, tangy air. This echoing vessel is occupied in a lonely way by the barge owners plus a half-dozen forestry engineers who are here for just one last phase, to pull out modular bridges and culverts.

And even they will be gone next week. We'll have our way with this place, and then, officially anyway, all of this will be returned to the wild.

SEYMOUR INLET and neighboring Belize Inlet share a mouth at Nakwakto Rapids, which is itself obscured from open ocean by an island—an uninhabited, tree-covered lump of land that sits like a stopper at the mouth of a bottle. If you didn't know that whole maritime worlds exist beyond, you would sail right by, none the wiser.

Nakwakto Rapids is a tidal narrows, notoriously tight and vicious in full gush. In the middle of the channel sits Turret Rock, which is said to tremble in the force of maximum flow. The trees on this tiny, vibrating island have been nailed with signs displaying the names of boats that have successfully shot these rapids. They look like those white highway crosses marking fatalities. Navigational disasters still occur here. Not so long ago, a tugboat sank while pushing through, and its crew only survived by climbing aboard the log barge they had in tow.

Nakwakto is one of the fastest tidal passages in the world. And yet behind this bottleneck lies a network of waterways, a kind of geographic womb. Behind the narrows, the ocean is so peacefully labyrinthine you might forget it is the ocean entirely. You might think of Venetian canals. At their narrowest point you could throw a stone across. Two centuries ago, hidden behind their gate keeping island, 'Nakwaxda'xw villages lay protected from intruders. The people thrived undisturbed on these shores long after curious Europeans had made contact with other coastal tribes. Nobody made a nautical chart back here until 1933. It is the southern boundary of a region, which even today lacks roads or cities, once called the Midcoast Timber Supply Area. A hunk of primeval woods now known around the world as the Great Bear Rainforest.

At the far reach of Seymour's long arm, inlets lead into smaller inlets, pockets inside pockets. Woods Lagoon is a purse of water ringed by an old cedar forest. The trees rise to dead white spars like wooden bayonets. It is a gnarled ecosystem, sprouted out of rock and thin dirt, pounded through maturity by cataracts of coastal rain. The forests here are something of a natural freak, a testament to the accreting tenacity of cedar, which will try to grow wherever their seeds find moisture. It smells and feels like a place uninterrupted by history, populated by hoary beings from the past. If pterodactyls swooped down from the canopy they'd hardly take us by surprise.

We used to come here every year, back when the logging camp ran full bore. It was a bustling place, an industrial village nestled in a bowl of forest with log booms lashed to the shore. The bottle-green water was so placid that in a pattering rain it came alive with perfectly circular ripples. Loggers slept in rows of bunkhouse trailers, their quarters connected by breezeways roofed with crenellated plastic. Boardwalks rutted over the years by thousands of footsteps, men going out or coming in, stomping in their caulk boots, formed avenues with names like Stagger Alley, scrawled in Magic Marker on the siding. Whoever had done the signage had the all-caps penmanship of someone more adept with brute tools than with writing instruments.

Clustered trailers, like a small suburb, organized around a cook house, a laundry room with washing machines labeled for two varieties of clothing, dirty bush garments and less-dirty bush garments—uptown wear, as loggers sometimes call it. A managerial office. Two al fresco living rooms with tweedy, sagging sofas. A satellite phone booth. The familiar bank of showers, toilet stalls, and urinals—for the men only. A dry room where we found a bucket of wax oil with a paintbrush in it, so you could marinate your boot leather without even troubling to unlace.

The camp was constructed mostly of particle board and two-by-fours. Topographic maps hung stapled to the walls. In the rafters sat huge bolts of industrial garbage bags, margarine tubs to catch the leaks, bales of pink insulation. Plus a cat, who stared down at the mousetraps in the hallways. Although the camp was not as far out in the wilderness as you might find yourself, it was hardly a day skip either. Men worked here in multiweek rotations. They commuted home in floatplanes operated with levers and knobs, with the analog simplicity of old-fashioned cigarette machines. Like the loggers we stayed two to a room, sharing ten square feet of floor space. We slept in narrow beds stretched tight with coarse white sheets, hospital corners done so severely by the camp's matrons that they cut off the circulation in our feet.

At night a black bear roamed the hallways looking for food. We could hear him wheezing outside our doors. In the evenings we watched him eat huckleberries from the bushes outside our windows. He was much more dexterously delicate than we imagined a bear could be. He stepped on the branches to lower them to the ground, then pursed his lips, like a human mouthing a string of grapes. We half expected him to unzip himself, like a man in a fur suit. We met a raven named Walter by the camp residents who flew alongside pickup trucks as they sped down the roads. If you rolled down the window, they said, he'd eat a sandwich from your hand.

If women worked here, they were cooks and custodial staff. The odd forestry professional or summer student. We shared a single, tiny bathroom with a note beneath the mirror that read: *This place is our oasis. Please keep it clean!!!* The sign featured a clip-art palm tree. This water closet of sparkly melamine and rusted porcelain was the only place in the entire camp that smelled remotely feminine. The shelves bowed with half-full bottles of fruity shampoo and pink cans of shaving cream, left behind by the females who'd come and gone.

We ate like men, like princely carnivores. Roast beef with mashed potatoes. Steak and mushrooms and baked potatoes. Ribs and macaroni salad. Caramelized protein char propped up with a side of carbs. No quiche, no curry, not a single asparagus spear. Once upon a time, in logging camps, there were no vegetables, no milk that didn't come from a can—nothing fresh at all that couldn't survive a long cargo trip. If we didn't know how to eat what was put before us, we learned quickly, without a peep of special vegetarian pleading.

Signs flashed everywhere reminding the residents of the social strictures. Use a fork, not your fingers. Take your hat off in the cook shack. No pissing in the bushes around camp. Drive school-zone speed until you get past the workshop. Beer everywhere, but nobody brought it into the cook shack. Mind on task. Safety is job one. Obvious back in the civilized world, but out here anarchy loomed in the leafy fringes. People required reminding.

Slightly apart and up the hill sat a bunkhouse referred to by the camp's residents as Heli-World. All the outbuildings were attached except for this one, which was removed, like a guest residence. It contained a private bathroom and a billiard table. Heli-loggers lived here. Men who bushwhacked their way through a forest nobody else could reach by road or boat.

Heli-loggers fall and buck their logs tree by tree, and then the trees are slung out by helicopter. Logs weighing tons swing overhead, out to the ocean from the hanging grapple of an air crane, whose booming rotors, even at a distance, are enough to give a weak heart palpitations. The logs are worth thousands of dollars each. They have to be, since the cost of running helicopters like these is hundreds of dollars every minute.

Helicopter logging wasn't one job, we learned, but an array of tasks so hideously dangerous it was a wonder they were even legal. Some fallers cut the tree trunks nearly all the way through, within inches of falling down. A helicopter came along later with a dangling hook and plucked these trees from their stumps like candles from a birthday cake. Some loggers wielded chain saws with cutting bars as long as a man is tall, in steep, cliffy terrain. Climbers bucked branches before the trees were even felled. They ran up a trunk with crampons and harnesses carrying half their body weight in gear—including the chain saws that dangled from their belts. They climbed high into the canopy, buzzing limbs as they went. Then they sawed through the spar, strapped to the tree by just one thin belt, which rested inches below the cut point. The treetop cracked away, and the trunk swayed with the force of the toppling stem. Sometimes they didn't even put a hand out to hang on. They were fit, strong, and slightly nuts. There must have been something at their cores, some hyped internal metronome. They felt right in sync pulsed up with adrenaline. They loved a vertiginous height.

The loggers we met were lean, wiry men. Or they were huge, with tough, beefy hands and necks like WWF champs. We met Crazy Bill, who wore white cowboy hats and, in his off-hours, had a passion for four-by-four driving at fatal speeds. We met guys with nicknames like Dog Balls and Bre-X and Shorty. Men who'd cut themselves open in the middle of nowhere or been strung up by the ankles with yarding cables. A burly man, delicately named Skyler, who got drunk during the Stanley Cup playoffs and ejected his TV through a window. Some of them started logging before they'd finished high school. Some had dads who'd done it, too.

They went to work before dawn and returned to camp by midafternoon. We trailed in a couple of hours later, and they were usually well into happy hour, killing time before dinner. They took off their boots and aired their sweat, sitting around in the sun on gutted vinyl benches and log rounds. They talked about the hideous contours of the land they worked—sheer and bluffy, impenetrable with understory brush. Salal so tight and tall they had to cut their way through. They were still in their bucking pants. T-shirts with the sleeves torn off, the cotton stretched loose at the neck holes.

Just wait till you see what's coming to you, they snorted.

We planted the land they'd cut the year before. We walked in their footsteps. It gave us a fleeting kinship, though probably they would disagree. Sometimes the loggers partied with us on the nights before our days off, even though they were paid to work every day they were in camp. They pulled beer cans from bottomless pockets. They laughed at us for needing days off to rest.

So weak, they scoffed.

We tried to explain how our bodies took a beating, how we never got more than one day of rest. In their off-shifts, they got a whole week. They were gorillas, and we were greyhounds. We busted out guitars, and they sang along with us out of key. We howled out tunes into the most sacred quiet of the night. Classic rock songs everyone knows by heart: "Sweet Home Alabama." "You Can't Always Get What You Want."

Eventually the fun came to an end. One morning, after a flamboyantly loud night, the camp foreman lumbered down the halls, looking to blast any one of us loitering in his sights.

Bastard tree planters, he cursed.

He was a big man in a trucker's cap. A solid paunch hung over his waistband. His feet were the size of bread boxes. But he drank chamomile tea from a white coffee mug with the tag looped around the handle.

Some of us remember our first time in this camp, nearly a decade ago. We were the first tree planters the loggers had ever seen. An old-timer once told me he thought it was good that girls worked in the woods now, alongside men, even though some of his co-workers weren't so keen. They like it simple, he said. Just men, the wives and kids stowed safely at home. They liked how it was in the time before policies and bureaucracies and environmental regulations, back in the days before rules.

Once, he said, he'd watched a pod of killer whales chase some porpoises into the lagoon.

A marine slaughter, right there, he said, pointing at the view.

For days and days, the water foamed pink with blood.

AROUND HERE we plant western red cedar, the celebrity species on the coast. A cedar stand is a climax community, often centuries older than a Douglas-fir forest. The bark of these trees is supple and soft. Stripped away from the trunks it looks like russet hair.

For the original peoples of the Pacific Northwest, cedar was a prime raw material. *Arbor vitae*, the tree of life. They used the roots for baskets and wove a rough linen from its fibrous bark. They had ways of cutting planks and peeling bark while leaving the tree standing. They made canoes from hollowed-out logs of cedar, which is prized for its decay-resistant qualities. The canoes were over sixty feet long and could carry forty people, plus provisions, over long stretches of cold, bad-tempered ocean. The coastal tribes were mariners, and they put out to sea in fleets of cedar canoes. These tribes became trading partners. And although the three major language families of the coastal aboriginal peoples comprise dozens of tongues, many are so similar they're often thought of as dialects. The history, the language, the geography, the cedar—all are intertwined.

In Coast Salish lore, cedar was bequeathed to humankind by the Great Spirit, who planted it on the grave of a kind and generous mortal. From the cedar tree the people made longhouses and weapons and tools. They made nets, harpoons, towels, and even diapers. They made totem poles and coffins and beautiful, smooth bentwood boxes. Cedar was the most versatile substance they had, as ubiquitous as plastic in our world.

One of the biggest red cedars of modern times once stood on Vancouver Island, in Cathedral Grove, a tiny preserve of virgin rainforest carved through by a tourist highway. The tree was over seven hundred years old and measured fifteen feet across, but it was set on fire by vandals in 1972. Today the world's largest known specimen is the Quinault Lake Cedar on Washington State's Olympic Peninsula. It's over twenty feet in diameter and contains 200,000 board feet of timber.

Everyone knows what cedar wood looks like, even if they have only seen photos. It's soft and lightweight with a silky finish. It has the reddish-brown hue of human skin bronzed by the sun. Fresh-cut cedar smells like Christmas and pencils, saunas and brand new shingles, like lemons and cinnamon and pepper. It is a luscious, expensive smell, too much and not enough all at once. The living tree has flat, ferny needles, if indeed they can be called needles, for they are more like tiny, waxy leaves. After a rain the branches grow heavy, until the tree takes on a weepy, downcast look. But on a fine, breezy day a cedar tree comes alive with movement. From a distance it looks like a woman wearing a dress made entirely of green feathers.

BEFORE THE white man arrived, the people of the Pacific Northwest lived next to the forest on the lip of the ocean. They dwelled among the trees, but they weren't averse to pushing against the wall of wood at their backs. They relied largely on the bountiful proteins of the sea, but more of their supplemental foods were found in clearings than beneath the darkened canopy. Berries grew in sunny openings, and game also foraged there. The people encouraged these meadows by starting fires, which were not always what we now call "controlled." From these man-made fields they dug camas, a lily bulb that tastes like sweet potatoes when roasted—a prized carbohydrate in a land without staple grains.

They logged, too, though theirs was a painstakingly selective version of the practice. Their fallers were experts. They knew how to choose precisely the right tree for their purposes and how to cut it down so that it toppled in a strategic direction. They did this without metal implements or domesticated animals. With any luck at all, they'd find a tree close to a river or near the beach, though sometimes they penetrated the forest for several miles to track down just the right one. The logging itself involved rites and ceremony. A faller would pray and fast to prepare. Before taking anything at all from a tree, the people talked to its spirit, to explain why they needed the wood, bark, or roots, and to thank it for its generosity.

For the coastal people, cutting was a team endeavor. They burned a tree at the base and chipped away at the trunk with stone adzes until it swayed and came down. The cutting alone might have taken days and days. Then they skidded the tree on rolling logs—each of which required cutting as well—with as many as sixty men pushing and groaning and tugging on ropes. These human drive teams were often composed of slaves. Without axes or band saws or teams of oxen, it was visceral, time-consuming work, expensive in calories and sweat and probably lives. Once they'd dragged the log into the water it took several canoes to tow it back to the village. Any kind of logging so strenuous and labor-intensive left a light mark on the land.

When Euro-American settlers reached the Pacific Northwest, they faced all of the same challenges and more. They were hell bent on bigger alterations, on clearing land to make way for farms. But cutting gigantic coastal trees proved a formidable task for people who'd come from easterly regions, where the trees stood like chopsticks by comparison. Where logs could be cut, hauled, and floated down rivers with relative ease. Rainforest trees were so big and unwieldy, and the terrain was so rough and dense, that preparing it for agriculture or grazing would have been a fight against the very composition of the land, a feat akin to moving mountains.

In the days before power tools it might have taken two men with axes several days to cut through an old rainforest tree, whose bark alone required hours of chipping and sawing. When such a tree fell it cut a swathe of sky into the surrounding canopy as it cracked through hundreds of branches. When it struck the ground the impact rumbled out like a tremor. The trunk might have bashed a crater into the soil several feet deep. The downed tree was so heavy it had to be cut into chunks and then dragged out, piece by piece, by horses or oxen. And behind the stump there would be dozens of other trees looming between homesteaders and a clean, tillable field. Once they'd finished cutting, they faced stumps with roots so thick, expansive, and tangled that the whole project must have seemed gruesomely overwhelming. It was easier just to set the whole thing alight.

In 1850, only a billion people walked the surface of the earth. The rainforest must have seemed wild and lonely and bereft of human company. As if what it badly needed was opening—order, light, and most of all, room—so that more people could come to live. Trees grew ubiquitously, in ironic abundance, since lumber was outrageously expensive. There was no ready way to cut, haul, or process wood without engaging the help of whole teams of men, all of whom required payment. And once the waterfront timber had been logged, further supply lay deep in the bush. And so forests were seen as something close to worthless, an impediment to the eye, plow, and cart. A stump field was a sign not of environmental violation but of progress, of nascent cosmopolitan cachet.

Small-time logging began on the west coast in the latter half of the nineteenth century, just as Canada came into being and the United States was in the throes of the Civil War. Independent hand-loggers employed teams of men with job titles like donkey punchers, whistle punks, and swampers, as well as the original teamsters, who were the foul-mouthed drivers of horse and oxen. These outfits cherry-picked old-growth trees near the shore, sometimes falling them straight into the ocean. The logs were then boomed and shipped to mills in the south. When this easily accessible wood was gone, the men used draft animals to drag logs out of the bush and down to the shore. Theirs was a rudimentary form of selective logging, or high-grading, some might say.

Lumberjacks cut notches into the tree trunks and hammered in their springboards—spiral staircases that allowed a man to cut above a tree's wide buttress. As time went on, they climbed higher up the mountains and farther into the bush. The deeper and steeper they went, the more brutal and risky the work became—sometimes it was literally crushing. They built skid roads. They hauled in steam donkeys to winch and inch and budge logs out. They built ever more complexly dangerous slides and flumes for the scudding of logs from mountainside to water. These chutes are the inspiration for rides at modern amusement parks—for Loggin' Toboggans, Zoom Phlooms, and Zambezi Water Splashes.

Early loggers were restricted by gravity and physics in practically every way, since they had no yarders or bulldozers or, for many years, even combustion engines. When disasters happened the victims might have been several days by boat from medical attention. An injured man either lived or he died, and everyone in camp would have known he met his fate without the aid of hospitals or doctors.

Archival photos from the early timber days show men who spent their lives squinting at inscrutable problems of mass and inertia. They were lean, mostly unsmiling men with moustaches and Popeye-sized forearms. Although they were solid, you might guess from their body shapes that they were also as agile as dogs. They owed their lives to an ability to sprint, to get out of the way of killer trees, which could roll and crash like runaway freight trains. You can still see their handiwork all over the Pacific Northwest. The old, notched stumps crumbled down by time in every kind of second-hand forest.

WOODS LAGOON hits us like a slap. All that land the loggers promised—the hairball gullies and snarled back corners. Cedar trees seem vengeful about their own demise, since they produce astronomical heaps of wreckage. Their branches swoop down before they grow up, and when cut they're shaped like sickles. The trunks themselves are often hollow inside, their heartwood rotted away. When these fall they blast apart into spears and shards.

This woody trash is infernally slippery, immune to the grip of our footwear. At the same time, it reaches out and snags us, like a field of giant fish hooks. A branch releases from pressure and whips us in the shins. We lose our balance and then fall into a garden of broken sticks. Our trousers tear apart at the inseams, then shred apart into hula skirts. All this slash is ensnarled in branched, woody webbings of salal, like that impenetrable briar in *Sleeping Beauty*. Salal is the world's floral greenery, the rubbery background foliage in bouquets. But here and now, I spend my days barging through it with my whole weight, as if through begrudging turnstiles. I travel in ups and downs, in French curls and hairpin turns, not so much walking as wading and stumbling. In this visual cacophony you can drive yourself mad trying to make a forest in neat, straight rows, and indeed Jake goes nuts every day. He curses at the top of his lungs with the regularity of a steam whistle, reminding us to glance down at our watches.

We find depths of exhaustion so profound they feel pleasurable—one of those brain-body paradoxes, as if we were drinking ourselves sober. Sometimes, when we tumble, our limbs refuse to push us back up again to vertical. Sometimes we don't even realize we've fallen, turtled on our backs with our seedlings escaping our bags. We catch ourselves with our faces to the sky, recognizing puffy forms in the clouds, feather pillows and sheep blobs. We've worn our steel blades down by inches. Our boot leather is chapped to a pulp.

A giddiness takes over, a deep, careless fatigue. It's not just Sly shaking his head and muttering. Brian is so sleep deprived his sentences come out in incomprehensible, rapid-fire stutters. One afternoon, he serenades me with an a cappella version of Neil Diamond's "Forever in Blue Jeans." We stand next to a truck on a crunchy stretch of rubble. A hot breeze blows over the land, flapping all the tarps. If I keep my lips open, the wind steals the moisture right off my tongue. The bugs struggle up in my lee. I listen to Brian sing the whole song with each of the verses and choruses. I wonder if it's a gift or I'm meant to join in or I'm simply to be held hostage by a song.

You're crazy, I say.

Money talks, he replies. But it don't sing and dance and it don't walk.

At the end of the day, on the drive back to the water's edge, the roads are eerily deserted. Adam drives as fast as physics will allow, as if he were trying to blast us into orbit. I guess we must love this sensation since we never complain, the white ribbon of road flying out beneath us, the spiky treetops blurring past. The soundtrack for our commute is Emily Haines singing: *Tu sais que je n'aime pas ma réalité.* The CD has been wedged in the drive for days, and no one has been able to coax it out. We jostle together in time to the music, to the rhythms of the chassis. We ramble out of words. And just like that, as a cloud runs out of water, we give up on our complaining. It must mean the end is near.

Blood crusts our temples. Black flies bounce on the windows, trying to escape. We crush them with our thumbs, leaving streaks of our own blood down the glass. We talk about the times we've rammed our shovels into hornets' nests by accident. The humiliations suffered because of insects—stung on the lips, the penis, the asshole—and the resulting elephantine swellings. We have a conversation, like the Frost poem, about whether we would rather die of hypothermia or burn up in flames.

K.T. says, When you freeze you feel euphoric at the end.

That's what they always say, Oakley responds, about the shitty ways to die.

We race toward our off-duty comforts, and the weary anticipation is palpable. The truck screams around bends, kicking up flumes of beige dust. As it hits the road bumps we settle into a nearly comfortable formation, like anchovies dovetailed into a can. Our cheeks are hot pink. Twigs and huckleberry leaves nestle in our hair. We are stunned and tired and indestructible.

Dirt. We're striped with it, smeared down the sides of our necks. We've found mud in all our crooks, washed it from every cranny. We've eaten it by accident and even on purpose just to see how it tasted. On our tongues it felt like sand stirred into cold butter. It tasted just like money.

Just outside the camp's boundary, the road rises like a cresting wave. This geographic feature seems to draw us in. Adam stomps on the gas, and all four tires leave the gravel. We feel a thrilling lightness in the bones, the looseness of skin, hair lifting from our scalps. For just those few seconds we escape the tug of gravity and the body's freight, and then we settle back down to Earth.

THE HEAD-FIRST plunge, the verbs before the nouns. If this quality were a substance, some blood-borne humor, Adam must have it in spades. He can be martially tidy in some ways and a magnificent slob in others. He moves into new locales seeking entrances and escapes. He has no superfluous flesh at all. He's the only person I've ever seen get four charley horses all at once.

We have noted his fondness for tight-fitting Lycra shirts. We have seen his teeth crumble out of his mouth. I've played dozens of Scrabble games with Adam, and I can never decide if he's cheating or winning or perhaps a little of both. We have come across him on a logging road lying under a car chassis with shop towels stained by transmission fluid. We horrified ourselves from a distance, mistaking the car's pink juice for blood. Once, on a foggy, out-of-the way cut block, he ate some wild berries to moisten his mouth. They were poisonous, and before long he puffed up and turned purple, crashing into anaphylactic shock. We strapped him to a basket stretcher with a bottle of oxygen and heaved him out, the whole crew tugging his formidable dead weight. The way rescues have been done since loggers started crushing and burning and gashing themselves open in the middle of nowhere.

We've seen Adam grind Ford trucks backwards through creeks and over stony beaches at low tide. Seen him MacGyver cooling systems with bits of hose and duct tape. Every year Adam can be counted on to flog at least one vehicle to death. He's even destroyed two trucks at once—one parked, one traveling fast in reverse. When he collided, he told me later, he still had his foot on the acccelerator. We've seen Adam so angry he charged up stairs, taking the risers three at a time. When he reached the top of the flight and flung a door open, we worried for the target individual, whose room he found at the end of the hall.

But on the other hand, if we need anything at all, he brings it without a moment's vacillation.

I need more, we'll shout.

One hundred pounds of trees on his shoulders, straight up if need be, undaunted by slopes or ravines, by distance or dizzying heights. And when he's dropped his cargo at our feet, sweating and wheezing, next thing he'll light a cigarette. If there is more than one Adam in the world, we're both grateful and chagrined he doesn't work with us. We make good money from the force of his turbojets.

There may be "slow food" and "slow travel," but there is no such thing as slow tree planting. Or logging gently, since tree-friendly wood has not yet been invented. Until then, if you want a piano or a paper plate or a hardwood floor—if you want an omelet, as they say, first you must break some eggs.

Adam lives in a little town on Vancouver Island where everyone knows everybody else, and you can walk practically anywhere in ten minutes. He spent his last night as a bachelor with so much nervous energy he built a rock wall with his bare hands by the light of headlight beams. Now he has a wife and two small boys. When he returns from his tours in the bush, does she make him strip down in the garage before setting foot in her house? Does she make him swear not to muddy up her washing machine? When we see her in town, Mrs. Adam, she can barely look at us, as if we are to blame.

WE ASSESS the damage in the gray light of our cabins. Bruises dot our thighs. They come in exactly the shape of the objects we fell upon, thin as a pencil or wide as a softball bat. We leave our shovels on the deck overnight, and they're rusted by the morning. Leaks in the roof and buckets in the galley. The bush makes attempts to digest us.

Aboard the *Daughters*, the hallmark of our resignation is the bathroom. We step on tree bark and hair and bits of gravel in the shower stalls. A dozen kinds of shampoo. A back-scrubbing brush. Lady razors. Assorted bars of gooey deodorant soap. Rose's panties hang from the towel rack. The rubbish bin overflows with crumpled sheets of brown paper towel, which means somebody's used them to dry off after a shower.

We are unsympathetic to the injured or the departed, since they've left us to carry out the deed. Our numbers have dwindled, our co-workers fled back to civilization on floatplanes summoned by satellite phone. They claim injuries, family passings, pets with cancer, and commitments to other bosses. Wherever they've gone, we are the stay-behinds. We imagine them planting on utopian plains, where the ground is flat and the air is cool and bug free, where there the logs are so slim you can step over them instead of detouring around. Where the rain, we like to say, is only practicing.

In trade we gain Julien, the boss's son. He's as burly as his dad but with the finesse of a trained athlete. He doesn't plant trees. He's a hockey player. Unlike us, he's symmetrically muscled. We can tell by the way he walks. He's here on a daily wage to chauffeur and unload, to gopher and ferry, to deliver tree boxes when the road's washed out or when the clear-cut's too deep to be feasible. He's always eating something lean and healthy, some form of low-fat vegetable roughage. He is educated, kinesiologically speaking, about fats and carbs, about fast- and slow-twitch fibers.

Our mental rubrics are more like on-off switches: it works or it's FUBAR. It hurts or it doesn't. Full or just plain empty. Julien does push-ups on the roads while we work. We watch with disgusted bemusement. What a strange luxury, this fanatic idea of our time—*the workout*—the superfluous wastage of calories.

Come on out here, we holler. We'll give you something to cry about.

Our job is immune to technology. We have GORE-TEX and fiberglass and PVC, but in the end it comes down to just us and our bodies and the trees. Researchers have studied us. They've swabbed our skin and drawn our blood into stoppered test tubes. They've strapped us with heart monitors and pricked us to measure our glucose levels. These experts want to quantify how far, how long, how hard a body can go. We've filled out their questionnaires. What do we eat? What kind of gloves do we wear? What kind of maniacs are we? But nobody has done a study on the contours of our minds.

If we could return ourselves like appliances from the Shopping Channel, surely we'd request different components. We could use better knees, for a start, secured with an extra ligament or two. Hands with tougher fingernails. We might ask for bigger feet and better balance. And if only we wore sharkskin, since we're stuck with an epidermis for an outer covering, not a carapace or fur. Our teeth are hard as rocks and our bones are as strong as wood, and yet we burn after a few short hours in the sun. It seems curious indeed that the toughest parts of us are on the *inside*. Our only consolation is the skin's sensitivity. For every blister and scratch, we gain sublime touches in trade—the sun on our shoulders or a puff of wind through our hair or even the texture of someone else's skin.

In our outdoor office there is no denying the merciless absurdities of the natural world. Plants grow, and small critters graze them, and other, bigger animals snap these victims in their jaws. It's a feudal arrangement, nature's energy chain, fraught with struggle and sacrifice. After the providers come the consumers, the emptiers, the raiders of seeds and roots and fruit. The stealers of honey, the grazers of the seas. And finally, the apex carnivores, the murderers, bloody in fang and claw. Topped by *Homo sapiens*, the only predator on the planet that straightens its teeth with brackets, wire, and glue.

Our genetic forebears weathered plagues, droughts, and famine. They fought and ate with their hands. Our bodies are still made to be flexed and worked. We have Achilles tendons—and thus a long-legged, springy step—though our closest primate relatives, chimps, do not. For two million years we chased down antelopes without the benefit of Nike or Adidas. Our bodies are still capable of traveling shockingly long distances, not in planes or in cars but on foot. We evolved to take a beating.

Although we're not the strongest or the fastest creatures on Earth, we are capable of incredible feats of relentless persistence. Humans have lived normal lives in extreme environments in nearly every corner of the world. The people of the Kalahari live in a place so dry and hot it has no lakes or running streams for several months of the year. The Inuit thrived in the High Arctic for generations without electricity, petroleum, or even smelted metal at temperatures that plunge to 40 degrees below freezing.

In their darkest months they have no sun at all to guide their way, only polar twilight.

At the same time, we're lazy. We'll eat the cheesecake instead of the spinach salad. We'll take the elevator before climbing the stairs. It is possible to live in our modern world without ever breaking a sweat. We suffer for it, since an estimated 1.5 billion people in the world are now overweight, an epidemic whose numbers have exceeded those of global hunger. Perhaps it's not entirely our fault. Cravings for delectable fats and for the sedentary life are the legacy of our hominid ancestors. For most of our prehistory, humans lived dangerously on the razor edge of nourishment and starvation. Eating involved a chase and a fight to the death. Or endurance contests of picking and gathering. Food had to be prized open or dug out from the ground. Or it hung high up on the end of a brittle branch. There were other animals to be outwitted who wanted these nutrients, too. No sweet, fatty substance came without exacting a toll nearly equal to its caloric reward.

In the modern world planting trees makes no sense at all. It shouldn't make us happy. And yet we were born with the tools at the end of our arms that are perfectly attuned to the task. Eyebrows catch our sweat before it runs down into our eyes. We can bend over two thousand times a day without complaint. We can lift and carry, toil and dig, from dawn to sunset after virtually no physical training at all.

Perhaps we feel something deep in our fibers that no one else seems to anymore. Our job isn't extreme or masochistic or backbreaking. It's not even all that hard. Actually, it's exquisitely *normal*. Our sore muscles are merely the equipment dusting itself off, exerting itself as it has done since naked apes picked themselves up off their forelimbs and began walking on two legs.

We can't help but feel we were made for fresh air and long hours of movement. For manual labor, whose simple rhythms match those of the breath and the fleshy *lub-dub* of the heart.

But how can we say for sure? We're not scientists or doctors. Our skills seem obsolete. Some of us never even graduated from high school. In just a few short months the planting season will be over. We'll head back indoors for the winter. And outside, beyond the windows, there will be that longed-for cold, that hunger we used to know.

PLANTING TREES is the opposite of instant gratification, since you must wait for each little sapling to show its signs. There are no guarantees against failure. All over the world the task is basically the same. From eucalypts in Brazil to the cedars in British Columbia to the teak plantations of Southeast Asia. There is something very old about the ritual, some kind of penance in the genuflection.

We have imbued trees with our metaphors. A planted tree symbolizes the wishful try. And new beginnings, since we plant a seedling when a baby comes into the world. Also when someone leaves it, so we have something lasting to remember the person by. It's a gesture of repair and good intentions. We sit in leafy shade when we need to pause, to meditate, or to wait for the storm to pass over. We plant trees to soothe our guilt when we fly in jumbo jetliners. Planting trees can be very sentimental.

Trees are community beings. They shelter one another from wind and weather. They communicate among themselves by secreting airborne chemicals. Underground, they hang onto each other with intertwined roots. A lone tree is almost certainly toppled in a big storm, but when a stiff wind blows through a clustered grove, they sway and bend together. Their roots move up and down in the soil, squeezing water through the subterranean passageways like a broad, pumping heart. The canopy combs fog and catches rain from clouds. In winter, snow gathers between the trunks, so that it may trickle out into the land during summer. Trees are nature's air conditioner. They calm the wind. It's why farmers plant them in rows at the edge of a field, to stop the dirt from sifting away. And as everyone knows but nobody can prove, where trees grow, the rain follows.

Plants possess a magic we lack. They spin matter out of air and light, photons into food and into living, breathing tissue. We talk to our Boston ferns and our African violets. We plant trees along the boulevards. We like to have them around us, benignly exhaling oxygen. Maybe we're a little envious. Kingdom Plantae, after all, is the reason we eat and breathe. Petroleum, too, is dinosaur vegetation, centuries of sunlight trapped deep in the earth's Carboniferous wafers like butterflies preserved between the pages of a book. And so we even owe our cars to the jungles of antiquity.

Seventeenth-century botanist Guy de La Brosse grew plants in sterile soil and distilled water. They died. He deduced some invisible force was at work in the dirt, some magical unseen element that caused life to root down and to grow up with unswerving tenacity. He called it manna. A tightly wrapped bundle of trees will try to grow when tossed out into a rocky ditch. Even then, left to dry out and die, the stalks will turn straight toward the sky. Their roots will push down in the opposite direction, fingering around for home. Trees are clever, as any plumber will tell you. Their roots strangle backyard pipes. They prize their way into weeping tiles as if they *know* there is water inside.

Trees move at a terrifically slow pace, and at the same time they have accumulated more biomass than any other organism

in the world. They are some of nature's most elegant engineer-
ing. As are we. We're creatures of the sun, too, in ways we are
only just coming to understand. And we're builders. When wood,
rock, and even steel are bashed and weathered, when they reach
the limits of strength and hardness, their surfaces wear down.
When we're chafed and exerted we don't wear down or wear out.
We grow a callus or a muscle. When we've strained so hard we
tear our most delicate fibers, by some biochemical feat we knit
back together, not broken but stronger. Who can say they know
for sure the giver of these gifts of adaptation?

{ 9 }

SUNSET

AS SUMMER APPROACHES, the sky fills with buzzing and flapping—bees and birds, dragonflies that swoop and clack like sticks knocked together. Hummingbirds dive bomb our heads as they buzz out their taunting calls. They mock our clumsy bones, our pitiful wingless existence.

In a clutch of weeks it will be the first day of summer, the shortest sleep of the year. The trees, triggered by just the right temperatures and just the right photoperiods, let rip. Their buds erupt into starbursts of tender needles. Conifers grow vertically from just one spot, the tip of the leader branch, which bolts skyward before it sprouts a crown of lateral branches. In good growing conditions a tree can shoot up a few feet in one summer; in bad years, scarcely an inch.

The spring plant in the rainforest must soon come to an end. Our seedlings need time to flush and grow, to root down before the onset of another winter. Our crew will disband. We'll spread out in twenty directions, moving on to inland parts that are just now pulling back their snow covers. We trade cedar and fir for their interior and sub-boreal cousins, ponderosa pine and black spruce. We'll live in tents for the hot months, in bush camps instead of motels. There will be cooks to serve us salads and enchiladas baked in lava flows of melted cheese. There will be bonfires and pretty girls—all the jubilations of summer camp with a little work thrown in on the side. We'll join the hordes of university students who flood the cut blocks each year once their final exams have been inked. Which is exactly how many of us started this job, once upon a time. It will feel like a welcome change, indeed like a party, because partying is exactly what nature is doing. Rutting and molting, burgeoning and ripening, throwing up its arms in euphoric celebration, a mambo on the grave of winter.

Hunter-gatherers of old tracked the movements of food animals, the herds or the flocks or the schools of fish. Millions of people still live this way. Planters of trees are also peripatetic creatures, though our quarry is just a paycheck. Come July, we travel in cars and trucks in search of an ever-unfolding spring. I've spent all the summers of my adulthood among the stumps, washing out to the clear-cuts with the rest of the tree-planting army. In my memory these months compile into thousands of bag-ups, and the summers merge into one long season, cut block after cut block, heat waves interrupted by winterludes. Each spring I packed my car with camping gear, sleeping bags, and spare tires, and I ventured outdoors, until the time came to head back inside in the autumn. Some years I lived nowhere. Home came with me in my Volvo station wagon, as a turtle carries its shell. Even now I don't kayak or rock-climb or visit the cottage. Summer has always meant work to me.

I planted trees at the edge of the northern prairie, in the

neighborhoods of pump jacks and gas wells. I planted in tall grass and clay, which after heavy rains turned to liquid gumbo, a substance so slippery you could glide a truck off the road without even turning the wheels. I planted the remnants of old forest fires, working among scorched trunks that covered the hills like blackened matchsticks.

I planted trees on northern plateaus where the land rose and dipped in swells of brown and rust. I passed through whole forests turned brassy by the mountain pine beetle, an insect that travels in biblical clouds like black sesame seeds tossed up in the air. A plague that has killed off a nation-sized forest, since the winters have grown too warm, with climate change, to kill the little insect. If you stood near the right clump of pine, you could hear them chewing. A sound, people said, like Rice Krispies popping in milk. A smell like inferno waiting to happen.

I toiled on dry hills overlooking the American border. The other side looked exactly the same in its geographical features, and yet here worked our Mexican counterparts, sweating it out with antiquated mattocks, for less than peanuts. Peanut shells. I planted cuts for the second and third times, where all the trees had been killed by bud worms or weevils or the roots had been infected with toxic fungi. Part of the job of refreshing these cut blocks involved pushing the old, dead trees to the ground so they wouldn't shade the new seedlings. Sometimes the roots were so rotten I toppled trees without even needing to lean into my hand. I replanted old clear-cuts where the seedlings had been trampled by cattle. All those years of replanting and trampling and replanting all over again. Sometimes I ran into cows in the field with their beamy ribcages, the grass clipped short as a putting green by their teeth. For a while I was sure I could make a job just replanting the tree farms that had died.

I planted trees on bilingually intermingled crews. Some people spoke no English and others spoke no French, and yet somehow we made our feelings known. I learned the curse words of the Québécois, which seemed to come at the end of sentences, like *amen*. In the evenings we built campfires. We sat cross-legged on flattened beer boxes with our hands put out to the heat. People brought out instruments from their glove compartments and their backpacks. Recorders, piccolos, bodhran, guitars, harmonicas, and instruments made of nothing more than gourd and wire. We listened to it dribbling out from cassette tapes, and then CDs, and as time passed, MP3s. It leaked from headphones. We walked to the showers humming. People sang on the block. There were notes in the air, always. That's how I knew that at the end of the world, we'd have music to keep us company.

Wherever I went, no matter how I traveled, I saw others of my kind in transit. Silvicultural workers crisscrossed the highways to get to their next destinations. I caught sight of their trucks mounted with fiberglass insulation boxes. I saw them on the ferries and hitchhiking on the roadsides. They were the ones in the beat-up cars with equipment piled up in the back seats. Foam mattresses and Silvicool sacs and guitars. I saw them loping down sidewalks with their shovels strapped to their backpacks. They were everywhere you'd find chain saws and feller-bunchers, wildfires, tree disease, and unkillable pestilent insects. Everywhere needed trees.

I found jobs near Prince George, the tree-planter gulag of Canada. A township in the middle of what had once been airy, undulating pineries. The local mascot was Mr. PeeGee, an effigy of a log-man wearing a hard hat. His head, I'd been told, was crafted from a septic tank. No matter where I walked, the town smelled like pulp-mill emissions, like brimstone. I didn't mind Prince George. At least it didn't hide what it was.

I planted trees in foothills and on high plateaus. Places seldom visited by tourists, by any people at all. I came to know the literal meaning of the word *panorama*—since clear-cuts made for unbroken views at once staggeringly beautiful and brazenly shorn. Some of these cut blocks were prehistoric upheaval sites, the remains of splendiferous tectonic clashes. Wafers of the earth's crust piled up in the distance, land rumpling like ice floes in a jam. The mountains sheared upward, baring the petrified sediment of former seas. I bashed open stones, and they came apart like clamshells, split into etchings of prehistoric marine worms. Snowflakes spiraled out of a blue sky. The creeks were a bright azure, cloudy with rock flour. The air was cold and dry, and it was electrifying just to breathe.

So rocky, I complained to my foreman.

He was a small, middle-aged man with a thick moustache. He wore the same pair of jeans every day. He smoked John Player Specials, which was the brand you chose when you planned to puff yourself into the grave.

Not rocky, he clarified. Just *stony*.

The price, at first, seemed incredible. A whole thirteen cents per tree. But alas, it was complicated. The soil lay hidden underneath moss, bark, and old forest floor, and it took most of this thirteen cents to free it from its coverings. This had to be done with a scalping procedure performed with the shovel blade. I swung my shovel high. I dug and scraped, like dogs dig holes in lawns. Once, I'd heard tree planting referred to as *backbreaking* and thought it was some kind of metaphor. *Screefing*, they called it. I didn't know the man who'd invented this task, but I knew he'd never planned to do the work himself.

Sometimes I went to bed without eating dinner, without even bothering to shower. I woke up in the morning with hunger knocking at my ribs. My body felt wooden, dried in a kiln overnight. It was a struggle just to pull my socks on. This was illuminating, in a way. A taste of what it might feel like to be old.

In these northern realms, nearly everyone on the crew had been recruited from parts of Canada too distant to know what they were getting into. A herd of robust prairie boys, blond and Christian. They grew excited with their knives and forks when the big hunks of meat emerged from the kitchen at dinnertime. There were east-coasters, Maritimers, whose dads had been lobstermen and brewery workers. They were by far the rowdiest, as if the distance they'd traveled had something to do with the force of their celebrations. They stuck together. I thought of them traveling as one, swinging from the rigging of a pirate ship across a raucous sea.

It's a bad year, said our bosses. Fewer trees, more of you.

That's why the prices had plummeted. They always said that. Work for less or don't work at all. They paid us according to complicated formulas. When our paychecks arrived we stood around tugging on our ears and scratching our scalps, comparing stubs. The accounting got so creative sometimes it ate away half our wages. Our foremen made a cut of our earnings, as deck hands net a portion of a fisherman's catch. They hired men as exclusively as possible, because men could be relied on to be competitive and hard earning. The result was a camp of mostly males, which led to a culture of furious contagion. Young men working like human pile drivers just to outdo each other. Even the women got caught up in work fever. Most of us were single. Unattached to places, people, and rules, and sometimes even to principled ideas.

In all that time I learned to think planting trees was whole-some and good, as long as you admired it from a distance. Trees made air. They sponged up the rains, and their roots held onto the dirt. From a distance it was the Mother Teresa of summer jobs. At the same time planting trees was a complicated gesture, a two-faced business. The locals seemed to know the difference. So did the loggers and the small-town residents whose view was our clear-cuts, who opened their windows to sulfurous pulp-mill fumes, though their noses had long since learned not to register it. They treated us like shoplifters and vandals and rowdy free-loaders, which sometimes, it must be said, we were. Unlike them we were temporary and transient. We didn't have to live on the shorn ridges or the pine-beetled plains. And we got paid, some-times handsomely, by the very same companies who supplied the town wages, the mortgages, the taxes, and the car payments. By the very same business that cut the trees down, which can-celed the altruism right out of the equation.

WHEN AUGUST rolled around the summers turned scorching. The work dried up, just like the water in the creeks. And so the tree planters edged out in search of further employment, as far north as you could go before tumbling over the border into Alaska, Yukon, or the Northwest Territories.

In the North, you could drive for hours between gas sta-tions. The roadside ditches brimmed with coffee-toned water. Organic fluff blew around in the wind, like summer snow. What the woods lacked in height they made up for in breadth. They seemed to be made of just a few ingredients. Water, sphagnum moss, trembling aspen, but mostly spruce, which is what we planted, almost exclusively. The land felt flat and endless and old as rock, as if mastodons might come crashing out of the underbrush. If you slipped into the bush and wandered in the wrong direction, you might turn in circles for days.

No way out but even fewer ways in. Up here, the land was so spongy and saturated during the warm months it was difficult to tell where terra firma ended and water began. The forest sprouted up out of muskeg—a soup of black muck topped by rafts of sphagnum moss. In many places the ground was so liquid and ever shifting that the only vehicular access was down ice tracks in the winter. Or along the seismic lines—long, treeless corridors used by the petroleum industry for their predrilling explorations. Camps were air-lifted into place, piece by piece, mess tents and cook stoves and all-terrain vehicles. These contracts began with helicopters, which might dip down by a random field or a strip of lonely road and pick up a major appliance in a cargo sling. You could watch a refrigerator levitate and disappear into the forests waiting beyond—a familiar thing in the wrong place, like a car floating down a river.

Until eventually, when no infrastructural pieces remained, the people became the cargo. I scurried to the helicopter with my duffel bags and shovel. I ducked my head under the whiffling blades, the sunlight strobing in my eyes, not knowing much about where I might be headed. Only that I'd call it home for as many weeks as it took to get the job done. I climbed in and buckled up, and the helicopter lifted over spiky green treetops. I looked down at orange-rimmed swamps with watery centers. They looked miniature, like puddles glistening with gasoline rainbows. Boreal forest stretched out in all directions, seemingly without end, like the pelt of an enormous sleeping monster.

The trees broke, and we hovered above a clear-cut so big I had to squint to see the edges. From the air it looked like a small prairie. The helicopter set down, and I got out with a group of my co-workers. The helicopter engine whined an octave higher and kicked up a blast radius of dust. We crouched and watched the chopper rise into the sky, taking with it our last chance for escape. The motor drained away. The sound was replaced by the buzz of a million mosquitoes, singing for our hot, red blood.

We lived on the edge of our worksite, like miners camped at the lip of a crater. We erected our dome tents in the leggy spruce that fringed the clear-cut. The forest floor was a timeless, mossy shag. When I stepped into it I sank to the ankles. I wondered how long it had taken for this living carpet to grow, how long before we killed it with our weight. It would take two days on foot to get to the nearest telephone, flush toilet, and electrical outlet, assuming you set off in the right direction.

We had no trucks, only an ATV. And so the crew walked to work like Snow White's dwarves in a line, all of us trudging through mud, woody chaff, tall grass, red paintbrush, and fire-weed in bloom. We shared footsteps, like people do in snow. When we arrived at our daily patch of the clear-cut, we filled our bags with spruce. We put ourselves to work in the coiling trenches like needles set down in vinyl grooves. We bent over at the start of our days and didn't stand up straight again until it was over. When I glanced back at my lines I could see the little trees leaning to one side or another. I knew it didn't matter. No company forester would venture all the way out here just to get down on his hands and knees to scrutinize my handiwork. So I kept on nailing them in with bleary abandon, scarcely wondering if they'd survive the winter.

The afternoons cooked. The sun baked our necks and shoulders. It seemed cruel that a place so savagely cold in winter could get so hot in summer. As if the land knew no middle ground, only extremes. The heat grew boggy and moist. Salt dusted our cheekbones. Our lips turned dry and white. Always the sweat ran, down the spine, through my scalp and down my cheeks. Every time I bent over it dripped off the tip of my nose. There was an insect for every hour of the day, as if they'd arranged their shifts. I spent a lot of time slapping myself across the face.

We carried our drinking water with us. If we ran out we could take our chances slurping out of a creek—if we could find one that ran clear. Mostly we went thirsty. In the distance I saw one tree left standing in the entire clear-cut, like a single point of stubble missed by a razor. It was a skinny thing with lopsided foliage waving in the air. In a few weeks we'd plant our way across the cut block and make it to that tree. Hundreds of dirty, sweaty man-hours would tick by before then, but at least there'd be something to mark the days. Some sign of progress in a cut block as featureless as a sand dune, where it seemed we could plant forever without making headway.

Back in camp, we had miles upon miles of forest to explore, but we stayed within twenty feet of the clearing. Nobody cared to penetrate the deep of it, where the woods grew dark and the breeze no longer penetrated. We pitched our tents as sailors swim at sea, never too far from the ship. At night, after the generator ran down, it was the kind of place that made you think of winter and loneliness, even at the height of summer. In the icy dark, when the temperatures dropped so low the wind could crack a face, the loggers came for the cutting and hauling.

We were so far north that the sun dipped in the middle of the night without ever descending completely. It dipped just under the horizon, a forever-twilight, moving from west back to east. Scalloped clouds drifted over milky sprinklings of stars. They weren't so much bright as everywhere, close and yet a

million light-years away. Aurora borealis sparked across the sky
so frequently that it became unremarkable. During the day, the
bush hummed with mitosis and reproduction. It was louder than
us, like the distant roar of a superhighway.

On our days off there was nowhere to go, nowhere to swim
in the heat. We lay down in the creek beds and let the water
gush over our naked shoulders. We slathered ourselves in clayey
mud and then crawled out like swamp creatures. We watched
ourselves dry out and crack. We breathed clouds of particulates,
pollen, insects, the dust of a billion things growing and dying
and disintegrating back down into the earth.

If we were lucky, a breeze blew through, combing the trees.
I liked to look up and watch them sway. They moved separately
and in tandem, like people leaning their heads together to talk
at a noisy party. They were old, survivor trees. I could wrap my
hands around many of the trunks. Examining the stumps, I
found growth rings so tight they were no thicker than paper. I
didn't know why anybody would take the trouble to roll out here
to hack them down. Maybe the land, despite its wild hackles,
was so flat it practically begged to be rolled over.

We planted trees until the clear-cut felt like our home turf,
until we'd filled it up completely with our footsteps and our
legions of orphan trees. Finally, we reached the timberline at
the far side. When its shadows fell across my face it felt as if I'd
planted right to the brink of some dense, monumental thing. It
occurred to me that this place under my feet was neither particularly north nor especially empty. The timberline was merely
the southern margin of a wilderness so big it felt galactic to stand
at the edge of it. It was the very same forest in which I'd learned
to plant trees—three provinces and a few thousand miles away.

OUR TIME aboard the *Lasqueti Daughters* is almost over. As spring turns the corner it feels as if the bush has kicked into high-powered production, as if it should be left alone, given privacy, to do its work. During these last weeks in the rainforest, Adam and Brian write up our crew lists on a portable whiteboard every day, as they have done for morning meetings since our season began in February. Now, as the days tick down, they draw with their dry-erase markers a thermometer of the sort charity campaigns use to show off the growth of their donations. This scale marks out our cumulative tree tally in increments of ten thousand trees. Once our red line hits the top, we'll be finished here in these backwoods. How many days will it take? We make guesses and wagers. We feel like bettors in a sports pool, only we're both the team and the gamblers.

Soon, we'll be free of the big slash and the Pacific slopes. We will leave here in search of summer diversions. Many of us will head off to fresh jobs and new crews. And when that stage is done, around Labor Day, some will return for one last tour on the coast with deep farmer's tans and our car trunks heavy with *objets trouvé*: moose antlers and interesting rocks and feathers collected from our cut-block travels. Hopefully we'll still be sane, because after one hundred days of full-throttle reforestation, we can come a little unmoored, a tad sunbaked about the brain.

By September those who've planted their way through three seasons will have tired of the bugs, the heat, and the unforgiving sun brought on by the North Pacific high, whose pressure system forces storms northward. Although the rest of the country has been camping and waterskiing and enjoying the heat, for tree planters the chilly months can't come fast enough.

Finally the mornings come coolly. The evenings arrive earlier and earlier by the day. The ground is dry and hard, shrunken like a cotton blanket gone around one too many times in the dryer. We ram our shovels down and cut it open. It puffs out dust and dried spores. Or we hit knobs of stubborn, toughened roots. The fireweed puffs out its downy cotton, which lets loose when we brush through. It clings to our sweat. After bashing around in the fields we look glued and feathered. The hornets are angry, and when we step even slightly in the wrong direction, they send out the Luftwaffe for attack. The conifers have set their buds— they'll grow from these points next year.

The blackberries ripen in the cut blocks. Our shirts are polka-dotted with purple juice, as if we had accidents with red wine. Our part of the world offers no starchy, luscious fruit. Native sweetness comes in the form of berries. The fields are a parade of tiny offerings, ripening one species after the other. Salmon, thimble, huckle, blue, salal, and black. As the seasons roll along the berries deepen in color from pale yellow to indigo. As with fireworks, nature saves the sweetest and the best for the end. A merciful touch, since they feed the animals who must fatten up before the coming of winter.

In autumn, our work takes us up to the saddles, the ridges, and the mountaintops, all the snow-mantled sites of March and April. At subalpine elevations, we encounter life-forms that thrive in penthouse locales—marmots, squirrels, and birds who spend the late season high up, far out on the limb. Tough, minuscule blooms muscle up from cracks in the rocks. Some of these flowers grow wild nowhere else on Earth, and they're in color for just a short wink in a year. Crusty lichens plaster the rocks—they've learned to suck moisture out of the air. Carpets of moss bristle with sporophytes, tiny reproductive stalks that look like miniature snakes charmed out of their baskets. There are spiny plants that look not like succulent rainforest vegetation but like blackened AstroTurf, like weeds that eke out a living in the desert. It's not so far from the truth, for these are exposed, fragile ecosystems. Summer comes late and winter returns early, and for much of the year, water is elusive or frozen. The fact that trees grow here is a small miracle. And even more miraculous is the sheer tenacity of the trees that might struggle to grow back.

The red cedar and the western hemlock of the valley bottoms give way to their hardier counterparts, mountain hemlock and yellow cedar. Yellow cedar grows widely on the coast, but seldom in thick concentrations. It nestles between other species or in tight groves in northern coastal rainforests, and for this reason it's also called Alaska cedar. It has flat, bluish foliage that grows in finer, lacier arrays than its red relative. A cut block with fresh yellow cedar stumps has a peppery, starchy smell. When these trees fall, they leave behind red-purple bark and splinters of yellow inner flesh.

Yellow cedar is a member of the cypress family. It's a hardy, admirable species. It grows in places others wouldn't dare, where snows are heavy or the soils rocky. Yellow cedars that find a home on high crags are sometimes so windblown and storm-thrashed that they become trained by the elements to crouch along the ground. Sometimes they sprout in pockets of dirt sandwiched between boulders. They may spend their whole lives hanging on for dear life. Yellow cedars are not prolific reproducers. They build with stubborn slowness, and their growth rings are tight and thin. But when they germinate in sheltered, fertile bowls, they can lift to magisterial heights.

Yellow cedar is my favorite kind of tree to plant. A load of yellow cedar will bully aside any other species in a set of planting bags. I can bash them around, and the roots never crumble. They aren't pretty, but a row of freshly planted yellow cedars looks satisfyingly upright and vigorous. They have fabulously obscene foliage, and I can spot them from twenty paces. When they are young, they're the green of a highlighter pen, as if nature was feeling flashy. And when I carry yellow cedar in my tree-planting bags, I'm usually someplace exotic and steep. There is typically a good breeze and an excellent vista. And if I'm at the top of a mountain and not trudging through snow, it means the end of tree-planting season is near.

Late one autumn afternoon we might look up and see geese flapping south in honking chevrons. Or we'll wake up to a morning that's as crisp as a finger snap. All at once, the balm of summer is over. An afternoon storm might close over. We'll yank out our rain gear from the very bottom of our backpacks, and when we shove our arms into the sleeves, foreign tree needles fall out of the folds. Shreds of dried moss and insect carcasses imported from other clear-cuts, hundreds of miles away. There is that smell again, our old friend, the punk of rain and rot, the aroma of the winter monsoons. Not an ending, but another kind of beginning, since our year is not a straight line of calendar days but a circle.

Green fades to oat-straw yellow. All is seedy and weedy and crackling. The plants have grown high, and reproduced. Now they wither and crust around the edges. Rodents burrow. They store caches of seeds they will soon forget. Maybe one day these will germinate—in this way, they too are tree planters. The summer rush is over, and the creatures of the forest have switched to reserve mode to make the best of what moisture is left. They hang out waiting for the rain to fall so that everyone might drink again. Nature has done its big job. Like a ball thrown up in the air, all has risen, crested, and begun its arc back down into earth. After many years spent outside we come to see this—the parabola—as the contour of life itself. It's the path the sun takes across the sky. The shape of a story. Ours included. Beginning, middle, and end.

Soon thoughts will turn to the off-season. Some of us will drive straight to the city, buy an airline ticket, and hop a plane to some international destination. Some will collect unemployment insurance, kick back in front of a wood stove, twist off a beer cap, and drink the winter away. Some will crack out paintbrushes and musical instruments. Adam and Brian will go home to their families.

By the time the autumn rolls around the natural world has fulfilled its promise, which is to grow, build, and propagate. Every species delivers its genetic legacy in the form of offspring, assuring a place in the future. At the end of our season, what has our purpose been? What about this broad seedling quilt we had a hand in making? These fledgling plantations will give us oxygen, in theory anyway. If all goes well, they'll draw carbon from the atmosphere. These infant organisms might live until the end of their crop rotation—around eighty years, as long as a human life. Or perhaps by some fluke or oversight, they'll be left to grow out their long natural lives. Some may live until the year 3000. In that time animals and languages will pass into extinction. The map of the world will be completely reinvented.

Perhaps a thousand years from now, some of our trees may approach old age. They'll begin to lose their needles. They may drop the last of their cones. Perhaps one might succumb to rot or infection until sap no longer flows. Over decades, its trunk will molder and soften. The tree will be dead but still full of life, since birds and insects will hollow the wood until it resembles swiss cheese. It will become a snag, a woodland condo for creatures small and smaller. This tree will eventually topple, so rotten in its roots that the wind may push it over. Different creatures will take up residence in the log, all the wet-skinned ground-dwellers, like salamanders and frogs, which need a summer refuge from the hot sun. Nest-dwelling rodents will tunnel inside and find shelter from the winter cold. Seeds might flutter down on the rotting bark and germinate, and our old tree will nurse new sprouts. Then eventually, perhaps after a century or more, this deadfall will melt into the earth, its stringy, decomposed fibers nearly unrecognizable as the xylem and phloem they once were.

DOES PLANTING trees work? Can it fulfill its many promises? It's a question of waiting around for a few hundred years to find out, since that is the basic difference between an ancient forest and a razed field studded with tender seedlings. Time. A primeval woodland is time incarnate. Sunlight made solid. Carbon turned to wood, molecules into cells. An old-growth tree needs centuries to build that bulk, which is why a natural forest stores more carbon than an engineered one. Trees run on cycles that span several human generations. They live in epic chronologies.

Until we learn how to fold up the centuries or to mimic photosynthesis there's no substitute for patience. Human hands can replace the trees but not necessarily the forest. Tree planting sets the stage, perhaps hastening a revival, but still we must wait. For something happens underneath an established canopy that we can neither replicate nor control. An ancient forest is a life-giving environment, like a coral reef or a wetland, where creatures flock to find shelter and nourishment. It's a biome defined by relationships—complexly layered, synergistic webs containing millions of organisms for every acre of space. How does everyone get along? Inside the apparent chaos is a precise and intricate order. Every plant, animal, and microorganism submits to a bio-evolutionary compact that equalizes rates of birth and death, immigration, and the evolution of old species into new ones. Countless beings dovetail together into limited space while sharing finite resources. This is biodiversity. A richness of community that, like any human neighborhood, is also deepened with time.

Scientists say we do ourselves a great disservice when we think of forests as lumber in waiting. In part, because we don't fully understand what we're extracting when we cut down the trees, especially in an old-growth forest. The boreal, for example, has long been considered an environment of low species diversity, characterized by vast swathes of monotonous, single-tree ecosystems. It's now believed that we've been looking in the wrong place for biodiversity all along. Nobody knows the entirety of creatures that live in northern, boreal soil. Many thousands of species of soil fauna are thought to exist that have not yet been discovered, let alone studied.

Mysteries exist not just underfoot but overhead as well. High in the canopy of the old forests of California and Oregon lives the red tree vole. A nocturnal rodent that builds its nests on tree branches a hundred feet in the air. This mouselike creature spends its entire lifetime in just one tree and never descends to the ground. It eats Douglas-fir needles exclusively. Its only water source is rain licked from the foliage. Generations of voles may live for centuries in a mature Douglas-fir. Although they're only six inches long, these rodents are a keystone species, a vital food source for martens, fishers, and endangered birds of prey. Beyond this not much more is known, since they are painfully shy animals. Hard to find—in the dark, halfway to the sky—and even harder to study.

Primary forests also moderate climate in ways that haven't been fully explored. Trees release water vapor through their foliage—evapotranspiration. In ecosystems like the Amazon rainforest an acre of canopy trees breathes out enough water to fill a swimming pool every year. The leaves release plant compounds, airborne hydrocarbons, that stick to water molecules in the atmosphere, thereby seeding the clouds. These clouds travel on the wind to drier regions in South America, delivering rain. They also moisten the Atlantic trade winds, influencing rainfall patterns as far afield as the corn belt in the American Midwest. Rainforests act like watering cans, soaking up heavy precipitation and redistributing it elsewhere.

It's always been thought that rainforests are the product of heavy precipitation. But a radical new hypothesis suggests that the converse may be true. According to this theory, mature, intact rainforests act like meteorological pumps, condensing water vapor from the air. A drop in local atmospheric pressure ensues. The rainforest, in turn, sucks in air and moisture from adjacent areas, in effect creating wind. This theory has not been fully studied or proven. But if it's true, then rainforests aren't just the beneficiaries of weather but also the makers of it. Climate is determined not just by convection currents and temperature shifts, but by living green processes, too. Thus, the consequences of sweeping deforestation might be much more far-reaching than anticipated.

Somewhere along the line we've come to believe that a tree is a just tree and that all forests must be equal. But a plantation does not necessarily a forest make. To begin with, tree seeds don't spread themselves like windblown spores or dandelion fluff, sailing over infinite distances. When a cone falls, it lands close to its parent, never too far from the canopy. Here it germinates under the cover of older, foster trees, protected from heat, wind, and snow. As the tree matures it needs others of its kind—competition—to grow up straight and tall, to reach toward the light. Tree communities were never designed to arise from bare earth. In this sense a forest is a prerequisite for itself.

Second-growth, tree farms, managed forests, plantations—that's what cut blocks are called once the planters have traveled through. As if the trees were widgets and forests could be thrown up as uniformly as subdivisions or coffee shop franchises. Trees are habitat providers and soil builders. They sponge up moisture and release it slowly. They're CO_2-scrubbing, living humidifiers. In this sense forests are the planet's great moderators. They soften the elements. We plant trees with high hopes, if not for a future timber supply, then for the natural perks—also known as "environmental services."

Trees provide carbon credits and environmental benefits, but only as long as they're alive. Silviculture is an imperfect discipline, and there are so many ways a tree can perish. Of root-rot plagues and insect infestations. From blight and mistletoe. Floods and landslides and long, hard winters. Fire and drought and climate change. Forests are just as susceptible to mortality as any human being, but when they die they become a liability. Carbon traffic begins to flow in the wrong direction. Its sequestered stores dumped into the biosphere by way of decomposition and fire.

It takes several years for a new forest to become a carbon sink. Planting trees in the Northern Hemisphere may be less beneficial than common sense suggests, perhaps even detrimental. A green canopy absorbs more heat than the open land it replaces, producing a net warming effect. We can plant too many of the same kinds of trees and wind up with a monoculture plantation, reducing habitat and increasing susceptibility to disease. We can sow exotic seeds in the wrong place, never knowing what kind of invasive, ineradicable monster we're creating. Not to mention operator failure. There are as many different ways to plant a tree as there are human moods or thoughts rattling around in one's brain. There are greedy trees and lazy trees and trees planted in fury or resignation.

There's no difference between old-growth and a forest made by hand once a few centuries have gone by. Primordial forests are not necessarily all that old, and neither are they all that virgin, much of the time. They've been killed off, over the planet's long history, and they've recovered. Strictly speaking, the earth doesn't care if the trees come and go. But perhaps, in the future, we will. There are more of us than ever before, and a few billion more to come. As the planet warms, we may come to see clearcuts as an obsolete extravagance. We may wish we'd looked at forests in a different way. Worth more standing than they are lying down, better off as trees than as logs.

PLANTING TREES, they say, is a young person's punishment. But even that isn't really quite right, because you can be a grandfather and still do the work. Indeed you might be a tree planter approaching senior citizenship and be able to keep up with the young bucks. You can be ninety-nine pounds and scarcely five feet tall and perform just as well as a football player. You can be a man or a woman; it makes no difference. Such are the ingenuities of the human body, which have as much to do with our brains as with our musculature.

Alas, no one can be a tree planter forever. Everyone must give it up. In fact every minute of the workday provides at least a few good reasons to hang up one's shovel. If none of the sensible factors are discouraging enough, surely our bodies will retire us one day. Some of us will burn our tatty boots in the last of the season's bonfires. Or we'll fling them unceremoniously into the cut block, one at a time, for some surveyor or logger or tree planter of the future to find.

After we quit we'll never stop wondering what it meant to the world, if anything at all, these little patches we made, our hectare groves that dot the countryside. In one hundred years there will be no sign of our crew, perhaps not even a trace of anything we made or did or built in our lives except perhaps our children's children. And yet, more seedlings have been planted in the province of British Columbia than there are people living on earth. It would take one person many lifetimes—more than one thousand years of walking—to touch a hand to every tree trunk.

Forests for the Future. Forests Forever, as the slogans and the T-shirts say. Not a salve or a fix for the planet, not exactly. We gave the trees some small purchase in the world, and they gave us the same in return.

{ 10 }

EXIT LINES

As the solstice approaches, the *Lasqueti Daughters* unties from her moorings. We retrace our watery footsteps, commencing our retreat toward civilization. We make but one more stop, dropping anchor along the edges of Seymour's main navigational channel. The water is placid. Seals thrash about near the shore. We see the occasional yacht motoring past, flapping the American flag.

We catch sight of another tree-planting crew in their boat, anchored on the other side of the inlet. We inspect them from afar with Skipper Peter's binoculars. We know this boat. We've seen the crew members lurking around on the wharves in Port McNeill. They steam back to town whenever their outlands are buried in snow. We've seen them surfing the Internet at The Haida-Way, caught them browsing the bulletin boards at the Laundromat.

Their boat is decrepit—at least it looks that way from a distance. We imagine a bunch of guys sleeping cheek by jowl in stacked berths, packed in as tightly as a submarine crew. Their boat has a moldy vinyl dodger, only ever half-zipped. They come out onto the deck carrying mugs and beer cans, wearing fleece pants and baggy sweaters. They look as if they haven't seen razors or barber shears in months.

There is only one woman aboard, the cook. She is a friend, we learn, of Keira's. One night this cook motors over in a skiff to pay a friendly visit. She looks like one of us, but different, too. She's wearing a bra, for starters. A ball cap, a baby doll T-shirt, and hiking boots. A pair of too-big sweatpants rolled up at the waistband and wet at the hems. She steps over the gunnels, strides into the galley, and leaps into Keira's arms. They hug like long-lost sisters. This cook, when it's time to return to her boat, takes one last look over her shoulder. A little forlornly, we think. Keira waves goodbye from the poop deck. Then she wipes her hands on the dishtowel tucked into her pants and heads back into the galley.

Keira's friend brought a note from our counterparts across the water. It was sent by a friend of K.T.'s. They are old buddies from Newfoundland, where they both grew up. They went to work together in their first years as tree planters. It was their escape from The Rock. They planted side by side nearly two decades ago.

The women among us are firm in our agreement that no matter how bad it gets, we'd rather be here than over there. Damp, narrow bunks. Nearly no women. At least we have doors that close. Our men start to speculate, as soon as the cook is gone, about how much money the other crew might be making. They all want to know how much their fastest horse is earning. It's the measure of something, of everything, we might say. There is talk of defection, jokes about the swim to the other side.

Few crews ever travel this far back, as if no one else could be bothered. This isn't the first time we've crossed paths with these familiar strangers across the water. We've seen their tree boxes piled up on our landings. Last year, we met them in a logging camp, a gang of men with work-worn smudges for eyes, pushing their plates toward the cookhouse steam trays. They went at the food as if they hadn't eaten in days. Their eyes grazed the naked shoulders of the girls among us, the spaces between the straps of halter tops. They kept their heads down and went to work at their plates, shoveling with their forks in their fists. They had the look of people who did nothing but *pound* and *slam*, who bled themselves out in tree-planting combat, who smoked pot all night to dull the ache of their battered bodies. We bantered across the tables, but we didn't intermingle. Like those vanishing clans who'd rather hold grudges than speak the last words of a dying tongue.

LASTLY, ADAM tells me, there's the matter of the cleanup back in Woods Lagoon. He sets his hand on my arm. I glance down at Adam's wrist. He wears a dive watch with a heavy stainless face, an altimeter, and a numbered bezel, as if there were both high climbing and deep diving to do. I know I've been assigned the garbage patrol.

Doug will go with you, he adds brightly.

We'll do this alone, a satellite crew of two. Julien will deliver us back down the channel in the skiff, which is printed with the name of the maker—aptly for Doug and me: Lifetimer.

Before breakfast, Peter gives Julien a hasty tutorial on the operation and troubleshooting of the skiff. It's an overcast morning, and the rain prattles lightly on the water. Doug and I kit up in our rain gear. We climb in, and Julien rips the cord on the outboard. The motor coughs. It takes more than a few smoky belches to get it to sing out into the morning.

Oh boy, I say.

I have done this dozens of times. Long, ridiculous bush-whacks on foot. Or in rowboats across scummy ponds. I've driven for hours to plant a handful of trees in a roadside, only to turn around and drive all the way back. I have commuted to work with fishing lodge crews, crammed in among pineapples, tiki torches, and six-foot plastic marlins. Game plans that can come to no good, that only highlight the daily absurdities of planting trees.

Now Doug and Julien and I zip across the water, which is green and gently rippled. We backtrack deeper into the inlet. The wind blasts our hair. My eyelashes flatten against my lids. It takes half an hour to return to Woods, and when we arrive we find it almost wholly depopulated. The big barge has gone. In its place floats a house, a cottage parked on a wooden deck with grass sprouting up through the planking.

The camp caretakers live here now. They come out to greet us as we putter up to the dock. A woman shuffles out onto the deck wearing tight pink bicycle shorts and a voluminous T-shirt. She smokes a long cigarette, holding the blue cardboard pack in her palm. She tells us her name is Carol. She wears tinted con-tact lenses, and they remind me of those glass-eyed dolls with lids that fall open and closed, depending on which way you hold them. Carol's husband joins us. His name is Darren. Carol is a smiley woman. We discover the farthest that Darren and Carol have ventured from the barge is about a hundred yards up the road. Mostly they hang out on the deck in Adirondack chairs, admiring what's left of the scenery.

We advise Darren and Carol of our plans for the day. We'll travel up the main line, out onto one of the claim's many dwindling spurs. We'll be back by lunchtime, we promise, at the latest. And as soon as this sentence leaves my mouth I know they're famous last words, though I can't yet say precisely why. There are a thousand reasons to get snagged, hung up, and waylaid planting trees. There's cake for dessert tonight, and chances are I'll never get to taste it.

What channel will you be on? asks Julien. Just in case.

Oh, says Carol. We don't have a radio.

I glance at Doug. His eyebrows rise up on his forehead, and his lips gather over to one side. Doug's a stoic sufferer. His spine has been dangerously compressed by years of bending double. Soon enough a doctor will make him choose between planting trees and walking.

We tear off down the road in a borrowed truck, one of two left behind by the logging company.

We roll up at a brushy cut block we'd started two weeks ago, which I'd hoped someone else would be sent back to finish. As we come over a rise we startle a chubby black bear. He stands up on his hind legs in the slash. Julien honks the horn. The bear waddles over the knoll, annoyed by the hassle of having to run away.

I shove my boots on, fill my bags, and follow the bear into the field. I climb a side hill of coarse woody trash and salal. I find the trees that I'd planted just two weeks ago. They look strange to me now, more tenuously alive than when they left my hands. I fill in where I left off. I make my way to the ridge top and peer over the edge at a down slope thatched with blowdown. My heart sinks. I'll have to go down there and make the best of it. At the bottom I glimpse a marsh, spiny at the shore with reeds. The distant reach of the sea laps against the flow of a creek, where salt merges with freshwater, the outflow stained by the tannic juices of cedar trees.

I pass the morning finishing what I started, weaving my way over and under the fallen trunks. By the time I crest the hill the sun burns behind the clouds. The air has grown muggy, and the black flies are out in a fury for every last drop of blood before the human mammals leave these woods. I find a long log protruding like a diving board from a slash pile. I know it will be springy, and so I step out onto it, balancing at the very end. I bounce there for a time, feeling the cool lick of the wind for the first time since the blast in the Lifetimer.

Out of this stillness comes an airy, muscular whoosh. I glance up at the underside of an animal with a giant wingspan, with feathers the gold-white of a vanilla candle. It glides just feet from my head, so close I could reach up and touch it. It passes over me, angles down, and skims the treetops that fringe the sea below. Then it skids gracefully down onto the water before blending into the textures of the forest. It's a strange-looking creature—a swan-like bird with a long, crooked neck. Part crane and part egret. It looks like no kind of goose or duck that flies around here, as if it had been blown far off course. One of those birds who roosts in the Arctic and winters in the tropics but outside of those two brief destinations spends most of its life on the wing.

In another hour of work I reach the top of the hill. I spot the truck with its hood propped open. At first I believe Julien has lifted it to create some shade so that he can sack out behind the steering wheel. But then he appears at the edge of the road.

Do you know anything about mechanics? he shouts.

It's not my strong suit, I call back.

And there it is, the inevitable snag. I drag my heels back to the truck, my footsteps cracking and crunching wood. Julien gets in behind the wheel to better demonstrate his difficulties. He turns the key. The dashboard lights up. And from somewhere deep in the guts of the engine comes a fatal clicking sound.

Doug returns.

Do you know that trick with a shovel and the solenoid? he asks.

I've seen it done, I say meekly.

We chuckle dryly. We ponder our predicament. Julien rubs his chin. He announces that he will jog back to the water's edge to get another truck.

Are you sure? I ask. Julien wears a windbreaker, cargo pants, and leather hiking boots. It's fourteen miles to the dock. I'm stabbed with a pang of that quintessential tree-planter desire, the supernatural wish to fly.

Yes, says Julien. He's sure he can go the distance without too much trouble at all. I'm abruptly grateful for the gift of his athletic training.

If you're not back in four hours, I tell him, we'll come looking.

Julien unzips his jacket, shrugs his shoulders, then punches a fist into his palm. He strides away from us, over a hump in the road, then breaks into a trot.

Doug and I refill our bags and return to our work. We finish according to our original estimate, just after noon. We sit in the narcoleptic truck and pick at our lunch tailings.

At the stroke of four, I turn to Doug. Time's up, I say.

A half an hour into our walk, we catch sight of a dust flume in the distance. We hear the rattle and squeak of a chassis, and finally a truck approaches. Darren sits at the wheel. Julien rides shotgun. They slow and then halt, and when Julien slides out to make room for us he's so chafed he can scarcely walk.

On the way back to the skiff Julien tells us about his jogging odyssey. On the way he ran into one cougar and two bears. He was more worried about the cougar. A movie popped into his mind: *The Gods Must Be Crazy*. He remembered that little boy of the desert who outsmarts a hyena by holding a scrap of wood above his head; a hyena won't attack a creature that looks big enough to put up a good fight. Julien wasn't totally sure if such a rule applied to cougars, but he scrabbled around in the slash and pulled out a foot-long piece of tree bark. Then he ran for a mile holding it high aloft.

As we clatter back to the dock, I catch sight of Walter, the local raven. He flaps into the truck's wake, flying from perch to perch, stump to stump, awaiting one last meal.

We return to the water's edge. Before we pull out Carol and Darren give us a bottle of cloudy liquid. They tell us it's vodka they made themselves with potatoes. As they wave us goodbye, the rain starts in again.

On our return to the *Daughters*, the skiff runs out of gas. In the process of changing tanks we flood the engine. Doug, Julien, and I sit there for a dozen minutes letting the gas line drain as the current pushes us down the channel. The hillsides are so tight with trees they absorb sound. I listen to the water lap the aluminum. Raindrops tap the water. We call out on our hand-held radio, the junior model that nobody wants to use, the one with the range of a baby monitor. Predictably, we get no answer.

Every few minutes we take another stab at the outboard's rip cord. It sputters and chokes. We wait another long while, flowing

the wrong way with the ocean's steady push. Julien gives the fuel
bulb a squeeze and then winds his arm up for one last shot.

I *hate* this shit, I curse. Although in fact this is a lie. I love
almost every part of it.

Well? says Doug.

Julien cracks his knuckles and reaches for the starter.

I cross my fingers and close my eyes.

THE FINAL day of the coastal season brings one of those late-
spring days when we can't decide what to wear. We're either
soaked and cold or stewing inside our raincoats. We spend the
day in clothes that are always on the verge of drying out in time
for it to rain again, our pants clinging to our inner thighs.

How many more to go? we shout.

We want to know the seedling countdown, though not even
Bradam know the right answer to that. In the eleventh hour, our
supervisors don't care what we do, just as long as we take out
the last of the trees and don't bring any back. We can hear their
mood over the airwaves. They discuss extraction plans. They
burn tree boxes and scrape up wet, plastic detritus from the
roads and fling our old banana peels into the slash. They scorch
our traces down to ash piles. We see towers of smoke. After today
they've got trucks to wash, maps to color-code with pencil cray-
ons, and spreadsheets to reconcile. More work than an ending
should really involve. It could be a separate job title in itself.
The After Planter.

The last day of a tree-planting season isn't something to be
filled up with wages but rather hours to be emptied of seedlings.
We plant the last of our bundles. We scoop out from our bags
all the cast-off dirt, the Styrofoam pellets and shiny flecks of

vermiculite. We fling it by the handfuls at the ground. We stagger our way down the block and then ski down the cut bank onto the road. We pop the buckles on our bags and slip the logger knots from our boots.

But then, inevitably, we catch sight of someone out there, slogging it out by herself while the rest of us sit on the roadside. It's Melissa. And although she's deep in the back, we sigh and bitch and clip back into our bags. We trudge out to meet her. She gives us a big, dirty grin. It might be Rose or Oakley or Jake or Rachel. It doesn't matter who it is, or even if we like them, because we're still going to head out to help them lighten their loads. It will get us all home that much faster.

How many do you have left? we ask.

They look into their left-hand pouches to count.

Doesn't matter, we say.

They give us half, and we do it for free. Until there is nobody left straggling. We reach down into our bags, and our fingers scrape the bottom. The last tree comes and goes without our even knowing it, just a blind pawing of the hand. This is how the finish arrives—over before it started, an anticlimactic dribble without ceremony or surprise. Now all our trees have been delivered to the ground. They've begun the wild life we'll never see, in this place we'll never revisit. Only later do we think about what it means, if we think of this final seedling at all. We never know if we'll feel that sensation again, the push of the left hand into the dirt. The tug of the right hand on the shovel handle, and that old, comforting grind in the rotator cuff. What if it was the last tree of our lives?

In the future we won't see a farmer's field or a roadside berm or a beach dune without wanting to nail it with seedlings. We'll hear the gurgling base notes of diesel engines, and a shiver will pass through our spines. We'll never understand why people need ski poles to go hiking. We'll confuse our dogs with people, since they were our cut-block sidekicks, our scouts and lookouts, for so long. Warm canned beer will suit us just fine. We might name our kids Willow or Cedar or Sequoia. At dinner parties, we'll be the first ones to clean our plates. We'll have a certain lasting appreciation for duct tape and Ziploc bags. For cashiers who whip our groceries past the laser, for highballers of all kinds. And deep in our storage cupboards we'll keep that old trinity—caulks, bags, and shovel—long after we've retired. One day we'll regain the feeling in our big toes, but our knees will never be the same.

What have we learned in all this time? How are we improved after a million stooping acts? We've cried in frustration, seen pain so brilliant it glowed. We've sobbed with laughter, submerged ourselves in paroxysms so violent our ribs were sore the next day. Does this happen elsewhere, in cubicles, in elevators? Is it possible in ironed attire? We know how to climb landslides. How to walk on the guts of the earth so that our feet never touch the ground. We know how to hang on by the fingernails and toe spikes. We know how to fall down backward and forward and also how to get up. Where will we take these skills at the end of our tenure? When we quit this miserable, beautiful life.

NOW, THE furious race to get back to the *Daughters*, to escape this wild place before it swallows us whole. We speed along at breakneck pace, only to reach our destination and wait some more. We stand around on shore counting minutes until the tide comes up so that we can drive the trucks aboard. On the beach we kick off our caulk boots. We pour out brown viscous water from our lefts and our rights. Finally, when the barge pushes up to the shore, we walk aboard in our stocking feet, tongues of wool slapping the planks. When we peel off our socks we find we've got pickled feet. Brad shows Keira his whitened, bloated toes. She retreats into the kitchen and comes back with her camera to take photos of these oddities.

When the last truck has driven aboard, the boat lifts and closes its prow and we begin the journey back to our many versions of home. As we travel down the long tube of Seymour Inlet, I sit with Peter in the wheelhouse. He's got a laptop stuffed with digital navigation charts. They flicker and re-orient as we move. On the way, a pod of white-sided dolphins leaps and frolics ahead of the bow.

By the time we reach Nakwakto Rapids the tide has turned, a bottle emptied and then filled again, yet never completely still. The *Daughters* struggles against the current. We chug along at less than half a knot. For a time I wonder if we'll make it through at all or if the tide will turn us back. After twenty minutes of grinding we pass through.

We watch the sun go down over the water. We motor past islets covered with trees. Stony reefs. Schools of jellyfish float near the surface. Summery air puffs against my face. It's almost too warm. If I close my eyes I can trick myself into thinking I'm no longer in Canada but in some clement, tropical clime. In my chest there's a heavy feeling, of melancholy no-return, since planting trees is an industry of perpetual, forward motion. I know I'll never have cause to come back here again, no matter how breathtaking it is.

Adam and Brian hustle around on the foredeck folding tarps, picking up spare tires, and lobbing them into teetering piles.

Those guys work really hard, says Peter. From the moment they get up in the morning until the middle of the night. And, he adds, they lie *all the time.*

At dusk we celebrate with Molotov cocktails contrived from Darren and Carol's homemade vodka. We mix it with the remains of the galley rations, powdered lemonade and coconut milk. We drink it from a mishmash of coffee mugs. We toast as the sun melts in a brilliant orange crush. The boat is alive with boisterous revelry. People laugh in the kitchen. Brad DJs at the CD player. There's another gathering almost directly beneath us in the smoking pit. Still another crowd on the poop deck murmuring and celebrating and getting slowly drunk, or trying to anyway. The big diesel engine hums. Later, when the sun goes down, Oakley will give Jake a mohawk with his clippers by the light of a Petzl headlamp. Pierre will make a video, and we will watch it even though no time at all has passed.

Soon we'll stop in Lund, a tiny coastal town, the northernmost on the Sunshine Coast. We'll get off at the government docks and find that summer has begun in our absence. We'll see townspeople walking dogs, tourists with sweaters tied around their shoulders. Citizens will stare at us as if we are a waterfront sideshow. Rose will leap from the boat and kiss the pavement. She wears her rabbit-fur vest, her cheek-covering sunglasses, and a cigarette pinched jauntily between her fingers. We'll crash into the bar for a single, pit-stop round. Bar hag cocktails—rye and ginger ales, whisky sours stuck with maraschino cherries. And then we'll scramble aboard again and head farther south to Powell River. Closer still to the rest of the world, like reentry into orbit.

Tomorrow we'll reach Egmont, and the same old thing will happen to us. Already it feels as if our minds have begun to shift. We'll tumble out onto dry land. There won't be time. We'll feel the pull of the highway, the deep need to arrive home, to arrive at some kind of destination before nightfall. We'll feel that same old desire to fall away from one another, as quickly as we can, after all that involuntary intimacy we grew.

Never again, we'll swear to each other.

See you in the fall, we'll sing.

Maybe we'll reunite. Maybe not. Planting life is only as sure as the strength of the wrist or the knee. For some of us there will never be a next time, even if we don't know it yet.

In Egmont we reacquaint ourselves with our cars. They're humid with must and condensation, the smell of our crumpled snacks on the day we left dry land. We find our vehicles right where we left them, parked in a patch of muddy grass near the wharf for commercial vessels. A yard full of scrap metal and concrete chunks, stray bits of steel scaffolding and rusty iron ship guts. Bales of pink fiberglass insulation wrapped in plastic. A gate will roll open, a strip of rusty corrugated metal on wheels. We'll gun our engines, ready for the open road.

Beyond the barge terminal there's a lineup of cars awaiting the ferry. Glossy sedans and leviathan white RVs glide down the lanes like pinballs in a rack. Normal folks in their minivans, talking on cell phones, standing around in windbreakers holding dog leashes or cardboard coffee cups. Small children dangle from their hands. We'll have to find a way to rejoin them. We'll zoom out onto tracts of open highway, the pavement a smooth, rediscovered luxury.

But after the initial burst of excitement, a wave of fatigue will creep over us. Later in the night we'll drop into beds like stones into water. When we wake up tomorrow we'll be different somehow, just a little bit. A change that yawns into the next day and the next. And soon enough, when we talk about tree planting, it will be in the past tense.

SELECTED BIBLIOGRAPHY

Cannings, Richard and Sydney Cannings. *British Columbia: A Natural History.* Vancouver/Toronto: Greystone, 2009.

Cohen, Shaul Ephraim. *Planting Nature: Trees and the Manipulation of Environmental Stewardship in America.* Berkeley/Los Angeles: University of California Press, 2004.

Drushka, Ken. *In the Bight: The B.C. Forest Industry Today.* Madeira Park, BC: Harbour Publishing, 1999.

Harrison, Robert Pogue. *Forests: The Shadow of Civilization.* Chicago: University of Chicago Press, 1992.

Kimmins, J.P. *Forest Ecology: A Foundation for Sustainable Management.* Upper Saddle River, NJ: Prentice Hall, 1997.

MacKay, Donald. *Empire of Wood: The MacMillan Bloedel Story.* Vancouver/Toronto: Douglas & McIntyre, 1982.

Mann, Charles C. *1491: New Revelations of the Americas before Columbus.* New York: Knopf, 2005.

Marchak, Patricia. *Falldown: Forest Policy in British Columbia.* Vancouver: David Suzuki Foundation, 1999.

———. *Green Gold: The Forest Industry in British Columbia.* Vancouver: University of British Columbia Press, 1983.

Maser, Chris. *Forest Primeval: The Natural History of an Ancient Forest.* San Francisco: Sierra Club Books, 1989.

May, Elizabeth. *At the Cutting Edge: The Crisis in Canada's Forests.* Toronto: Key Porter, 1998.

McDougall, Christopher. *Born to Run: A Hidden Tribe, Superathletes, and the Greatest Race the World Has Never Seen.* New York: Knopf, 2009.

Montgomery, David R. *Dirt: The Erosion of Civilizations.* Berkeley/ Los Angeles: University of California Press, 2007.

Peattie, Donald Culross. *A Natural History of Western Trees.* Boston: Houghton Mifflin, 1953.

Pojar, Jim and Andy MacKinnon. *Plants of Coastal British Columbia.* Vancouver: Lone Pine Publishing, 2005.

Power, Michael J. and Jay Schulkin. *The Evolution of Obesity.* Baltimore: The Johns Hopkins University Press, 2009.

Puettmann, Klaus J., K. David Coates, and Christian C. Messier. *A Critique of Silviculture: Managing for Complexity.* Washington, DC: Island Press, 2009.

Rajala, Richard. *Clearcutting the Pacific Rainforest: Production, Science, and Regulation.* Vancouver: University of British Columbia Press, 1998.

Sands, Roger. *Forestry in a Global Context.* Cambridge, MA: CABI Publishing, 2005.

Schwantes, Carlos Arnaldo. *The Pacific Northwest: An Interpretive History.* Lincoln/London: University of Nebraska Press, 1996.

Stewart, Hilary. *Cedar: Tree of Life to the Northwest Coast Indians.* Vancouver/Toronto: Douglas & McIntyre, 1984.

Suzuki, David and Wayne Grady. *Tree: A Life Story.* Vancouver/ Toronto: Greystone, 2004.

Taylor, G.W. *Timber: History of the Forest Industry in B.C.* Vancouver: J.J. Douglas, 1975.

Thomas, Peter. *Trees: Their Natural History.* Cambridge, UK: Cambridge University Press, 2000.

Vancouver, George. *A Voyage of Discovery to the North Pacific Ocean and Round the World, 1791–1795.* Ed. W. Kaye Lamb. London: Hakluyt Society, 1984.

Van Pelt, Robert. *Forest Giants of the Pacific Coast.* Seattle/London: University of Washington Press, 2001.

Williams, Claire G. *Conifer Reproductive Biology.* Dordrecht: Springer, 2009.

Williams, Michael. *Deforesting the Earth: From Prehistory to Global Crisis.* Chicago/London: University of Chicago Press, 2006.

ACKNOWLEDGMENTS

THANKS ARE OWED to Marni Jackson, Ian Pearson, and Moira Farr, mentors in the Literary Journalism program at the Banff Centre. I'm grateful for support from the Canada Council for the Arts. Allan Markin and Jackie Flanagan, benefactors of the Markin-Flanagan writer-in-residence program at the University of Calgary. Gudrun Will at the *Vancouver Review*, who published part of this book in earlier form. Juliet Gill, my mother, a proofer of the highest order. Scott and Shana at Wagner Reforestation, who kept me employed during much of the writing. Peter Lironi, who welcomed us aboard. John Vigna, author, planter, ideal reader. Zsuzsi Gartner, dear friend and test kitchen guru. Rob Sanders at Greystone. Nancy Flight, for her wisdom and guidance, and Lara Kordic, for her sharp-eyed copyedit. Kevin Turpin, physiology advisor and exemplary tree-planting man. Not one word would exist without my extended silvicultural family. Roland and crew, especially.

OTHER TITLES *from the* DAVID SUZUKI
FOUNDATION *and* GREYSTONE BOOKS

. . . . .

Sacred Headwaters: The Fight to Save the Stikine, Skeena, and Nass
by Wade Davis, photography by Carr Clifton, Paul Colangelo and
members of the ILCP, foreword by David Suzuki, afterword by
Robert F. Kennedy Jr.

*Empire of the Beetle: How Human Folly and a Tiny Bug Are Killing
the Great Forests of the West* by Andrew Nikiforuk

*Beneath Cold Seas: The Underwater Wilderness
of the Pacific Northwest* by David Hall,
introduction from Sarika Cullis-Suzuki

The Atlantic Coast: A Natural History by Harry Thurston

*You Are the Earth: Know Your World So You Can Help
Make It Better* by David Suzuki and Kathy Vanderlinden,
art by Wallace Edwards

Arctic Eden: Journeys through the Changing High Arctic
by Jerry Kobalenko

The Legacy: An Elder's Vision for Our Sustainable Future
by David Suzuki

*Dodging the Toxic Bullet: How to Protect Yourself from Everyday
Environmental Health Hazards* by David R. Boyd

Tar Sands: Dirty Oil and the Future of a Continent,
revised and updated 2nd edition by Andrew Nikiforuk

The Declaration of Interdependence: A Pledge to Planet Earth
by Tara Cullis and David Suzuki with Wade Davis,
Guujaaw, and Raffi Cavoukian

More Good News: Real Solutions to the Global Eco-Crisis
by David Suzuki and Holly Dressel

Lakeland: Ballad of a Freshwater Country by Allan Casey

The Sea: A Literary Companion edited by Wayne Grady

Night: A Literary Companion edited by Merilyn Simonds

The Big Picture: Reflections on Science, Humanity, and a Quickly Changing Planet by David Suzuki and Dave Robert Taylor

A Good Catch: Sustainable Seafood Recipes from Canada's Top Chefs by Jill Lambert

David Suzuki's Green Guide by David Suzuki and David R. Boyd

Bees: Nature's Little Wonders by Candace Savage

The Hot Topic: What We Can Do about Global Warming by Gabrielle Walker and Sir David King

Gardens: A Literary Companion edited by Merilyn Simonds

Deserts: A Literary Companion edited by Wayne Grady

A Passion for This Earth: Writers, Scientists, and Activists Explore Our Relationship with Nature and the Environment edited by Michelle Benjamin

The Great Lakes: The Natural History of a Changing Region by Wayne Grady

The Sacred Balance: Rediscovering Our Place in Nature by David Suzuki, Amanda McConnell, and Adrienne Mason

An Enchantment of Birds: Memories from a Birder's Life
by Richard Cannings

Where the Silence Rings: A Literary Companion to Mountains
edited by Wayne Grady

*Dark Waters Dancing to a Breeze: A Literary Companion to Rivers
and Lakes* edited by Wayne Grady

*Wisdom of the Elders: Native and Scientific Ways of Knowing about
Nature* by Peter Knudtson and David Suzuki

The Rockies: A Natural History by Richard Cannings

Wild Prairie: A Photographer's Personal Journey
by James R. Page

Prairie: A Natural History by Candace Savage

Tree: A Life Story by David Suzuki and Wayne Grady

The Sacred Balance: A Visual Celebration of Our Place in Nature
by David Suzuki and Amanda McConnell with Maria DeCambra

*From Naked Ape to Superspecies: Humanity and the
Global Eco-Crisis* by David Suzuki and Holly Dressel

The David Suzuki Reader by David Suzuki

*When the Wild Comes Leaping Up: Personal Encounters
with Nature* edited by David Suzuki

*Good News for a Change: How Everyday People Are Helping
the Planet* by David Suzuki and Holly Dressel

*The Last Great Sea: A Voyage Through the Human and
Natural History of the North Pacific Ocean* by Terry Glavin

Northern Wild: Best Contemporary Canadian Nature Writing edited by David R. Boyd

Greenhouse: The 200-Year Story of Global Warming by Gale E. Christianson

Vanishing Halo: Saving the Boreal Forest by Daniel Gawthrop

Dead Reckoning: Confirming the Crisis in Pacific Fisheries by Terry Glavin

Delgamuukw: The Supreme Court of Canada Decision on Aboriginal Title by Stan Persky

DAVID SUZUKI FOUNDATION CHILDREN'S TITLES

You Are the Earth by David Suzuki and Kathy Vanderlinden

There's a Barnyard in My Bedroom by David Suzuki; illustrated by Eugenie Fernandes

Salmon Forest by David Suzuki and Sarah Ellis; illustrated by Sheena Lott

Eco-Fun by David Suzuki and Kathy Vanderlinden

Photo by: Kevin Turpin

CHARLOTTE GILL IS the author of the story collection *Lady-killer*, a finalist for the Governor General's Literary Award and winner of the Danuta Gleed Award and the B.C. Book Prize for fiction. Her work has appeared in *Best Canadian Stories*, *The Journey Prize Stories*, and many magazines. She spent nearly two decades working in the forests of Canada and has planted more than a million trees. She lives in Vancouver, British Columbia.

THE DAVID SUZUKI FOUNDATION

The David Suzuki Foundation works through science and education to protect the diversity of nature and our quality of life, now and for the future.

With a goal of achieving sustainability within a generation, the Foundation collaborates with scientists, business and industry, academia, government and non-governmental organizations. We seek the best research to provide innovative solutions that will help build a clean, competitive economy that does not threaten the natural services that support all life.

The Foundation is a federally registered independent charity that is supported with the help of over 50,000 individual donors across Canada and around the world.

We invite you to become a member. For more information on how you can support our work, please contact us:

The David Suzuki Foundation
219–2211 West 4th Avenue
Vancouver, BC
Canada V6K 4S2
www.davidsuzuki.org
contact@davidsuzuki.org
Tel: 604-732-4228
Fax: 604-732-0752

Checks can be made payable to The David Suzuki Foundation. All donations are tax-deductible.

Canadian charitable registration: (BN) 12775 6716 RR0001
U.S. charitable registration: #94-3204049